D0875907

Modern European History

A Garland Series of Outstanding Dissertations

General Editor
William H. McNeill
University of Chicago

Associate Editors

Eastern Europe
Charles Jelavich
Indiana University

Great Britain
Peter Stansky
Stanford University

France
David H. Pinkney
University of Washington

Russia
Barbara Jelavich
Indiana University

Germany
Enno E. Kraehe
University of Virginia

MODERN EUROPEAN HISTORY

How Shall We Govern India?

A Controversy Among British Administrators,
1800–1882

Ann B. Callender

Université d'Ottawa
BIBLIOTHÈQUES
LIBRARIES
University of Ottawa

Garland Publishing, Inc.
New York and London 1987

8800023041

Copyright © 1987 Ann B. Callender
All rights reserved

Library of Congress Cataloging-in-Publication Data

Callender, Ann.
  How shall we govern India? : a controversy among
British administrators, 1800–1882 / Ann B. Callender.
  p.   cm.—(Modern European history)
  Bibliography: p.
  Includes index.
  ISBN 0-8240-7801-2 (alk. paper)
  1. India—Politics and government, 1765–1947.
2. India—Constitutional history. 3. Great Britain—
Colonies—Asia-Administration—History. 4. India—
Officials and employees—History. 5. India—
History—British occupation, 1754–1947. I. Title.
II. Series.
JQ211.C35   1987
320.954—dc19   87-26004

JQ
211
.C35
1987

All volumes in this series are printed on acid-
free, 250-year-life paper.

Printed in the United States of America

TABLE OF CONTENTS

LIST OF ILLUSTRATIONS

I N T R O D U C T I O N

Ruling India in the 19th century raised many unique problems. But in the widest sense it raised the difficulty which the British found in every alien territory added to the Empire: how to govern in lands of vastly different traditions and opaque cultures. It was one thing for British soldiers to capture forts and conquer principalities. It was quite another to set up civil administrations which made a measurable impact on everyday life. Those who looked out through the windows of the East India Company in Calcutta upon this sprawling sub-continent of self-governing villages were faced with an essentially practical, not theoretical, problem. How could 773 servants of the East India Company govern, in any meaningful sense of the word, an imperial outpost of 461,000 square miles?[1]

It was an aspiration which looked ludicrous when set against the sheer numbers of the Indians, their ancient and resistant religions, their immobile caste system, their ossified village traditions. To the British observer Indian life had remained unchanged for centuries, unaffected in most

---

[1]Figures compiled from the East India Register, 1825.

of its social forms by the succession of invasions and
empires. Previous conquerors, with limited exceptions such
as the Mahrattas in early 18th century Maharashtra, had
succeeded in imposing only a military presence upon the
countryside; their power to govern the domestic and
economic life of the ryot (cultivator) had proved vacuous.
For the new British authorities, therefore, their problems
increased by the strangeness of the country, it seemed
historically best advised to rule from barracks, to be
content with the establishment of peace and the conqueror's
exactions of money from the people. Yet the distinctive
ambition of the British was quite different. They aspired --
quixotically, it seemed -- to govern through a civil rather
than military administration, to raise taxes by district
officers rather than by soldiers. It looked, in the 1780's,
an impossible task to the detached observer. Yet remarkably
by 1825 Bengal, Bombay and Madras had been brought under
varying forms of effective civil government; and further
administrations were set up with the step by step conquest of
British India.

        There are several constitutional histories of this
process, treating the development of both national and local
government under British imperial rule. Some of them are

commendable; four, are excellent.[2] But their limitations

have long been clear. They are confined, for the most part,

to factual expositions of what happened, and cover, in several

instances, only limited periods. None, remarkably, offers any

detailed report or analysis of the debate (to use what at

some points of this story can only be called a polite term)

among British administrators over how to proceed, over the

merits of rival forms of government.

Into this gap this book tries to step. The story it

relates is one of surprising passion and fervor, surprisingly

neglected by the writers in the field. Indian historians can

perhaps be forgiven their uninterest in the internecine warfare

of British bureaucrats, but the failure to attend to competing

points of view is rather less explicable in the two major

works of Hugh Tinker and Cecil Cross.[3] One assumes that both

authors confronted an impossible problem of scale: the task

of simple exposition of the history of local and national

government in India is a monumental one, akin to writing the

---

[2] Reginald Coupland, The Indian Problem, 1833-1935,
London, 1943; Sir C.P. Ilbert, The Government of India,
Oxford, 1915; B.B. Misra, The Central Administration of the
East India Company, 1773-1834, Manchester, 1959; and its
companion volume, The Administrative History of India, 1834-
1947, Oxford, 1970.

[3] Hugh Tinker, The Foundations of Local Self-Government
in India, Pakistan and Burma, New York, 1968; Cecil Cross,
The Development of Local Self-Government in India, 1858-1914,
Chicago, 1922.

history of local government in Western Europe, and to add
to this a full explanation of competing viewpoints on how
best to proceed might have proved a Herculean labor one
likely to produce a book of impossible size.

Something must here be said of the important facts
which govern the debate. The common feature of British
administrations throughout India -- and the main reason for
their success -- was the recognition of a series of Indian
"home truths". These were that acceptance was only possible if
government was limited; that progress was possible only after
careful social preparation; and that laying waste in the manner
of 18th century military rulers was calculated to create nothing
except hostility. Effective civil government depended, it was
seen, upon building on existing foundations. In practice this
meant a succession of compromises between British despotism
above and self-ruling village communities below; it meant the
recognition of practical limits to imperial ambitions. It was in
fact the only option, it was perceived as such, and it worked.

From the first days of conquest (Bengal, 1765) these
realities were respected. Cautious British governors understood
they were reliant upon the traditional village governments
to keep the peace, to dispense justice, and to collect
taxes. They made attempts -- appalling in their ineptitude,
as will be described below -- to strengthen village institutions.
The only reforms they tried in these early years, such as

weeding out corrupt village leaders, were directed to this end.
There were no constitutional landmarks in this process, no
dates which define dramatic leaps forward. Between 1800 and
1840 what was happening in the three presidencies and two
provinces under British rule was the increased delegation of
work to village officials and the gradual incorporation of
self-ruling village institutions into the framework of the
British Raj. This meant, for example, the empowering of
village officials to collect British land taxes, to decide
small claims cases, to supervize policing, and to aid British
district officers in famine relief. It was the only way
these jobs could be done, given the limited capacities of the
East India Company; it also had the merit of making allies
rather than enemies of village leaders.

That this policy of devolution of power did not remain
a settled one gives rise to the controversy raised in the
title of this book, "how shall we govern India?". It was
a question posed in differing forms and with varying answers
throughout the century. As a problem it is examined below
in three separate periods, 1800-1840, 1840-1870, 1870-1882.
Something of the relevant historical background is briefly
given now.

From 1800 to 1840 the dominant policy for the government
of India (the Utilitarians dissenting) was to strengthen
Indian rule in the villages and to strengthen British rule

in Calcutta. But this policy was voided as a permanent
option when the traditional institutions of village self-
government collapsed almost everywhere. This unplanned
development occurred as British district officers, while
upholding the traditional forms, expected Indian village
leaders and councils to respect procedures more appropriate
to (say) the Mayor and Councillors of Stow-in-the-Wold in
performing their traditional responsibilities. The
consequences look obvious in retrospect but were not so at
the time. Indian village leaders were incapable of acting like
sturdy Cotswold farmers, and were increasingly bypassed by
district officers who preferred to deal directly with the
individual cultivators. Those few who did meet British
expectations were absorbed into the British way of doing
things. In either case village leaders lost their influence.
Their historical responsibilities were altered or diminished,
and their offices became hollow forms. On a separate front
village courts were bankrupted of importance by the British
appeal system. The outcome was the almost complete breakdown
of local self-government across India by 1840; and the problem
of how to govern India became, for the next thirty years, not
a choice between Britons or Indians but of devising an
effective administrative system ex nihilo.

This task stirred up -- in the normally placid waters
of constitutional history -- a quite remarkable degree of

passion, disagreement and bad blood. "The provincial
jealousies and rivalries of our civil service here are
lamentable," was the impression of Lord Lytton[4] within hours
of his arrival as Viceroy, in his first letter home in
1876.[5] British quarrels in this period were generated by
bitter disagreement over two key words: "centralization"
and "decentralization". On one side stood the victors of
1840-70, the advocates of tight control from Calcutta. Led
by the Governor-General, Lord Canning,[6] and his financial
advisor, James Wilson,[7] they believed that efficient
government depended on maintaining a clear line of command
from the Government of India to the districts; and they
attempted to dictate imperial policy to district officers
who were accustomed to deciding issues sitting alone under
a banyan tree. On the other side stood the victors of 1870
(and ever thereafter) who argued that the official closest

---

[4]Edward Robert Bulwer Lytton, 1st Earl (1831-1891);
Held diplomatic appointments by Washington, Florence, Belgrade,
Vienna, Copenhagen, Athens, Lisbon, Madrid and Paris;
Viceroy of India, 1876-1880.

[5]Lady Betty Balfour, ed., Personal and Literary Letters
of Robert, 1st Earl of Lytton, London, 1906, vol. II, p. 9,
(Lytton to Fitzjames Stephen, 14 April 1876).

[6]Charles John Canning, 1st Earl (1812-1862) MP 1836;
Viscount Canning of Kilbraham 1827; Under-Secretary of State
for Foreign Affairs 1841-1845; Postmaster-General 1853;
Governor-General of India 1855; Viceroy 1858-1861; Earl
Canning 1859.

[7]James Wilson (1805-1860) Influences of the Corn Laws,
1839; Fluctuations of Currency, 1840; The Revenue, 1841;
established the Economist, 1843; MP 1847-1859; Joint Secretary
of the Board of Control, 1848-1852; Financial Secretary to the
Treasury, 1853-1858; Vice-President of the Board of Trade and
Paymaster-General, 1859; first Finance Member of the Supreme
Council of India, 1859-1860.

to the people governed best. Led by the Governors of
Madras and Bombay, Trevelyan[8] and Frere,[9] this group --
chiefly men in the presidency and provincial capitals --
fought with determination in the 1860s to sabotage rule from
Calcutta, and fought with fervent backing from district
officers in the field. Their triumph was sealed in 1870 when
Mayo,[10] as Viceroy, handed back to the presidencies and provinces
a large measure of the powers seized by the central
bureaucracy over the previous half century.

It is possible, and tempting, to record the history of
this dispute as little more than a cheap ower struggle among
bureaucrats. But this was only a small part of the truth,
and not the important point. The practical problem of

---

[8]Charles Edward Trevelyan (1807-1886) entered East
India Company's Bengal Civil Service as a writer, 1826;
Assistant to Sir Charles Metcalfe, Commissioner at Delhi,
1827-1831; Deputy-Secretary to the Government of India in
the Political Department, 1831; Secretary to the Sudder
Board of Revenue, 1836-1838; 'On the Education of the People
of India', 1838; Assistant Secretary to the Treasury, 1840-
1859; administered the Irish famine relief works, 1845-1847;
KCB, 1848; 'The Organization of the Permanent Civil Service'
with Sir Stafford Northcote, 1853; Governor of Madras,
1859-1860; Finance Member of the Supreme Council of India,
1862-1865.

[9]Henry Bartle Edward Frere (1815-1884) entered the
Bombay Civil Service, 1834; Assistant to the Collector at
Poona, 1835; Private Secretary to Sir George Arthur,
Governor of Bombay, 1842; Political Resident at Sattara, 1845;
Commissioner of Sind, 1850; KCB, 1859; Member of the Council
of the Governor-General, 1859; Governor of Bombay, 1862-1865;
Member of the Council of India, 1867; Baronetcy, 1876;
Governor of the Cape, 1877-1880.

[10]Richard Southwell Bourke, Earl of Mayo (1822-1872)
Chief Secretary for Ireland, 1852-1866; Viceroy of India,
1869-1872.

governing a difficult and -- after the Mutiny of 1858-59 --
a rebellious country, was still foremost: the practical
possibility of effective British government, of actually
carrying on, was still in doubt. Questions of nearness or
remoteness "to the people" were not questions of idealized
political theory. They were questions about how government
was to be exercized if it were to be viable at all. Hence
the degree of passion and commitment in the answers raised
-- a commitment which without any doubt superseded the
personal animosity which arose. The tone of debate,
especially after 1860, was not so much of backbiting and
jealousy as of almost religious fervor, of moral rectitude,
of haranguing and sermon-preaching and self-righteousness
bred of the sincere feeling that the other side was misguided,
that the powers in Calcutta really did not know how to
govern Indians, that the district officers (as it appeared
from the capital) somehow believed that you could govern
India under 327 local law codes. Naturally the element
of recrimination crept in over district officers who failed
to fill in forms and obey Calcutta's orders. But this was
a symptom of the problem, not the problem itself. The
very future and continuance of British government in
India was at stake. No voices were raised demanding a
return home, but the fear of a further Mutiny, if mistakes
were made, lurked in every mind.

After 1870 "how shall we govern India?" reverted,
as before 1840, to a question of Indians versus Britons. The

controversy widened beyond the rival aspirations of central, presidency and provincial governments to the involvement of the Indians themselves. The people who responded to Indian pressure for greater participation included the same decentralizers, led by Trevelyan and Frere, who urged the cause of officialdom closer to the people in the 1860s: and they did so for many of the same reasons. The efficiency of British government in India was once again in question, threatened by the magnitude of the programs of moral and material improvement undertaken in the wake of the Mutiny. To some in the Indian Civil Service (ICS) it seemed that the mounting responsibilities of government could only be shouldered with the aid of Indians.

The practical efficiency of British government was no longer, however, the topic of fiercest debate. Battle lines were now drawn over Indian self-rule -- over the merits and demerits of power-sharing. In the 1870s a program of political education for the Indians raised passionate ideological support among Radicals and non-authoritarian Liberals, who viewed it as a first move towards ultimate democratic self-government. Their opponents, the majority of the ICS, responded with disgust and recrimination and with the warning the inexperienced Indians could only complicate the work of British officials and impede the implementation of imperial policies designed to improve Indian standards of living. They also clearly saw and disliked the long-term goals of political education --

democracy and independence from Britain -- and they took

considerable consolation from the prediction of their

leading spokesman, Sir Henry Maine,[11] that total self-rule

was at least a century away.[12] By 1882, when Lord Ripon[13]

instituted a limited measure of municipal self-government,

the question "how shall we govern India?" had become an

issue of nationalism rather than efficiency. A revolution

in opinion separated those who championed Indian self-rule

after 1870 from those who did so before 1840. This book

will explore that tremendous change of thought.

---

[11]Henry James Sumner Maine (1822-1888) Tutor at
Trinity Hall, 1845-1847; Regius Professor of Civil Law at
Cambridge, 1847-1854; Reader in Roman Law and Jurisprudence
at the Inns of Court, 1852; Law Member of the Supreme Council,
1862-1869; Corpus Professor of Jurisprudence, 1871-1878;
Member of the Council of India, 1871-1888; Whewell Professor
of International Law at Cambridge, 1887.

[12]Sir M.E. Grant Duff, Life and Speeches of Sir Henry
Maine, London, 1892, "Speech on Indian Municipalities",
p. 266.

[13]George Frederick Samuel, 1st Marquis of Ripon
(1827-1909) MP 1852-1859; Under-Secretary of State for War,
1859-1861; for India, 1861-1863; Secretary of State for War,
1863-1866; for India, 1866; Lord President of the Council,
1868-1873; Viceroy of India, 1880-1884.

CHAPTER ONE

CULTURAL ASSUMPTIONS UNDERLYING THE DEBATE ON INDIAN
GOVERNMENT

Before examining in detail British theories about Indian
government, it would be helpful to examine the racial and
cultural assumptions which underlay these theories. Among the
numerous writers on Indian topics between 1780 and 1880,
three can be singled out as advancing original, comprehensive
and vastly influential surveys of Indian society: Sir
William Jones, a Judge of the Supreme Court at Culcutta
(1783-1794), a distinguished Indologist, translator of
religious, legal and literary works in Persian, Sanskrit
and Arabic and author of important books and articles on
the history, language and literature of ancient India;
James Mill, Assistant Examiner of the East India Company in
London (1819-1829). Examiner (1830-1836) and author of
The History of British India, the most important historical
survey of Indian civilization written in English in our
period; and Charles Grant, a high-ranking official of the
East India Company in India (1767-1790), a Director of the
Company (1793-1823), Chairman (1805, 1809 and 1815), Member
of Parliament (1802-1818) and the author of Observations
on the State of Society among the Asiatic Subjects of Great
Britain, particularly with respect to Morals and on the
Means of Improving It (sic), a Christian indictment of
Indian society. Each of these three men founded a 'school'

of thought on Indian history. Jones presided over a
clique of Indophiles known as Orientalists; Mill, as
Jeremy Bentham's closest disciple, directed the smaller but
equally important band of Utilitarians; and Grant, as a
zealous Evangelical, led a vast army of Christian soldiers
in Britain and India. Every young man recruited to Indian
service in the nineteenth century was required to read the
scholarly works of Jones and Mill at Haileybury College in
Hertfordshire, the staff-training center for the East India
Company and subsequently for the Crown. None was obliged
to read Grant's polemic, but given its publicity and
widespread dissemination in Evangelical organizations
throughout Great Britain, it would have been difficult -- if
not impossible -- for anyone interested in India to be
ignorant of its message.

In the closing decades of the eighteenth century
William Jones introduced Europeans to Sanskritic literature
and Indian history. Ever since Queen Elizabeth had
chartered the East India Company in 1600, Englishmen
visiting India had written travelogues and diaries, some
of which had been published in limited editions. But Jones
was the first to translate religious, literary and legal
books from Persian and Sanskrit into English and make them
widely available to readers on the Continent, as well as in
Britain. Further, he was the first to examine the "cloud
of fables" (his words) which astrologers had compiled to
explain India's past, and the first to postulate a proper

chronology of Indian history.[1] Quite rightly, he has been
called the 'father of Indology' and credited with interesting
Europeans in Indian culture.

Jones was an Oriental scholar of distinction before he
ever reached India. This was important, because it ensured
an eager and receptive audience for his subsequent discoveries
about India. While a schoolboy at Harrow in the 1750s he
taught himself Arabic script, and, equally remarkably, while
at Oxford in the 60s he housed an Arab at his own expense in
return for lessons in Arabic.[2] At Oxford he learned Persian,
and in 1792 he wrote a Persian grammar, which earned him
election to the Royal Society.[3] In quick succession he
completed A Short History of Persia, A History of the Turks
and A History of the Life of Nader Shah, all winning him an
international reputation.[4] In 1794 he was called to the Bar,

---

[1] Jones, William, "The Third Discourse, Delivered
2 February 1786 by the President, Asiatic Society of Bengal",
Asiatick Researches, London, 1801, vol. I, p. 421.

[2] Mukherjee, Soumyendra Nath, Sir William Jones: A Study
in Eighteenth Century British Attitudes to India, Cambridge,
1968, pp. 20-22.

[3] Ibid., p. 31.

[4] Ibid., p. 39.

and in 1780 he took up the post of Supreme Judge in Calcutta
to facilitate acquiring and studying Indian materials and --
like most of his contemporaries -- to make his fortune by
living simply and remitting most of his substantial salary
home for investment.[5]

Following Voltaire, whose hypotheses about the Chinese
had sparked off European curiosity about Asia a half century
earlier, Jones admired Oriental civilization and set about
discovering links between it and the Occident. Within a few
months of arriving in Calcutta he began to trace cognates and
structural parallels between Sanskrit, Greek and Latin.
"The Sanskrit language", he postulated,

> whatever be its antiquity, is of a wonderful structure;
> more perfect than the Greek, more copious than the
> Latin, and more exquisitely refined than either; yet
> bearing to both of them a stronger affinity, both in
> the roots of verbs, and in the forms of grammar, than
> could possibly have been produced by accident; so
> strong, indeed, that no philologer could examine them
> all three without believing them to have sprung from
> some common source, which, perhaps, no longer exists.[6]

Further, he conjectured "that Phythagoras and Plato derived
their sublime theories from the same fountain with the sages
of India".[7] Neither the hypothesis of a common Indo-European
language, nor of a common culture, was original to Jones. He
was, however, the first eminent scholar to take up these ideas

---

[5]Ibid., p. 35.

[6]Jones, op. cit. p. 423.

[7]Ibid., p. 425.

and prove them to the satisfaction of contemporaries and
later generations (including Goethe, Herder, Schlegel,
Michelet and Hugo).[8] Culling evidence from treatises on
law, music, philosophy, religion and science as well as
from art and architecture, he correlated his findings with
Greek, Roman and Persian remains and arranged them according
to Ussher's dating of the Old Testament chronology.[9] Through
this feat of comparative history he linked India's past to
that of the ancient Near East and Europe. Though a Deist,
Jones accepted the Biblical assertion that all men spoke
one language until the Flood, after which Noah's children
scattered throughout the world and the original mother tongue
of mankind was forever lost. He speculated that after the
Flood Noah settled in Iran, and his descendants there spoke
a derivative of the original language, which eventually
became Persian. Two of his sons migrated to the West,
while his third son, Ham, settled in India and spoke another
derivative of the world's first language, which became
Sanskrit.[10] Ham's descendants, in Jones' opinion, never
reached "the transcendently majestick"[11] heights of civilization

---

[8]Marshall, Peter J., The British Discovery of Hinduism
in the Eighteenth Century, Cambridge, 1970, p. 16.

[9]Mukherjee, op. cit., p. 98.

[10]Ibid., p. 99.

[11]Jones, William, "The Second Anniversary Discourse,
Delivered 24 February 1785 by the President, Asiatic Society
of Bengal", Asiatick Researches, loc. cit., p. 406

achieved by his brothers' progeny in Europe, yet they
nonetheless produced epics "magnificent and sublime in the
highest degree"[12] and made music "on truer principles than
our own".[13] Jones' translations of plays like <u>Sacontala</u>,
or the Fatal Ring as well as law codes like The Institutes
of Hindu Law, or, The Ordinances of Menu, substantiated
these and similar claims for the previously unrecognized
achievements of the ancient Indians and stimulated further
research in Europe and India.[14]

Such research was of more than academic interest: it
was of inestimable use to the East India Company. Ever since
the Company had begun accruing political power on the
subcontinent in 1765, the need to understand the customs and
institutions of the country had become increasingly acute.
To encourage Company servants to undertake studies which would
aid the Company in governing this strange and regionally-
diverse land, Jones founded the Asiatick Society of Bengal
in Calcutta in 1784. In the course of the next decade its
membership grew to over one hundred, and its publications
stretched to five volumes of <u>Asiatick</u> <u>Researches</u>, including
one which was pirated and avidly read in Europe.[15] Three

---

[12]Jones, "The Third Discourse", <u>loc</u>. <u>cit</u>., p. 429.

[13]Jones, "The Second Anniversary Discourse", <u>loc</u>. <u>cit</u>., p. 410

[14]Marshall, <u>op</u>. <u>cit</u>., p. 16.

[15]Kopf, David, <u>British</u> <u>Orientalism</u> <u>and</u> <u>the</u> <u>Bengal</u>
<u>Renaissance</u>, Berkeley and Los Angeles, 1969, p. 34.

Governors-General -- Hastings, Cornwallis and Shore --
actively promoted the Society,[16] and some of the Company's
most distinguished servants submitted articles to Asiatick
Researches, including Charles Wilkins (who was knighted for
his translation of the Bhagavat Gita and other contributions
to Indology),[17] Jonathan Duncan (Governor of Bombay, 1795-1811),
who wrote on Bengali and Persian literature)[18] and most
notably, H.T. Colebrook (a Supreme Court Judge and then
Professor of Sanskrit at the College of Fort William, who
studied the Vedas).[19]   Jones, as President of the Society,
delivered an annual 'Discourse' in the manner of
Sir Joshua Reynolds at the Royal Academy of Art, explaining
his own work and co-ordinating the findings of members for
easy reference by Company servants.

The aim of Jones and his fellow Orientalists in the
1780s and 90s was to teach the British how to step into the
Mughul's footsteps and rule India in the traditional manner.
Perceiving themselves as belonging to the most recent of a
long line of foreign dynasties, they aspired to keep the
peace, collect taxes and make as reasonable a profit as
possible for themselves. They reckoned to rule through
existing institutions and leave Indian society in tact.
Their attitude was best displayed by Jones' good friend,
Warren Hasting, Governor of Bengal in 1772 and Governor-

---

[16] Marshall, op. cit., p. 124.

[17] Kopf, op. cit., p. 27.

[18] Ibid., p. 30.

[19] Ibid., p. 39.

General from 1772 to 1785, who aspired "to adapt our
Regulations to the Manners and Understanding of the People,
and Exigencies of the Country, adhering, as closely as we
are able, to their Ancient Usages and Institutions".[20]
Hastings saw that the key to operating indigenous political
and judicial bodies was mastering Indian languages. To this
end he became proficient in Persian and competent in Urdu
and the Bengali dialects;[21] he also founded the Calcutta
Madrassa, a center for Arabic and Persian studies,[22] supported
the Asiatick Society, patronized Indian pundits translating
Sanskritic documents into the vernacular languages, and
befriended British Indologists, who -- like Jones -- dedicated
works to him in gratitude for his encouragement.[23]

Fundamental to Hastings' and Jones' Orientalist ethos
was both racial and cultural tolerance. Its sources were
threefold: their humility in response to an ancient, and as
yet still largely uncomprehended, civilization; their limited
ambitions for British rule; and their experience of permissive
Georgian society, where calls for political reform, religious
revival and moral probity were as yet barely audible and

---

[20]Hastings to the Court of Directors, 3 November 1772,
quoted by G.W. Forrest, Selections from the State Papers of
the Governors-General of India: Warren Hastings, Oxford, 1910,
vol. II, p. 277.

[21]Kopf, op. cit., p. 21.

[22]Marshall, op. cit., p. 13.

[23]Mukherjee, op. cit., p. 79.

rarely heeded. This same lack of prejudice enabled Company
servants of the 70s, 80s and 90s to parade shamelessly behind
standards portraying Hindu gods and goddesses and to open
Company offices on Sundays yet close them for Hindu and
Muslim festivals, displaying an indifference to British morés
which later generations would find totally unacceptable.[24]

Tolerance also led the Orientalists to regard such
practices as infanticide, suttee (the burning of widows on
their husbands' funeral pyres), thuggee (ritual murder) and
the caste system as lamentable but acceptable -- at least
for the time being. Reforming Indian society by eliminating
these customs was not outside their vision of the future,
but they conceived it as a task for the Indians. Jones
and his colleagues saw their role as purely advisory: by
delineating the contours of ancient India, they would provide
a model for Indian reformers to emulate. Jones conjectured
that once upon a time -- sometime after Ham and his
descendants reached the subcontinent -- India has enjoyed
a civilization markedly similar in all essential features
to contemporary societies around the Mediterranean. "How
degenerate and absurd soever the Hindus may now appear", he
stated, "... in some early age they were splendid in arts
and arms, happy in government, wise in legislation, and
eminent in various knowledge..."[25] Jones' colleague,

---

[24]Forbes, Duncan, "James Mill and India", _Cambridge Journal_, vol. V (1951), p. 22.

[25]Jones, "Third Discourse", _loc. cit._, p. 421.

Colebrook, fixed this golden age at the second millenium B.C.,
when the Vedas revealed that the Indians were hearty meat-
eaters, unsuperstitious monotheists and dedicated
egalitarians. To his understanding of history, idolotry,
vegetarianism, caste and disregard for human life were all
latter-day accretions, ones which the Indians could eliminate
over time without damaging the fundamental characteristics
in their society.[26] Orientalist hopes that the Indians would
launch their own Vedic reform movement were not ill-founded,
for the Brahmo Samaj, the Prarthana Samaj and the Arya Samaj
were all established in the first half of the nineteenth
century to purify Indian society according to Vedic
prescriptions; and all were relatively successful.

The Orientalist posture of cultural relativity did not
go unchallenged. The first prominent official to undermine
it was Earl Cornwallis, appointed Governor-General in 1786
to stop Company servants from 'shaking the pagoda tree'.
Scandals like the Resident of Benares receiving a salary of
Rs. 12,000 a year and illegally augmenting it by another
Rs. 400,000 not only robbed unwitting peasants and bankrupted
princes: they also deprived the Company of legitimate
revenue and brought it into disrepute in Parliament and the
City of London.[27] Cornwallis' remedy was to reverse
Hastings' policy of ruling through Indian intermediaries:

---

[26]Kopf, op. cit., p. 41.

[27]Thompson, Edward and Garratt, G.T., Rise and Fulfilment
of British Rule in India, Allahabad, 1966, p. 172.

to reorganize the entire administrative and judicial
structure by reserving all senior positions for Europeans,
paying them generous salaries, forbidding them to accept
gratuities of any sort and requiring anyone suspected of
graft to submit, under oath, an inventory of all his property
before leaving India.[28] He excluded Indians not so much
because they were morally lax as because they could not be
controlled so easily as their equally venal European
colleagues; and to his mind, rigid control was essential if
corruption and misgovernment were to be halted.[29] Anglicization
seems both revolutionary and racist in retrospect, but
Cornwallis intended it to be neither. As a Whig, he aimed at
stopping the breakdown of Indian society under the pressue of
greedy and unscrupulous Europeans. And as an Orientalist, he
employed Sir William Jones to compile Hindu and Muslim laws
into a code which European judges could use to uphold
traditional values and institutions.

If Cornwallis pursued conservative ends by revolutionary
means, his friend, Charles Grant, possessed a thorough radical
disposition towards India. He not only believed that
Orientalism was both wrong and evil: he convinced Parliament

---

[28]Ibid., p. 174.

[29]Stokes, Eric, The English Utilitarians and India,
Oxford, 1959, p. 26.

that his charges were valid. The inspiration for his
crusade against Orientalism was Christianity. In 1776
he experienced a dramatic and highly emotional conversion,
and overnight his tolerance of Indian social and religious
customs gave way to a fanatical desire to convert the
Indians to Christianity.[30] He envisaged this mission as
far more than a religious exercise: it was to be a moral,
intellectual and social revolution as well. In 1784 he
began A Proposal for Establishing a Protestant Mission in
Bengal and Bihar with the startling assertion that reforming
the administration would do no good unless common values
united the rulers and the ruled; for so long as there was
"a universal want of those qualities that cement society --
of integrity, truth and faithfulness", the people could
neither participate in government nor even benefit from
good laws.[31] The only mechanisms for creating the essential
common bond were the Christian Gospel, Western thought and
Western technology. And the best agents for launching this
monumental undertaking were Christian missionaries, whom
Grant demanded the Company admit to India for the first time
and support financially.[32] Cornwallis was too much a Whig
and Orientalist to endorse such a scheme, and the Court of

---

[30]Embree, Ainslie, Charles Grant and British Rule in
India, New York, 1962, p. 54.

[31]The Proposal, itself, has never been found; but it
was quoted extensively by Grant in a letter to
William Wilberforce, 17 September 1787. See Morris, Henry,
The Life of Charles Grant, London, 1904, p. 112.

[32]Ibid., p. 113.

Directors were too wary of jeopardizing their investment
to allow British missionaries to upset Indian sensibilities.[33]

Undeterred by his failure to win the Company's
approval for his Proposal, Grant wrote an even more
impassioned plea in 1797, Observations on the State of
Society among the Asiatic Subjects of Great Britain,
particularly with respect to Morals and on the Means of
Improving it. This pamphlet was pivotal in changing British
attitudes to India in three ways: first, by portraying the
Indians as depraved victims of Brahminical tyranny rather
than as heirs to a once great, if now fallen, civilization;
second, by advancing the policy of assimilation -- of making
Indians into 'black Englishmen', as Macaulay was to put it
thirty years later -- to replace the policy of preserving
indigenous institutions; and third, by persuading Parliament
to accept this analysis of the Indians and support Christian
missions.

At the heart of Grant's case lay his condemnation of
the East India Company's Orientalist policy of shielding
Indian society from change. He argued forthrightly that
this laissez-faire stance led the Company Directors to
shirk their responsibility as Christian gentlemen to seek
"the general welfare of the many millions under /the Company's/

---

[33]Embree, op.cit., p. 119.

government".[34]   Grant believed that Britain's conquest of
India was providential: that God meant Britain to benefit
materially from the association and the Indians to reap
moral as well as material rewards. Adding self-interest to
religious obligation, he repeated the Proposal's assertion
that British government would never be effective until
common values united the British and the Indians.[35] The
elevation of the Indians to Christian standards of morality
was thus a matter of practical administration as much as a
God-given duty.

To prove his case Grant demonstrated the appalling
rift between Indian and British social values. "The Hindus
are a people exceedingly depraved" and "they exhibit human
nature in a very degraded humiliating state",[36] he boldly
asserted: "they want truth, honesty, and good faith in
extreme, of which European society offers no example".[37]

---

[34]Grant, Charles, Observations on the State of Society
among the Asiatic Subjects of Great Britain, particularly
with respect to Morals; and on the Means of Improving It.
Parliamentary Papers, 1812-1813, vol. X, paper 282, p. 1.

[35]Ibid., p. 89.

[36]Ibid., p. 25.

[37]Ibid., p. 26.

The hallmark of their depravity was "selfishness...
unrestrained by principle, operat/ing/ universally".[38]
"Money, the grand instrument of selfish gratification" was
their "supreme idol";[39] robberies were "exceedingly
common";[40] and families were hopelessly divided by
individuals pursuing their own selfish ambitions -- men
exhibiting "the insensibility of brutes",[41] women, "held
in slavish subjection by men, ris/ing/ in furious passion
against each other"[42] and parents even selling their
children for money.[43] Grant carefully documented each of
these allegations with long quotations from travelogues
and Company records to confirm the wretchedness of the
Indians and shock his readers to support his proposals.

Though sunk in misery, the Indians could be saved
according to Grant, for the cause of their depravity was
social rather than racial. Hinduism was "a despotism, the
most remarkable for its power and duration that the world

---

[38]Ibid., p. 47.

[39]Ibid.

[40]Ibid., p. 28.

[41]Ibid., p. 53.

[42]Ibid., p. 28.

[43]Ibid., p. 29.

has ever seen."[44] It

> has undoubtedly had a very considerable influence
> on the formation of their character. When a man
> finds himself dependent on the will and caprice of
> another, he thinks and acts as a degraded being...
> Fear necessarily becomes his great princple of action...
> The arts of deception, suppleness, and servility are
> resorted to, and thus a system of falsehood and
> narrow selfishness is generated.

Through the caste system Brahmin priests subjected the Hindus
to "perpetual abasement and unlimited subjection".[45] Worse
yet, they exercised a tyranny over the Hindu mind, keeping it
ignorant through superstition and destroying all possibility
of virtue by depriving the individual of freedom of choice
and action.[46] Grant's solution was to expose the Hindus to
the error of their socio-religious system, "for the Hindoos
err because they are ignorant; and their errors have never
fairly been laid before them".[47] He confidently predicted
that once they had appreciated the cause of their plight,
they would exercise free choice, abandon caste and idolotry
and accept the Christian Gospel, and through it go on to
assimilate the entire Western approach to life. Missionaries
bringing the Bible in English, an English library and
British technology would create the identity of religious,

---

[44] Ibid., p. 40.

[45] Ibid., p. 44.

[46] Ibid., p. 40.

[47] Ibid., p. 76.

moral and social values which was the prerequisite to
efficient British rule.[48] Furthermore, they would bring
profit to the East India Company, for "wherever our
principles and our language are introduced," he confidently
concluded, "our commerce will follow".[49]

   To publicize the Observation and gain parliamentary
support for Christian missions to India, Grant enlisted
the invaluable aid of his Evangelical friends of the
Clapham Sect. Having persuaded the group's leader,
William Wilberforce, to sponsor the measure in the House of
Commons, he encouraged the Church Missionary Society
(chaired by Grant, himself) and the Bible Society (chaired
by Lord Teignmouth, who, as Sir John Shore, had succeeded
Cornwallis as Governor-General of India) to flood Parliament
with petitions. Through the remarkable network of branch
associations as well as ladies', juvenile and penny
associations of these two societies in every county in
Great Britain, 1500 petitions were delivered to Parliament.[50]
In response Parliament inserted the so-called 'Pious Clause'
into the East India Company Charter when it was renewed
in 1813, requiring the Company to permit missionaries into
India, establishing an Anglican bishopric and providing
£10,000 a year from public funds for education.

---

[48]Ibid., pp. 75-80.

[49]Ibid., p. 111.

[50]Embree, op. cit., p. 272.

Grant's Observation was one of the most successful
pieces of propaganda ever written in England. Privately
printed by Wilberforce in 1797, it was circulated not
only to the Directors of the East India Company and MPs,
but also to members of the Bible and Church Mission
Societies and the Society for the Propagation of Christian
Knowledge.[51] Before the Charter renewal debates of 1813
its message was conveyed in sermons, pamphlets and The
Missionary Register, a newspaper devoted to impressing the
British public with the depravity of the Indians and their
need for Christianity and Western enlightenment.[52] In
1813 and in 1832, when the Company's Charter was again
reviewed by Parliament, the Observation was printed as a
Parliamentary paper. Although it is impossible to quantify
how many copies were printed in entirety or excerpted,
circulated and read in the early decades of the nineteenth
century, it is possible to assume that a large portion of
the literate British public became acquainted with its
content. On one day alone in 1813 twelve hundred people
attended the annual general meeting of the St. Pancras
Branch of the Bible Society to discuss Grant's proposals
-- an impressive but not uniquely high turn-out for an

---

[51] Ibid.

[52] Ibid.

important Evangelical meeting of the period.[53] By the
1820s there were thousands of branches of the Bible and
Church Missionary Societies in Great Britain, distributing
Bibles to India, sponsoring missionaries and accepting
Grant's diagnosis of Indian society as axiomatic.[54]

If Grant turned British admiration for Indian society
into contempt, James Mill assembled a weighty body of
information in support of the new point of view. Between
1806 and 1817 he wrote his History of British India for the
same reason Jones and Grant had pursued their investigations:
to ascertain how Indian society functioned as a preliminary
to advising the British authorities on the best means of
governing it. Although he endorsed Grant's assessment of
the Indians as benighted and in need of Western enlightenment,
he dismissed Christianity as inimical to this program. As
a rationalist and scholar, he addressed his arguments to
Jones rather than to Grant, the religious polemicist.
Criticizing Jones for being "crude" in his approach to
Indian history,[55] he denigrated his hypothesis about Indians
of an earlier age as "far surpass/ing/ the rhapsodies of

---

[53]Brown, Ford K., Fathers of the Victorians: The Age
of Wilberforce, Cambridge, 1961, p. 249.

[54]Ibid., p. 318.

[55]Mill, James, The History of British India, London, 1840,
vol. II, p. 156.

Rousseau on the happiness and virtue of savage life".[56]
To his mind Jones' basic error was to use the word
'civilization' without bothering to ascertain what it meant.[57]

For Mill, equipped with Bentham's Principle of
Utility, the term 'civilization' meant a society which
realized the greatest happiness of the greatest number. He
labelled the society in which the few enjoyed pleasure at
the expense of the many as barbarous and the one in which
every citizen was capable of discovering and pursuing his
own self-interest, and thereby realizing happiness, as
civilized. According to his calculations Britain was the
apogee of civilization and India the nadir. Despite the
fact that the unreformed House of Commons was still far too
aristocratic to his taste, and despite his and Bentham's
long-standing campaign to enshrine the Principle of
Utility more clearly in British statute law, Mill nonetheless
believed that the greatest happiness of the greatest number
was achieved more successfully in Britain than anywhere
else in the world. India, in contrast, was "barbarous
and semi-civilized"[58] "Despotism" on the one hand and
"priestcraft" on the other had made the "Hindus, in mind

---

[56] Ibid., p. 157.

[57] Ibid., p. 156.

[58] Mill, James, "Affairs in India", Edinburgh Review,
vol. XVI, (1810), p. 147.

and body,... the most enslaved portion of the human race".[59]
Domination by a rigid and tyrannical political and
religious elite over centuries had reduced them to a
hideous state of degradation never experienced by Europeans,
even in the darkest years of the feudal period.[60] Deprived
of political and economic power as well as social mobility,
the overwhelming majority was uninspired to work; and as
a consequence of this crippling lack of motivation, they
were poor, apathetic, listless, servile, and even more
ignobly, superstitious and cruel as well.

Mill's solution for this degraded condition was British
rule. As early as 1810 he boldly asserted in the Edinburgh
Review that "English government in India, with all its vices,
is a blessing of unspeakable magnitude... We wish its
prolongation for the sake of the natives, not of England".[61]
Neither he nor his son, John Stuart Mill, who entered the
service of the East India Company in 1823 and remained there
until the Company's abolition in 1858, ever changed his
mind. In the first instance James Mill demanded that the

[59]Mill, History, loc. cit., vol. II, p. 187.

[60]Ibid., II, pp. 210-211.

[61]Mill, James, "'Voyages aux Indes Orientales' by
Barthelemy", Edinburgh Review, vol. XV, (1810), pp. 371-372.

British provide India with an administration proficient at
realizing the greatest happiness of the greatest number as
swiftly and efficiently as possible. Because the Indians
were too enslaved in mind and body to calculate their own
happiness, British administrators would have to remain in
sole control of the country until the Indians had been
educated to assess their own self-interest rationally, and
could therefore be entrusted to discover their own happiness.
Next, Mill required the British to equip India with a law
code designed to free the individual from the fetters of
priest and caste -- two major sources of unhappiness for the
many -- and courts competent to dispense these laws cheaply
and impartially. Third, he instructed the British to
design a land revenue system instituting private property;
for only the enjoyment of private property would vanquish
sloth and with it poverty, to Mill's understanding the root
cause of the Indians' moral vices. (See Chapter II for an
analysis of Mill's land revenue policy.) Surprisingly,
Mill did not advise the British to launch a national
education program immediately. This was because he believed
ignorance sprang from poverty, and that before education
could be effective, poverty would have to be eliminated
through good laws, sound administration and private property.[62]

The History of British India was as polemical in its
espousal of Utilitarianism as Grant's Observations were of

---

[62]Stokes, op. cit., pp. 56-58.

Christianity. In the memorable words of one modern
historian, it was "alive with the sound of grinding axes".[63]
H.H. Wilson, a leading Orientalist, sought to arm the
reader against Mill's 'prejudices' by supplying a lengthy
preface and footnotes in 1840 to the fourth edition of
the History.[64] Besides accusing Mill of being a blatant
panegyrist of Bentham,[65] Wilson charged him with arrogantly
refusing to consult Indian documents and relying
exclusively on European ones. This limitation of sources
ensured a one-sided view, and a hostile one at that; for
Mill used missionary accounts extensively, and these were
hardly impartial. "The missionaries", Wilson despaired,
"are so on the watch for vice that they often discover it
where it does not exist...."[66] In exasperation with the
enormity of Mill's prejudices and the deficiency of his
evidence, Wilson savaged Mill's entire chapter on the Hindu

------

[63]Burrow, J.W., Evolution and Society, Cambridge,
1966, p. 43.

[64]Wilson, H.H. 'Preface' to James Mill's The History
of British India, loc. cit., vol. I, pp. vii-ix.

[65]Ibid., p. vi.

[66]Ibid., vol. I, p. 464.

religion in his final footnote:

> The whole of this review of the religion, as of the
> laws of the Hindus, is full of very serious defects,
> arising from inveterate prejudices and imperfect
> knowledge. Every text, every circumstance, that
> makes against the Hindu character, is most assiduously
> cited, and everything in its favour as carefully kept
> out of sight, whilst a total neglect is displayed
> of the History of Hindu belief. The doctrines of
> various periods and of opposing sects, have been forced
> into one time and one system, and the whole charged
> with an incongruity, which is the creation of the
> writer. Had he been more impartially disposed, indeed,
> it would not have been easy to have given an
> unobjectionable account of the Hindu religion, as his
> materials were exceedingly defective. Manu is a good
> authority for the time to which it refers, and
> Mr. Colebrooke's essays furnish authentic details
> of particular parts of the ritual, but the different
> travellers who are given as authorities of equal
> weight, are utterly unworthy of regard.[67]

Wilson's defence of Indian culture was as passionate in tone
as Mill's denunciation, but it rested on familiar criticism.
In the 1820s T.B. Macaulay accused Mill of deducing his
conclusions from Utilitarian principles rather than inducing
them from the broadest possible array of evidence;[68] and ever
since then, philosophers and historians have been repeating
the charge and proving its validity.[69] Equally significantly,
it must be pointed out that Mill paid far less attention to
the particular circumstances of society than his mentor,
Bentham, let alone Macaulay. Whereas Bentham recognized the

---

[67]Ibid., vol. I, pp. 436-437.

[68]Clive, John, Macaulay; The Shaping of the Historian,
New York, 1973, p. 130.

[69]See Eli Halevy, The Growth of Philosophic Radicalism,
London, 1928, p. 271.

necessity of discovering local customs and tailoring
Utilitarian practices to the specific social, economic and
intellectual conditions of a given society at a given time,[70]
Mill dispensed with this tedious exercise by devising a
convenient short-cut -- his 'scale of civilization'.
Designed according to British specifications, this universal
measuring rod was used to assess the degree of civilization
any society had reached in relation to Britain: religion
was judged according to the tenets of Deism and Newtonian
physics; law was rated according to Utilitarian standards
of completeness and exactness; and social behaviour was
gauged according to the status of women.[71] Employing these
criteria to fix India on the scale of civilization, Mill
proved that India was 'uncivilized'.

Bentham and Mill had few totally committed and
thoroughly knowledgeable followers in the Indian
administration, not because the tenets of Utilitarianism
were unattractive, but rather because the philosophy of mind
underlying it was unintelligible to the practically-minded
officials of the East India Company (as to those of the
Indian Civil Service after the Company's abolition in 1858).

---

[70]Bentham, Jeremy, "Essay on the Influence of Time and
Place in matters of Legislation" in The Works of Jeremy Bentham,
ed. by Sir John Bowring, Oxford, 1910, vol. I, pp. 169-194.

[71]Forbes, op. cit., p. 29.

Most notable among the cognoscenti who understood
Utilitarian principles and tried to put them into practice
in a comprehensive fashion were: in London, James Mill,
his son, John Stuart, and his fellow Examiner in the
1820s, Edward Strachey; and in India, Holt Mackenzie,
India's leading revenue expert from 1819 to 1831, and
H.E. Goldsmid and Sir George Wingate, architects of Bombay's
revenue scheme (see Ch. II for the Utilitarian experiments
of all three). The most famous official who respected
Mill, understood Utilitarian philosophy and instituted some
of Mill's legal aspirations for India was T.B. Macaulay.
"The History of India", he judged, "though not free from
faults, is, I think, on the whole, the greatest historical
work which has appeared in our language since that of
Gibbon"[72] -- praise, indeed, from England's most popular
historian of the nineteenth century. Ironically, Mill and
Macaulay were old enemies, having waged war in the
Westminster and Edinburgh Review, respectively, over Mill's
allegedly deductive methods of writing history. Nevertheless,
in 1833 Mill recommended Macaulay for the new post of
Legal Member of the Governor-General's Council, because
his old adversary was well-versed in philosophy and
government.[73] It would overstate Mill's influence on
Macaulay to describe Macaulay's Minute on Education (which

---

[72]Quoted by John Clive, op. cit., p. 310.

[73]Ibid., p. 311.

substituted English for Persian as the medium of higher
education) as "James Mill's philosophy expressed in
Macaulayese";[74] for Mill did not share the Evangelical
Macaulay's optimism about elevating the Indians through
education.[75] Yet as Legal Member he imposed English legal
principles -- approved by the Utilitarians -- on
Sir William Jones' codes of Hindu and Muslim law and
transformed them into vehicles for lifting the Indians up
Mill's scale of civilization.

Many men in the East India Company and Indian Civil
Service failed to grasp the underlying premises of
Utilitarianism but nonetheless read Mill's History,
accepted his analysis of Indian society and supported his
general policies for moral and material regeneration. The
most influential of these camp followers was
Lord William Bentinck, who flattered Mill, in person,
before leaving London in 1829 with the testimony: "I am
going to British India, but I shall not be Governor-General.
It is you who will be Governor-General".[76] Bentinck
possessed neither the mind nor the temperament of a
philosophic radical, but he admired Mill and pleased both

---

[74]Forbes, op. cit., p. 23.

[75]Stokes, op. cit., p. 55.

[76]Quoted by John Rosselli, Lord William Bentinck: The
Making of a Liberal Imperialist, 1774-1839, London, 1974, p. 84.

Mill and Bentham by ordering the abolition of suttee and
thuggee and the institution of English language education.
The corps of Mill's camp followers learned Utilitarian
principles from William Empson, Professor of Political
Economy at Haileybury from the 1820s through the 1840s,
and employed the Principle of Utility as the credal
statement of the new ethos of reform instituted by Bentinck
and Macaulay.[77] With the defeat of the Marathas -- the
last powerful Indian challengers to British rule -- in
1818, Company officials consolidated the territories of
British India and attained a security of hegemony unknown
since the rule of Aurangzeb, the Mughul emperor, in the
seventeenth century. With possession and peace came the
opportunity to tackle the causes of India's degradation
by making the fundamental changes in Indian society
prescribed by Mill. "The greatest happiness of the greatest
number" animated the new generation of men in the 20s and
30s who rejected Orientalism and set about the laborious
task of remaking India in the image of Britain.

As early as 1800 the Orientalists recognized that
their campaign to elevate Indian society in the eyes of
Western observers and preserve it from Westernization was
doomed to failure. Warren Hastings, having watched Grant's

------

[77]Stokes, op. cit., p. 52.

propaganda campaign win widespread popular support as well
as parliamentary endorsement, moaned to Lord Hastings
(Governor-General, 1813-1823): "our Indian subjects having
been represented as sunk in grossest brutality... it is
therefore said that as we possess the power, so it is our
duty to reform them, nay, to 'coerce' them into goodness
by introducing our faith among them".[78] The Orientalist,
H.H. Wilson, blamed Mill rather than Grant for the defeat
of the magnanimous, respectful stance towards Indian society
displayed by Warren Hastings and the earliest British
administrators. He condemned Mill's History as a book whose

> tendency is evil: it is calculated to destroy all
> sympathy between the rulers and the ruled; to
> preoccupy the minds of those who issue annually from
> Great Britain, to monopolise the posts of honour and
> power in Hindustan, with an unfounded aversion
> towards those over whom they exercise that power...
> There is reason to fear... that the harsh and
> illiberal spirit /which/ has of late years prevailed
> in the conduct and councils of the rising service in
> India... owes its origin to impressions imbibed in
> early life from the History of Mr. Mill.[79]

In 1882 Max Müller (the eminent Indologist who became Professor
of Comparative Philology at Oxford in 1868, discovered links
between the Celtic and Indian language and played the same
role as Sir William Jones a century earlier in interesting

---

[78]Moon, Penderel, Warren Hastings and British India,
London, 1947, p. 349.

[79]Wilson's 'Preface' to Mill's History, loc. cit.,
pp. viii-ix.

Europeans in Indian studies) lamented that recruits to the
Indian Civil Service believed that Indians were "not amenable
to the recognized principles of self-respect, uprightness,
veracity..., never restrained in their dealings by any
regard for the truth, never to be trusted on their word".[80]
Most of the civil servants studied in this book were
jaundiced by Grant and Mill before they ever reached India.
Few rejected them in favour of Jones and the Orientalists
in the 1830s and 40s, and even fewer after the Mutiny of
1858. (See Chapter VI for an analysis of the effect of
Mill's concept of civilization on the debate on the Indian
capacity for self-rule).

With their visions of the Indians as barbarous and
in need of Westernization, Grant and Mill altered the terms
of debate on Indian government. Jones and the Orientalists
had been content to see Britain keep the peace, collect
tribute in the form of land revenue, leave the Indians to
reform their own society, and allow them to govern themselves
in all but the top positions in the administration.
Instructing East India Company officials to imitate Indian
princes, they advocated an enlightened despotism above and
village self-government below. To their understanding
Indian law expressed the common will and corporate wisdom
of the Indian people over centuries. If the British

---

[80]Müller, F. Max, *India, What Can It Teach Us?*,
London, 1883, p. 35.

ignored it and replaced it with a Western code and Western patterns of government, the East India Company would become the cruelest tyrant ever to conquer India.[81] Grant and Mill utterly disagreed. They demanded that the British firmly assume the reins of government at all levels and impose reforms on an inert population. Grant saw the chasm between rulers and ruled as unbridgeable and sought in his Observations to discover how the relationship between Britain and India could be made "permanent and secure".[82] To his mind Indian self-government was an absurdity. India was a despotism; British settlers and officials were denied the franchise; and there was no reason to grant the Indians a voice in government when the British had none.[83] Further, from his upper middle class Evangelical perspective, Grant assumed that the Indians -- like the lower orders in Britain -- would forever remain in a subordinate position allocated by God, for neither group displayed the honesty, industry and intellectual vigour necessary to democracy.[84] (See Chapter VI for an

---

[81] Marshall, op. cit., pp. 130-131.

[82] Grant, Observations, loc. cit., p. 5.

[83] Ibid., pp. 97-98.

[84] Hutchins, Francis, The Illusion of Permanence: British Imperialism in India, Princeton, 1967, p. 13.

extension of this argument.) Mill, in contrast, saw
Britain's mission as being self-limiting and looked forward
to the day when British administrators could relinquish
their power, having accomplished the Utilitarian mission
of training the Indians to ascertain and realize their own
happiness. Yet both he and his son, John Stuart, saw the
British Empire as surviving indefinitely, given the
ambitious nature of the Utilitarian undertaking.
Significantly, they eschewed Indian participation in government
until an educated, property-owning elite had been 'civilized';
and they dismissed full Indian self-rule until that
distant day when Britain's job was complete. In the
meantime, they placed their hopes for Indian advancement up
the scale of civilization in a corps of enlightened,
progressive and disinterested Britons -- i.e. officials of
the East India Company, and subsequently, of the Indian
Civil Service.[85] Convinced that good government was more
important than self-government, they articulated a
trade-off between efficiency and self-rule which defined
that basis of all future discussions on the government of
India.

[85]See John Stuart Mill's Memorandum on the improvement
in the administration of India during the last thirty years
and the Petition of the East India Company to Parliament,
London, 1858.

CHAPTER TWO

THE DEBATE ON
THE ORGANIZATION OF GOVERNMENT AND INDIAN FITNESS FOR
SELF-RULE:

1800 - 1850

The debate on how to govern India began when the British conquered the subcontinent in the 18th century. By 1800 a major controversy had developed within the East India Company over the nature and merits of traditional village government. Opposing factions appealed for authority to differing versions of Indian history, establishing a pattern for the debate for the rest of the century. The opponents of village self-rule drew, in addition, on deductive theories of the best form of local government for India (as, indeed, for any other part of the world). A brief description of the workings of the village community in the late 18th and early 19th centuries is given below to acquaint the reader with the terms used, and problems discussed, throughout the debate on the governance of India.

I. THE DECCAN VILLAGE COMMUNITY

To do justice to the vast array of Indian village institutions would take a lengthy volume, as Baden-Powell

discovered a century ago.[1] Numerous types of rural settlement then existed, so the sketch which follows cannot pur-
port to be comprehensive. The village community of Western
India, specifically that of the Deccan plateau, differed
in detail from that of the South, North or East; yet it
sufficiently resembled these other regional variations to
be representative and to serve here as a clear example of
the issues raised in the debate on local self-government.

British administrators became interested in the
Deccan pattern of village self-rule in 1818 when the huge
plateau of Maharashtra was annexed to the Bombay Presidency.[2]
They were immediately impressed by the peace and order in
the village communities, by the vitality of the system of
local self-government and by the connection between them;
for during the preceding century of warfare the Mahratta
Empire had been destroyed, the countryside laid waste, and
the cultivators impoverished. Nevertheless the Maharashtrian villages had remained stable with the aid of enduring

---

[1]B.H. Baden Powell, The Indian Village Community,
London, 1896.

[2]See map p. 46.

MARATHA EMPIRE

and traditional institutions.[3]

The first characteristic of the Deccan village which struck British administrators was the concentration of power in the hands of the thulwaheeks (proprietor-cultivators), who were descended from the original settlers of the village. Their distinguished ancestry brought with it a permanent claim to village land (so long as tax was paid on it) and the right to sit on the village panchayet (council).[4] Beneath this privileged thulwaheek minority were the upris (tenants-at-will). Possessing no recognized claim to the soil, they leased allotments of the arable waste on an annual basis from the co-parcenary brotherhood of thulwaheeks who controlled the village. Excluded from the panchayet, the upris were obliged either to abide by its rules or to emigrate.[5]

---

[3]Founded by Shivaji between 1645 and 1675, the Maratha Empire was a confederacy of Hindu states centered in Poona and extending over the Deccan plateau of Maharashtra. Over the next century it was expanded by its rulers (called peshwas, or prime ministers) as far north as the Punjab, east as Central India, and south as Madras; and between the 1690's and the 1750's it posed a serious threat to the Mughul Empire based at Agra. Beginning with the battle of Panipat in 1761, it suffered a series of crippling military defeats; and in the 1780s and 90's it was further weakend by internal feuds. The Anglo-Maratha wars of 1775, 1802 and 1816-17 further diminished the peshwa's territories and troops. In 1816, when Baji Rao II surrendered to Sir John Malcom, the peshwaship was abolished and the Deccan was annexed by the British.

[4]Ravinder Kumar, Western India in the Nineteenth Century, London, 1968, p. 20.

[5]B.B. Misra, The Administrative History of India, 1834-1914, Oxford, 1970, p. 464.

In Maharashtrian village communities, and throughout the subcontinent, the distinction between those who owned property
and those who did not was more important than any diversity
of caste or occupation.

Executive authority was vested entirely in the patil,
the oldest and most respected member of one of the village's
leading thulwaheek families.   Customarily there was only
one patil per village, and the office was passed from father
to son.   In times of distress, however, the patil's duties.
and privileges were sold off in whole or in part; and the
office was either circulated among the different thulwaheek
patriarchs or shared simultaneously by several of them.[6]
As the official link between the village and the region's
higher authorities, the Deccan patil represented village
interests to the government of the day -- Mughul, Mahratta
or British.   Whenever a land revenue settlement was renewed
before 1818, the patil advised Maratha district officers
(called mamlatdars) about local crop and living conditions
and negotiated the rate of assessment with them.   If his
suggestions, almost invariably for a low rate, were not
heeded, he protested; and if his objections to a high rate
were ignored, he ceremoniously left the village so that

[6]Surendranath Sen, The Administrative History of the
Mahrattas, Calcutta, 1925, 2nd ed., p. 216.

collection of the revenue became impossible.[7]   Sooner or
later an acceptable demand was agreed and the patil then
required the thulwaheeks to pay by jathas (family groups)
and the upris to pay individually.   At harvest time he
collected the requisite amounts and passed the total on to
the mamlatdar.[8]

For his services the patil was handsomely rewarded.
As the most socially distinguished person in the village,
he signed all documents first and went first in all
processions.   Payment in kind -- in grain, cotton, shoes,
fodder, oil, betel leaves, sugar cane, goats, cloth,
vegetables, salt and seasonal perishables -- was so generous
that one Maratha historian has computed that his living
standards in the 18th century exceeded those of a contemporary British Deputy Collector in Bengal.[9]   Assisting him

---

[7]These negotiations had their amusing aspects.   Lionel
Ashburnham, a Deccan Collector of the 1830's, recorded that
under the British, as under the Mahrattas, the patils tried a
number of ingenious ploys to secure a low assessment.
Frequently they begged for a reduction in the figure fixed by
the government on the excuse that the monsoons had failed; or
that locusts or wild dogs had destroyed the crops;   or that
tigers had eaten the village cattle;   or that a neighbouring
village had stolen the water supply.   If the government
official refused to lower the assessment, the patil would not
sign the revenue contract for his village until he had been
formally sent off to prison.   He would then sign under protest
and boast to his village about his great fights with the
Collectors Sahibs.   John Martineau, Sir Bartle Frere, London,
1895, 2nd ed., vol. I, p. 28.

[8]Kumar, op. cit., pp. 26-27.

[9]Sen, op. cit., pp. 217-219.

were a kulkarni (accountant) who kept the village
records and a mahar (watchman) who variously guarded
the village against marauders, served as the patil's bailiff
and looked after village sanitation.

   The primary organ of justice in the village community
was the panchayet. Nominally composed of five (paunch)
men, this court actually consisted of five to twelve leading
thulwaheeks. A panchayet was convened by the patil whenever he was unable to persuade quarrelling villagers to
reach an amicable settlement of their differences. Members
were selected not for their impartiality, but rather for
their acquaintance with the contestants and their
familiarity with the matter at issue. Before evidence was
heard both parties signed an agreement (rajinama) to abide
by the decision of the panchayet; and unless corruption
of members of the court could be proved, the contestants
were required by custom and forced by community pressure to
accept the panchayet's verdict. Court procedure was simple,
there being neither judge nor codified law to guide the
inquiry. The panchayet listened to the evidence of
witnesses called by both sides, examined written documents
and, when guilt or innocence remained unclear, submitted
the disputants to ordeal by fire and water. Because the
right to sit on the panchayet was limited to respected
members of the village community, the court's authority to
interpret customary law and apply it to particular disputes
was generally accepted by the inhabitants. And

because the panchayet dispensed justice cheaply and in a manner understood by all, its popularity was great.[10]

Through the operations of the patil and the panchayet the village community conducted all its own affairs; and through the workings of the village artisans (twelve hereditary ballutodars) and cultivators, it was self-sufficient as well.[11] Before 1818 its only regular link to whomever governed the Deccan plateau -- Mughul or Mahratta -- was the annual collection of the land revenue. This tax was gathered by two sets of intermediaries posed between the village and the ruling power, the deshmukhs and deshpandes on the one hand, and the mamlatdars on the other. The former were petty rajahs who had held sway over zillahs, or small tracts of land, since time immemorial.[12] They had been granted, in recognition of their intimate knowledge of the land and their close relations with the ryots, five per cent of the tax returns by the Mughuls for supervising revenue assessment and collection. Because this enhanceable form of payment

---

[10]Kumar, op. cit., pp. 30-33.

[11]Robertson to Elphinstone, 4 December 1818, "Memorandum on the Administration of Justice under the Mahrattas", R.D. Choksey, The Aftermath of Revolt, Bombay, 1950, pp. 292-294.

[12]Kumar, op. cit., p. 12.

imbued its receivers with a permanent interest in the
prosperity of the area, the deshmukhs and deshpandes dealt
with the ryots fairly; and because they were just, they were
traditionally regarded as protectors of the village
communities under their jurisdiction.[13]

This sympathy between the deshmukhs and deshpandes
and the ryots (cultivators) was so strong that Shivaji,[14]
who conquered the Deccan for the Marathas in 1690, feared
that collusion might lead to tax evasion.   To insure
against this he divided the Deccan into talukas, or revenue
districts, and appointed one mamlatdar to preside over each.
His job was to direct local police, settle disputes
unresolved by the village panchayet, and supervise tax
collection.   Every time the peshwa (the Maratha ruler)
enhanced the rate of assessment, each mamlatdar was ordered
to consult the deshmukhs and deshpandes of his taluka
about local agricultural conditions.   He was then instructed
to negotiate a new settlement with them; and they in turn

---

[13]Chaplin to Warden, 18 November 1820, Choksey, op.
cit., p. 205.

[14]Shivaji (1630-1680) son of a rich jagirdar of the
Western Ghats (bounding the Deccan plateau on the West);
began capturing the hill fortresses of the Ghats held by the
Delhi Sultanate in 1646 and holding them by force, bribery and
trickery; routed the Mughul Governor of the Deccan, 1663;
captured Surat, 1664; formally crowned himself Chhatrapati
(King of Kings), 1674; established a stable civil administration for the Mahratta Empire, which he effectively founded.

were required to reach agreements with individual village
patils.[15] An unjust demand brought the deshmukhs and
deshpandes to the peshwa's court in Poona, where they
pleaded the cause of the village under their auspices.
Their appearance at court achieved two important ends:
it proved an immediate recourse to grievance, and it
reminded the offending mamlatdar of the wisdom of
judicious conduct towards the village communities in
his taluka.[16]

So long as there was a strong government at Poona
to direct the mamlatdars' activities and respond to the
deshmukhs and deshpandes' petitions, a balance of power
existed between those responsible for the welfare of the
Deccan village communites. This beneficial equilibrium
of forces broke down between 1785 and 1802, however, under
the strain of dynastic squabbles. The victorious Baji
Rao,[17] an imprudent and devious ruler, secured money for

[15]Kumar, op. cit., pp. 13-14.

[16]Sen, op. cit., pp. 252-256.

[17]Baji Rao II became the peshwa in 1795; devoid of
military skill and fond of intrigue, he set the Maratha military and civil leaders against each other and made the Maratha
Empire vulnerable to attack by Indian rulers and the British;
accepted a subsidiary alliance with the British under the
Treaty of Bassein in 1802 to secure protection from his enemies;
in return for this he was forced to yield territories worth
26 lacs of rupees and to agree to British direction of Maratha
foreign policy; forced to accept a British Resident at Poona
in 1811 and to renounce his position as head of the Maratha
Empire in 1817 with the Treaty of Poona.

his private wars by farming out revenue collection to the highest bidders. The post of mamlatdar was filled by men unacquainted with local agricultural conditions, uninterested in the needs of the village communities, and disinclined to treat the ryots leniently. Besides realizing as high an annual assessment as possible, they regularly levied taxes which had traditionally been demanded only for specific purposes.[18] Moreover, they imposed excessive fines, exacted forfeitures of property in default of payment, and imprisoned recalcitrant ryots. Because they controlled the courts of appeal for all revenue cases, they were able to subvert the normal course of justice for their own ends; and because the peshwa benefitted from their extortion, cries of distress from the deshmukhs and deshpandes were ignored. Thirty years of such oppression reduced the ryots to penury, upset the traditional system of justice, and transferred political and economic power from the village communities to this new class of tyrants.[19] In this way the indigenous system of local self-government was seriously disrupted, though not totally destroyed.

The Deccan pattern -- of vitality in the 17th and early 18th centuries followed by disintegration during the

---

[18]Misra, op. cit., p. 466.

[19]Parliamentary Papers (House of Commons) 1853, vol. III, no. 445, evidence of Elphinstone, Grant Duff and Chaplin, 1832.

decades of warfare preceding the establishment of British rule -- was repeated to a greater or lesser extent throughout Western and Southern India. The village communities of Madras suffered a greater decline than those of Bombay; while those of the North-West Provinces emerged surprisingly unscathed from the wars of conquest. Nowhere did they totally disappear, yet nowhere did they survive intact.

II. THE DEBATES OF ORIENTALISTS AND UTILITARIANS ON LOCAL SELF-GOVERNMENT

During the half-century preceding the Mutiny a spirited debate on the merits of local self-government was waged between and among leading Orientalist and Utilitarian administrators. The Orientalists -- so-called because of their respect for Indian society and their anxiety to preserve it against overly extensive or hasty Western innovation -- were great admirers of the self-ruling village community. Led by Thomas Munro (Governor of Madras from 1819 to 1827),[20] Mountstuart Elphinstone (Governor of

---

[20]Thomas Munro (1761-1827) entered the East India Company's Madras Army, 1780; served in Baramahal in the civil line under Captain Read after 1792; ruled the Ceded Districts, 1800-1807; in England 1807-1813; Governor of Madras, 1819-1827.

Bombay from 1819 to 1827)[21] and Charles Metcalfe (Lieutenant-
Governor of Agra in 1834 and of the North-West   Provinces
from 1836 to 1838),[22] they campaigned relentlessly to shield
the ancient village communities from the forces of change:
from petty modifications designed by local officials as well
as from sweeping changes imposed by the introduction of
Western concepts of law and patterns of administration.
In opposition to the Orientalists stood the Utilitarians led
by James Mill, Assistant Examiner for the East India Company
from 1819 to 1830 and Examiner from 1830 to 1836.
Condemning the village community as a major obstacle to the
realization of the greatest happiness for the greatest number
of the rural population, they resolved to destroy the
indigenous system of local self-government in the cause of
reform.

---

[21]Mountstuart Elphinstone (1779-1859) ICS; went to
Bengal as a writer in the East India Company, 1795; Assistant
to the Resident at the court of Baji Rao at Poona, 1801-1804;
Resident at Nagpur, 1804-1808; Envoy to Kabul, 1809-1810;
Resident at Poona, 1811-1817; Chief Commissioner of the
Deccan, 1817-1818; Governor of Bombay, 1819-1827.

[22]Charles Metcalfe (1785-1846) ICS; to Calcutta as a
writer, 1801; Assistant Resident at Daulat Rao Sindia's
court, 1801-1802; in the Governor-General's office, 1803;
Political Officer in the Mahratta War, 1804; Assistant to
the Resident at Delhi, 1806; on special mission to Ranjit
Singh at Lahore, 1808-1809; Deputy Secretary to Lord Minto,
1809-1810; Resident at Gwalior, 1810; Resident at Delhi,
1811-1819; Secretary in the Secret and Political Department
and Private Secretary to the Governor-General, 1819-1820;
Resident at Hyderabad, 1820-1827; member of the Supreme
Council, 1827-1834; Governor at Agra, 1834; acting
Governor-General, 1835-1836; Lieutenant-Governor of the
North-West   Provinces, 1836-1838.

This fundamental policy disagreement arose from the
different methods by which the Orientalists and Utilitarians
analyzed Indian society.   The Orientalists examined
institutions like the village community in terms of past
history and present circumstance.   As practically-minded
men -- imbued with more common sense than imagination --
they were more adept at dealing with concrete facts than with
abstract theories.   Experienced in devising workable
solutions to everyday problems of administration, they
assessed village institutions by pragmatic standards such
as their suitability to the Indian character and their
capacity to meet the inhabitants' needs.   By contrast the
Utilitarians studied Indian society in terms of political
economy and judged village government according to notions
like accountability, rationality, simplicity and
intelligibility, which were completely alien to traditional
Indian values.   Ricardo's economic theories and Bentham's
constitutional thought provided Mill in London and Mackenzie[23]
and Pringle[24], his principal followers in India, with guides
for remodelling customary society to meet Utilitarian
requirements.

----

[23]Holt Mackenzie (1787-1876) ICS; to India, 1808;
Secretary to the Government in the Territorial Department,
1817; member (1820) then President of the Council of the
College of Fort William, 1825; Secretary to the Governor-
General, 1826-1831.

[24]Robert Keith Pringle (1802-1897) ICS; joined the
Bombay Civil Service, 1820; Chief Secretary to the
Government of Bombay and then Master of the Mint; Acting
Member of the Bombay Council; officer in charge of Sind,
1847-1854.

The Orientalists were by definition opposed to remaking India in the image of the West. Intimate with Indian history and Indian habits, they were convinced that it was impossible for a British trading company to govern effectively several million people -- all but a few thousand of whom lived in small villages scattered across half a million square miles. Faced with the difficult task of establishing British rule in areas recently conquered from Indian princes, they recognized the practical necessity of relying on the Indians to govern themselves through indigenous village institutions. Repeatedly they extolled the durability, stability and self-sufficiency which had enabled the village community to survive through countless invasions and changes of regional and central government; and they expressed the hope that village self-rule could be maintained after the new British administration had been firmly established. Their respect for the Indian system of local self-government rested, therefore, on two grounds: first, that the village communities had grown organically out of Indian society over hundreds of years; and secondly, that they had guaranteed a tolerable measure of peace and freedom to all.

Two striking odes to the village community, the first written by Munro in 1806 and the second by Metcalfe in 1832, capture their esteem for the traditional mode of self-rule. Munro's minute provides both a clear exposition of the merits

of self-rule as he saw them and also a key concept -- that
of the "little republic" -- which Orientalist sympathizers
of later generations repeated in defence of village
institutions.

> The Village Communities are little Republics,
> having nearly everything that they want within
> themselves, and almost independent of any
> foreign relations. They seem to last where
> nothing else lasts. Dynasty after dynasty tumbles
> down; revolution succeeds to revolution; Hindu,
> Pathan, Moghal, Mahratta, Sikh, English, are
> masters in turn; but the Village Communities
> remain the same. In times of trouble they arm
> and fortify themselves; a hostile army passes
> through the country; the Village Community
> collect their cattle within their walls, and let
> the enemy pass unprovoked. If plunder and
> devastation be directed against themselves and
> the force employed be irresistible, they flee
> to friendly villages at a distance, but when
> the storm has passed over they return and assume
> their occupations. If a country remain for a
> series of years the scene of continued pillage
> and massacre, so that the villages cannot be
> inhabited, the scattered villagers nevertheless
> return whenever the power of peaceable possession
> revives. A generation may pass away, but the
> succeeding generation will return. The sons will
> take the places of their fathers, the same site
> for the village, the same position for the
> houses, the same lands, will be reoccupied by the
> descendants of those who were driven out when
> the village was depopulated; and it is not a
> trifling matter that will drive them out, for they
> will often maintain their post through times of
> disturbance and convulsion, and acquire strength
> sufficient to resist pillage and oppression with
> success.[25]

Metcalfe amplified upon why the Orientalists admired these

---

[25]Quoted by Mark Wilkes, Historical Sketches of the
South of India, Mysore, 1810, p. 140.

"little republics":

> The union of the Village Communities, each one
> forming a separate little State in itself, has,
> I conceive, contributed more than any other
> cause to the preservation of the people of
> India through all revolutions and changes which
> they have suffered, and it is in a high degree
> conducive to their happiness and to the enjoy-
> ment of a great portion of freedom and
> independence.[26]

Considered as strict history, this was far from honest. The Orientalists proved themselves capable of much romantic historical invention, which served as propaganda in their disputes with Utilitarians. Their most influential fantasy was that of the "golden age" of the "village republic", which was looked to as a kind of Court of Appeal when controversial policy was to be decided. The exact nature of this original pure form was never made clear. It was admired for its early display of representative government; for the Orientalists regarded the panchayet as a court which took the interests of the entire community into consideration. It was said further to be a commonwealth in miniature, self-sufficient, guaranteeing the freedom of all inhabitants from slavery and autocracy, bestowing equal political and economic rights on the property-owning minority (though not on the landless tenants). A blind eye was turned among Orientalists to the lack of elected leaders and of

---

[26]Parliamentary Papers (House of Commons) 1832, vol. III, Revenue, Minute of 7 November 1830, p. 333.

equality among its members, to its inherent oligarchic
rule.   Munro, Metcalfe and Elphinstone all recognized
the emotive quality of the term "republic" and played on
it skillfully to enhance their arguments.

The Utilitarians were barely impressed.   Not only,
they declared, had this "golden age" never existed: there
could be nothing democratic or socially just about a "village
republic" which deprived the majority of political rights
and economic power.   Any golden age lay in the future
alone, when village oligarchies and institutions had been
broken up and villagers allowed the free pursuit of their
own interests.   Rejecting even the limited proposition
that the "little republics" assured a good if simple life
for the rural population, the Utilitarians measured the
worth of village government upon the scales of political
economy and concluded that the village community was a
repressive body which restricted personal liberty and
deprived the cultivators of the produce of their labor.
In their opinion these were more than temporary
derangements of an otherwise admirable system: they
were the inescapable consequences of a system of government which placed an illusory "social interest" above
that of individuals, and which retarded justice to ensure
the dominance of the co-parcenary brotherhoods.   Declaring
the village community to be inimical to the Principle of
Utility, they called for the destruction of village
government and the atomization of rural society in the name
of progress and social justice.

Utilitarians and Orientalists alike recognized the land revenue system as the key to achieving their opposite ends. Their opportunities arose with the conquest of each new state (from Madras in 1780 to the North-West Provinces in 1834) and the immediate need to find taxpayers to support the British administration. Both groups were hostile to the "permanent settlement" instituted by Cornwallis in Bengal in 1793.[27] The Utilitarians, out to destroy the village community, supported a "ryotwari settlement" on the land, by which the government vested proprietary rights in the peasant-cultivators and directly contracted the revenue demand with them, thus doing away with the village rulers as an institutional link. They correctly foresaw that if government officials took over the jobs of tax assessor and collector, and village leaders were deprived of their highest dignity as intermediaries between the state and people, then the village community would lose its cohesion and exist increasingly only in name.

The Utilitarians were unanimous in this view. In contrast the Orientalists, anxious to buttress local self-government, failed to agree on the land revenue

---

[27]Charles Cornwallis, 1st Marquis (1738-1805) entered the Guards and served in Germany, 1758-1762; MP for Eye; Earl, 1872; Major General, 1775; served in the American war, 1776-1781; Governor-General of India, 1786-1793; 1805.

policy which would achieve this. Metcalfe and Elphinstone backed the "mahalwari settlement" by which the
government vested proprietary rights in the members of the
village community as a group and negotiated a revenue
contract with their representatives at regular intervals.
They believed that the employment of village officers to
assess and collect taxes for the British administration
would strengthen village institutions.   But Munro in
Madras took a very different line.   Observing that the
vitality of the village communities had been sapped by
incessant warfare in the 18th century, he insisted that
reinvigoration would only come if the ryots were given
an economic stake in the villages' survival.   Hence a
ryotwari settlement was thrust upon Madras with Munro's
stipulation that "every ryot, so long as he pays the rent
of his land /̄ i.e. the land revenue_7 , shall be considered
as the complete owner of the soil and shall be at liberty
to let it to a tenant without limitations as to rent, and
to sell it as he pleases".[28]   The theory was to stimulate
the village economies, mysteriously awaken among the
cultivators an interest in village affairs, and thus
revitalize corporate bonds.

Land revenue policy -- and with it, the survival or

---

[28] R.C. Dutt, Economic History of India in the
Victorian Age, 7th ed., London, 1950, p. 111.

destruction of the village government -- hung on more than
these abstract calculations, however.   It varied from
region to region with Orientalist attitudes to another
problem which was central to the debate on village self-
rule: the mounting power of the patils.   Throughout
India the British took over village societies in which
traditional ryot rights to the land had to their
understanding been surrendered to powerful rajas,
zemindars and patils in the preceding century of warfare
and anarchy.   Confronted with widespread oppression of
the ryots, the Orientalists realized that the village
communities could not be preserved in their existing state
and that action would have to be taken against the patils.
But it was utterly unclear how far the powers of the
patils ought to be undermined; it was quite unclear how
long traditional village government could last if the
patils were stripped of power; and it was quite impossible
to calculate, even if objectives were set, how the various
options of land revenue policy would react upon the patils
and the villages.

On this critical problem Elphinstone, Governor of
Bombay, took a defiantly conservative stance.   Labelling
the patils "the most important functionaries in the village
and perhaps the most important class in the country", he
pointed out that they were instrumental in serving as a

link between the ryots and the state.[29]   He reminded his subordinates that without their co-operation the British administration could neither collect the revenue nor dispense justice nor protect property; and he advised them not to probe too closely into their activities. "Too much care cannot be taken," he cautioned,

> to prevent their duty becoming irksome and
> their influence impaired by bringing their
> conduct too often under the correction of
> their superiors.   I would lend a ready ear
> to all complaints against them for oppres-
> sion, but I would not disturb them for
> inattention to forms; and I would leave
> them at liberty to settle petty complaints
> their own way, provided no serious
> punishment were inflicted on either party.[30]

In his opinion the power and prestige of the patils should be effectively buttressed by allowing them a wide latitude in determining the expenditure of village funds, in settling disputes, and in collecting the land revenue.[31]

From this it naturally followed that Elphinstone should choose a mahalwari rather than ryotwari land settlement for Bombay.   "I am not democratic enough to insist on a ryotwari system," he declared; "I think that the aristocracy of the country whether it consists of heads

---

[29]Ibid., p. 138.

[30]Ibid., p. 350.

[31]Ibid.

of villages or heads of zemindarees should be kept up".[32]
He nevertheless deemed it necessary to make a thorough
study of Maratha tenurial relations before imposing any
tax scheme. He instructed the Deccan Commissioners to
carry out a ryotwari survey in order to discover the
extent of each cultivator's holdings; and he ordered
them to negotiate the revenue demand with the patils, to
fix a sum for each village as a whole, and to let the
patils assess the individual ryots and collect the agreed
sum.[33] This land policy was based on two expectations:
first, that the definition and registration of all property
rights would dissuade if not prevent the patils from
overassessing the ryots and generally abusing their trust;
secondly, that the agreement of revenue contracts between
state officials and village leaders would affirm corporate
responsibility for the tax burden and strengthen local
self-government.

Similar expectations -- that a combined mahalwari
settlement and ryotwari survey would stimulate village
institutions and prevent corruption and oppression --
were held by Charles Metcalfe in the North-West

---

[32]Quoted by Kenneth Ballhatchet, Social Policy and
Social Change in Western India, 1817-1830, London, 1957,
p. 32.

[33]Dutt, op. cit., p. 350.

Provinces. Like Elphinstone, he regarded the village
community as "the greatest blessing possessed by India",
and vowed to protect it from injudicious innovation.[34]
"I wish that the Village Constitutions may never be
disturbed," he declared forthrightly, "and I dread
everything that has a tendency to break them up".[35]   To
this end he argued that the co-parcenary brotherhoods who
ruled each community should be allowed to continue to
divide the tax burden by local custom. He believed that
any attempt by the government either to impose a plan for
sharing the revenue demand or to contract directly with
the ryots would irreparably disrupt the fabric of rural
society. He also held that villagers should be allowed to
manage their internal affairs in traditional ways; for
interference by British officials would "subvert the Village
Constitution, sever the link by which the community is bound
together, and cause its dissolution".[36]

All this conceded, however, Metcalfe advocated a
drastic reduction of the patils' remaining powers.
A reading of Rousseau -- hardly to Elphinstone's taste --
imbued him with democratic sympathies and the notion that

---

[34]Parliamentary Papers (House of Commons) 1832, vol.
III, Revenue, Minute of 7 November 1830, p. 333.

[35]Quoted by D.N. Panigrahi, Charles Metcalfe in India,
Delhi, 1968, p. 90.

[36]Ibid.

aristrocracies who misbehave should be replaced by popular representatives.[37]   Rousseau led him both to support the cause of parliamentary reform in Britain and to call for the redistribution of the patils' powers in India.   In 1830 he complained that British officials had forgotten that the patil was no more than a representative of the village community when it came to the negotation of new land revenue contracts.   They had instead begun to treat him as the sole landowner of the village and to disregard all other property rights.[38]   This over-rating, Metcalfe believed, had two undesirable consequences: first, it distorted the patil's position in the eyes of the village and invited oppression; secondly, it upset the customary balance of power among the fraternal proprietors who controlled village affairs and thereby weakened the traditional system of local self-government.   Convinced that the patils were capable of seriously undermining the ancient village constitution, Metcalfe advised his subordinates to be alert to all spurious property claims put forward by the patil and to treat him as the first among equals -- not as the village zemindar.   He had visible cause for alarm.   In certain villages the patil's

[37]Ibid., p. 76.

[38]Parliamentary Papers (House of Commons) 1832, vol. III, Revenue, Minute of 7 November 1830, p. 333.

tyrannous reign had already totally destroyed corporate feeling, and here Metcalfe was forced to recognize that the traditional village and its institutions were béyond revival. In these areas (which to his relief were small in size and few in number) he advised -- with regret -- the institution of a ryotwari settlement.

In Madras, there was a much more serious breaking of ranks among the Orientalists than the differences between Elphinstone and Metcalfe in Bombay and the North-West. Thomas Munro, Governor from 1819 to 1827, accepted that the transformation of the patil into an oppressive zemindar had debilitated the system of local self-govern-ment. But he did not believe that a ryotwari survey was in itself sufficient to re-establish the ryot's rights on the land, by setting individual claims to property on the official record. Such analysis of Indian history, Munro believed, mistook the historical reality of the village community and misunderstood the real significance of the patils' ascendancy. After careful study he announced his conclusion that the "natural state" and ancient condition of Indian society was "a great body of individu-al Ryats".[39] To his understanding the village was a latter-day accretion, an "artificial state", an oligarchy,

[39]G.R. Gleig, Life of Sir Thomas Munro, London, 1830, vol. III, p. 320, Minute of 31 December 1824.

which vested property rights in the co-parcenary brotherhoods from whom the patils were selected, and which
reduced the great mass of ryots to the status of tenants
and sub-tenants.[40]   If the patils were to be dealt with
and a healthy system of local self-government created --
one which rested on popular consensus and joint responsibility -- the ryots must be restored to their proper
position of peasant proprietors.   Munro claimed (though
few people in India or Britain agreed with him) that a
ryotwari rather than a mahalwari settlement was the conservative
solution needed in the villages, the one guaranteed to
regenerate ancient social ties and promote viable local
self-government.

Only two figures on either side were able to lift
the problems of land revenue and village government from
the example to the theory and provide some intellectual
counterpoint to the wranglings of practical men:
Elphinstone and James Mill.   Mill was the leader of a
brash army of radical reform whose weapon was the ryotwari
settlement, which the Utilitarians regarded as the agent
of final destruction of village self-government.   Their
prediction was that the ryotwari settlement would shake
out land from group control and inaugurate an open

---

[40]Ibid.

property market. This would in turn provoke important
social and economic changes: the individual would be
freed from community obligations; corporate bonds of
every sort would be loosened; corporate practices would
be eliminated; and traditional local self-rule would
wither away.

Political economy yielded two straightforward, and
to James Mill's mind irrefutable, arguments in favor of
these revolutionary changes. The first was that the
greatest happiness of the greatest number could never be
achieved so long as the interests of the patil were at
odds with those of the cultivator. With the patil
profiting from exacting as much as possible from the ryots
and pocketing the difference between the gross village
collection and the amount surrendered to the government,
extortion and over-assessment were predictably widespread.[41]
What was original in this analysis was Mill's conclusion
that the ryots did not submit to the rule of the patils
because they benefitted from it, as the Orientalists
contended.   Rather, they accepted tyranny because they
were too illiterate and superstitious to make a rational
choice in favor of a new and better system.   In 1831 Mill
warned a House of Commons Select Committee that what
masqueraded as village co-operation was nothing more than

---

[41]Parliamentary Papers (House of Commons) 1831, vol.
V, evidence of 2 August 1831, pp. 292-293.

a thinly disguised system of mass exploitation; and
he advised Committee members not to interpret the ryots'
passive acceptance of the status quo as enlightened
choice.[42]

Mill's second argument was that no acceptable means
of rewarding the patil for acting as the state's revenue
agent was compatible with the dictates of political
economy. If, as Ricardo postulated, the state as landlord was entitled to all of the rent (the surplus remaining
after the cost of wages and the ordinary rate of profit
were subtracted from the gross produce),[43] no margin of
profit was available with which to pay the patil for
assessing and collecting the land revenue. Should the
state claim any amount in excess of the rent in order to
reimburse him, it would force the cultivators' standard
of living to plummet below subsistence level. This would
cause immediate hardship and impede the cultivators from
meeting the revenue demand in the future. Should the
state instead deduct the patil's pay from the rent,
government programs would be jeopardized and the cultivators

---

[42]Ibid.

[43]Stokes, op. cit., p. 88.

would again be the losers.[44] Thus the prosperity of the
ryots and the advancement of the country depended upon the
elimination of all sycophantic village officials and the
destruction of traditional local self-government.

Somewhat against his natural habits (for the wholly
deductive Essay on Government was now well behind him) Mill
in 1831 turned to history to buttress his case for a
ryotwari settlement. Here there were difficulties. An
examination of 18th century documents revealed that
hereditary middlemen -- be they zemindars, patils or whatever -- had probably been interposed between the cultivator
and the central or regional government since the beginning
of recorded history. Mill was forced to conclude that
if the direct contractual relationship between the
cultivator and the state which he championed had ever
existed in India, it had done so in the period before
historical documents were available. Citing uncertain
historical facts was dangerous, if widely indulged in
British argument on India; but in the absence of actual
evidence of a ryotwari system Mill had no alternative.
In uncharacteristically tentative tones, therefore, he
"conceived" to the Select Committee "that generally, at
one time,

---

[44]James Mill, "Observations on the Land Revenue in
India", Parliamentary Papers (House of Commons) 1832, vol.
IV, pp. 48-49.

> the lands of India were occupied by ryots who had
> a right of perpetual occupancy; they were the
> hereditary tenants and cultivators of the land;
> I conceive that from them the revenue was collected
> by the officers of government, and that to the
> demand of government there was no limit ....
> It frequently happened, from the disposition to
> collect the rent in a summary manner, that middle-
> men were interposed in the shape of mere renters:
> a certain district was rented, and the man held it
> only for such length of time as he was entitled
> by lease .... From the tendency in India of almost
> all things to become hereditary, those zemindars
> often continued from father to son ... and the head
> of the village became a sort of hereditary
> collector.[45]

Mill's supposition that the ideal relationship between the

ryots as hereditary tenants and the state as universal

landlord had been wrecked by the intervention of greedy

headmen was at least plausible as a theory of Indian

history. It found numerous adherents in India and in

Britain. But as a cynical exercise in historical deceit,

it was to prove an awkward tool in Utilitarian hands.

Among Orientalists, Elphinstone alone provided

sophisticated answers to the questions of theory threaded

through the problems raised by village government: how much

change is desirable and possible when administering a people

of unfamiliar traditions? and how much change is undesirable

yet unavoidable? His response was Scottish and extra-

ordinarily conservative. Despite his moderate Whiggism at

home, his concern to eliminate the abuse of power in India,

---

[45]Parliamentary Papers (House of Commons) 1831, vol.
V, evidence of 4 August 1831, pp. 307-308.

and his fleeting interest in Bentham's constitutional
theories, he was far more reluctant to tamper with the
structure of traditional society than any other leading
Orientalist.   The motto of his administration in Bombay
presidency was "scrupulously to avoid all innovations....
I am anxious," he informed the Governor-General in 1818,

> ...to endeavour to show the people that they
> are to expect no change but in the better
> administration of their former laws.
>   No body of regulations could indeed
> be introduced into a State, the component
> parts of which are at present so unsettled,
> and at all times so complicated.[46]

In his opinion the most commendable and gradual reforms
were to be abhorred if they diverged too widely from
traditional ways; for "even just government", he asserted,
would "not be a blessing if at variance with the habits and
character of the nation".[47]

        Wide reading in the Edinburgh philosophers of the
late 18th century persuaded Elphinstone that societies
develop in stages and that specific civil institutions
are appropriate to each successive state.[48]   He deemed
the Maratha system of local self-government to be worthy
of preservation not because it was good or just, but because

---

[46]Elphinstone to Hastings, 18 June 1818, Choksey, op.
cit., p. 171.

[47]Ibid., p. 172.

[48]R.D.Choksey, Mountstuart Elphinstone, Bombay, 1971,
p.11.

it suited the peoples' needs and was familiar to them.
"The present system," he observed,

> is probably not bad in itself as the country
> has prospered under it, notwithstanding the
> feebleness and corruption with which it was
> administered. At all events it is generally
> known and understood. It suits the people
> whom indeed it has helped to form, and it
> probably is capable of being made tolerably
> perfect by gradual improvements introduced
> as they appear to be called for.[49]

Elphinstone feared that if reform programs were pressed
too vigorously, the Indians would be left "without any
known objects by which they would direct their course".[50]
Further, "odium", "prejudice" and "disgust" towards the
British would be aroused, and hostility towards beneficial
change of every sort would be provoked.[51] Accordingly,
he advised his colleagues not to meddle with customary
institutions before carrying out a full-scale inquiry into
Maratha society and determining the precise extent of reform
which could be tolerated without opposition.[52] Scottish
philosophy of history taught the cautious Elphinstone that
governments are rarely the wisest agents of social reform,
and that much innovation and progress in society is
uncalculated and at times unconscious. Hence his warning

---

[49]Elphinstone to Hastings, 18 June 1818, Choksey,
The Aftermath of Revolt, p. 173.

[50]Ibid.

[51]Ibid., p. 172.

[52]Dutt, op. cit., p. 350.

to the Deccan Commissioners against disturbing customary
relations: "everything even in the details of the civil
administration must be done on a general view of all its
bearings; and improvements can only be made by degrees
after a separate consideration of each individual measure".[53]
Even then they must proceed with care: the consequences of
administrative measures could not always be forseen; the
spontaneous "novelties /‾which‾/ must accompany every
revolution" would inevitably lead to unpredicted and unwanted
results.[54] It was a potent -- and largely unheeded -- warning
applicable throughout India, against the elevation of too
much ideology over practice.

III.   THE FATE OF THE VILLAGE COMMUNITY IN MADRAS,
       THE NORTH-WEST   PROVINCES AND BOMBAY

It is a paradox of the British presence in India
that under Orientalist rule the institutions of village
government underwent the alternative fates of summary
execution or slow death.   The former fate was dealt out by
Munro to Southern India, where with a simple ryotwari
settlement the villages disintegrated as early as the 1820's.
The latter fate occurred in Bombay and the North-West
Provinces, where the mixed system of a ryotwari survey and

[53]Elphinstone to Hastings, 18 June 1818, Choksey, The
Aftermath of Revolt, p. 171.

[54]Ibid., p. 172.

a mahalwari settlement proved a slow-acting poison for the
village community.   In Bombay Presidency Elphinstone and
his mahalwari settlement were outmaneuvered by the Deccan
Commissioners, whose sympathy with the ryotwari system
led them to deal directly with the cultivators and simply
to ignore village leaders.   In the North-West   Provinces
anxiety among the Orientalist administrators to preserve the
village was no less than Elphinstone's; but there, too,
misjudgment at the highest level (to call it gross incompe-
tence would be unfair in this complex and foreign culture)
proved fatal.

The slow disappearance of village institutions in
Bombay and the North-West Provinces illustrates the sad
but undeniable truth that the Orientalists did as much
inadvertently to destroy the traditional system of local
self-government as the Utilitarians did intentially.   In
the North-West   Provinces the architect of destruction was
Holt Mackenzie, who exhibited the conservatism of an
Orientalist and open admiration for Ricardian economics.
He was the author of a scheme dating from 1819 which attempted
to marry Ricardian rent theory with Orientalist social hopes.
These were, in Mackenzie's words, "to avoid as much as
possible any direct interference with the village communities";
and, in a language reminiscent of Elphinstone, "to avoid those
sudden revolutions which our operations appear to have so
strong a tendency to produce, even where no change has been

distinctly contemplated".[55] Mackenzie had no intention
of granting greater economic freedom to the individual
cultivator: for him, village government was sacred. But,
like Elphinstone, he miscalculated. His first mistake came
with the imposition of a ryotwari survey in an attempt to
reach a fair assessment of individual tax liabilities.
Mackenzie had a fair grasp of the implications of a ryotwari
survey for village institutions -- more so than the naive
Elphinstone and Metcalfe: he clearly understood that a
register of individual property rights would eliminate the
patils' role as tax assessor and would create a ryotwari
settlement in fact if not in name. Nevertheless he trusted,
wrongly, that a mahalwari settlement based on the principle
of corporate responsibility for the land revenue and executed
between the state and village leaders (here called lambardars,
or persons holding a lambar or number in the Collector's
register) would effectively preserve the indigenous system
of local self-government.[56]

This half-baked scheme became law in the early 1820's
when Mackenzie decided to apply Ricardo's net produce
criterion to the ryotwari field survey. But the whole

---

[55]Holt Mackenzie, Memorandum of 1 July 1819, Selections
from the Revenue Records of the North-Western Provinces, 1818-
1820, p. 130.

[56]Dutt, op. cit., p. 191.

system quickly showed itself to be unworkable.   Within a
few years Mackenzie realized that a comprehensive survey
could not be completed within any reasonable period of time.
He also discovered that a uniform formula of revenue
assessment throughout Northern India entailed the destruction
of the great variety of local assessment and collection
procedures which ensured the viability of the village
communities.   He therefore backtracked on the whole original
plan and advised the District Collectors of the province to
use the net produce criterion only as a check on figures
computed from past collections and present revenue resources.[57]
This recommendation was incorporated into Regulation VII of
1822, the first land revenue law for the North-West
Provinces, which shows Mackenzie still trying to have the
best of all worlds.   To preserve village institutions, the
new law required that property rights be vested exclusively
in the village community and that all claims to superior
tenures established as a consequence of tax farming in the
18th century be ignored.   Mackenzie sought to guarantee
the survival of traditional practices by two further
stipulations: first, that the patils be formally empowered
to distribute the village tax burden and collect it for the
state;   secondly, that the co-parceners be entitled to claim
for the village the land of anyone who failed to pay his due

---

[57]Stokes, op. cit., p. 97.

share of the revenue.[58]   Through this Regulation Mackenzie
hoped to preserve Munro's "little republics" as economic
units and to maintain the apparatus of village self-rule.

He was doomed to disappointment.   The ryotwari
survey introduced in 1818 slowly killed off corporate
patterns of tenure and cultivation by introducing -- quite
inadvertently -- a free market in land.   It was a short step
from compiling a register of legally recognized individual
property holdings to the introduction of a market in them
and to the dissolution of the village's sole right of
ownership.   This trend was accelerated throughout the
1820's by Regulation VII, which (incomphrehensibly from one
exhibiting Orientalist sympathies) granted every co-parcener
the right to apply for the separation of his property
interests from those of the group, and which facilitated the
transfer of land by instituting a simple procedure for alien-
ation and sale.   Joint responsibility for the land revenue
was further undermined by the District Collector's practice
of registering all co-parceners as lambardars and by making
contracts with each of them individually.   For example, in
1820 eighty lambardars were appointed in one village, where
collective holdings were completely obliterated.[59]

---

[58]Ibid. p. 119.

[59]Misra, op. cit., p. 417.

In 1833 the Governor-General, Lord William Bentinck,[60]
tried to arrest the subdivision of tenurial rights by
ordering that villages be organized into mahals (or estates)
and that a single lambardar be engaged to represent each one.
But the transfer of property titles continued unabated.[61]
In the 1840's and 50's the sale of land gathered momentum
under the influence of a new generation of Company servants
for whom Orientalist awe at thousand year-old institutions
meant little and for whom the Utilitarian vision of an
atomized society held great appeal. By 1855 the battle to
save village institutions in the North-West   Provinces had
been lost when one such recruit, John Strachey,[62] the young
Collector of Moradabad, could claim their destruction as
positive progress and observe that

> no great changes can be brought about without
> some cause for regret. That the full recog-
> nition of private property rights will bring
> with it, as one of its inevitable results,
> the dissolution of the ancient village institu-

---

[60]William Cavendish Bentinck (1774-1839) Governor of
Madras, 1803-1807; Commander in Chief in Sicily, 1814;
Governor of Bengal, 1829; Commander in Chief in India, 1833-
1834; Governor-General, 1834-1835.

[61]Stokes, op. cit., p. 103.

[62]John Strachey (1823-1907) ICS; went to India in
1842; served in the North-West   Provinces, Judicial
Commissioner of the Central Provinces, 1862; President of
the Sanitary Commission, 1864; Officiating Chief Commissioner
of Oudh, 1866-1867; Member of the Governor-General's Council,
1868-1872; Lieutenant-Governor of the North-West   Provinces, 1874-1876; Finance Member of the Supreme Council,
1876-1880; Member of the Council of India, 1885-1895.

tions of the country seems indisputable, but
they are necessarily doomed to decay with the
establishment of good government and the
progress of civilization. The objects which
they were so admirably adapted to fulfill are
gradually passing away. The power which
their constitution gave them of powerful passive
resistance to oppression is now no longer needed.
As long as such institutions form the basis of
society, any large amount of progress is
impossible; and I believe that one of the
greatest advantages which the proceedings
connected with the last settlement conferred
upon these provinces was this possibility
before almost unknown, of disposing freely of
land like any other property.[63]

This was the voice of the mid-century, expressing the firm

conviction that the indigenous system of village self-rule

had outlived its usefulness.

In Bombay, Elphinstone was more alive than Mackenzie

in the North-West Provinces to the potential damage to the

village from a ryotwari survey; and he was also much more

conservative. Why, then, did village government collapse

more quickly in Bombay than it did in the North-West? The

short answer is that Elphinstone was outmaneuvered by his

own subordinates (who had different political goals), was

quite unable to supervise their activities in detail over an

area of 200,000 square miles, and was preoccupied with other

responsibilities as Governor. Despite lengthy and minute

advice from him, the Deccan Commissioners -- though faithfully

---

[63]John Strachey, "Frequency of Transfer of Proprietary
Title", 16 July 1855, Selections from the Records of the North-
Western Provinces, vol. IV, pp. 333-335.

administering a mahalwari settlement -- went their own way
on many other matters; and Elphinstone was seemingly
uncomprehending, uninformed and ineffective in stopping them.
When he eventually realized how widely they were destroying
village self-rule, his protests were too late.

The process was begun in 1818 while Elphinstone was
still Chief Commissioner of the Deccan. He was anxious to
preserve the institutions of village self-government at any
cost: upon them, he believed, social stability depended.
But this Olympian view was not shared as the priority of
policy by the Commissioners, who saw disturbing social
injustices under the rule of the patils in many of the
villages they visited. For them protection of the ryots
from oppression was more important than the maintenance of
traditional institutions. Although they followed the
Governor's instructions (he succeeded in 1819) to fix the
revenue demand on the village as a unit, they refused to
acknowledge the customary authority of the patils, deshmukhs,
and deshpandes where they deemed the ryots' interests to be
at risk. By thus ignoring traditional elites, they
reduced the ryots' respect for and reliance on them; and
they thereby began the destruction of the Maratha system of
local self-government.

Between 1818 and 1822 the Deccan Commissioners
simultaneously instituted a mahalwari settlement and
surreptitiously introduced innovovations which crippled the

village officials on whom it depended. First, they reduced
the patils' control over the village economy. They stripped
them of the authority to offer leases on preferential terms
in order to attract upris to the village; and they forbade
them to dispose of wasteland without government permission.[64]
Secondly, they diminished the patils' status within the
villages by limiting their dues and allowances and by
restricting their control of village expenses.[65] Next, they
curtailed the rights, prerogatives and responsibilities of
the deshmukhs and deshpandes, whom they considered "the fit
agents of despotic rule"[66] and whom they chastised as a
parasitic class steeped in extortion and deception, hostile
to the interests of both the cultivators and the state.
They wrote to Elphinstone -- who hoped otherwise -- that under
no circumstances would they either consult the deshmukhs and
deshpandes during revenue negotiations or pay them for
unsolicited advice.[67] Thus did the Deccan Commissioners
evade the spirit if not the letter of Elphinstone's land
revenue policy.

---

[64]Kumar, op. cit., p. 58.

[65]Ballhatchet, op. cit., p. 118.

[66]J. Briggs, "Revenue Report On Khandesh", 31 October
1821, Selection of Papers from the Records at the East India
House, relating to the Revenue, Police, and Civil and Criminal
Justice under the Company's Government in India, vol. IV, 1826,
p. 346.

[67]Ballhatchet, op. cit., p. 122.

Utilitarian officials in Bombay were in a decided
minority in relation to their Orientalist colleagues; but
three of them were able to shake the very foundations of
village self-rule from positions of high influence.   Foremost among them was the Superintendent of Revenue, Robert
Keith Pringle, appointed by Elphinstone in 1826 during a
brief flirtation with Benthamite constitutional thought.
Pringle succeeded in dealing an even heavier blow to the
solidarity of the Deccan village community than that meted
out surreptitiously by the Commissioners.   He regarded the
rivaj survey, which had been instituted by the peshwas at
the beginning of the 18th century and which was used by the
Commissioners as a rough guide to village assessment, as
grossly inaccurate and unfair.   Condemning it as "obscure,
fluctuating and unequal",[68] he proposed the substitution of
a rational plan based on Ricardo's rent theory.   What in
fact he devised was in immensely complicated procedure for
calculating the net produce of the land (by estimating the
gross produce of each biga -- or 2/3 acre -- for nine different
soil types, converting this into a money figure, deducting
overhead costs, and then fixing the state revenue demand at
55 per cent of the resultant sum).[69]

[68]R.K. Pringle, "Report on the Survey and Assessment
of the Deccan", 6 September 1828, Revenue Letters from Bombay,
vol. VIII, 1829-1830, p. 214.

[69]Stokes, op. cit., p. 100.

This eleborate survey scheme was applied in the taluka of Indapur, a revenue subdivision of Poona, between 1828 and 1830. Its consequences filled presidency officials with alarm. As the assessments for each village were slowly compiled, it emerged that the new survey would substantially lower the revenue obligation of the thulwaheeks while doubling that of the upris.[70] This surprised Pringle who, with Metcalfe and Munro, had assumed that village leaders throughout India had been arbitrarily transferring their village revenue obligations to the non-proprietary ryots. The Indapur survey demonstrated how limited the scope for exploitation had been in face of the staggering poverty of the ryots. Where the patils had demanded an excessive amount from them, they had fled to other villages which required lower contributions; and under the old system, the thulwaheeks had been obliged to shoulder their defaulted share of the tax burden.[71] By eliminating corporate responsibility Pringle's new plan removed the thulwaheeks' duty to assume a large percentage of the upris' taxes. It also increased the upris' tax burden to a degree that one-third chose to emigrate from the taluka.[72] Many who remained were tortured by Indian revenue officers but still paid less

---

[70]Kumar, op. cit., p. 104.

[71]Ibid., pp. 102-111.

[72]Dutt, op. cit., p. 375.

than one-half the estimated revenue in the first year.[73] As
a result, Bombay officials labelled Pringle's survey an
unmitigated disaster.

Indapur was but a small revenue unit within the Bombay
Presidency. It was, however, seen by the Utilitarians as a
crucible for the testing of Ricardian rent theory, and it was
watched by Orientalists with horrified fascination. Nothing
was done by them to inhibit this most notorious of
Utilitarian experiments in India: Pringle was followed in
Indapur in 1835 by two officials, H.E. Goldsmid[74] and George
Wingate,[75] who like him were appointed on the basis of sheer
competence and who rapidly brought their Utilitarian
convictions into play. In an attempt to resolve the
disaster bequeathed by Pringle yet remain faithful to Ricardo,
they simplified his method of calculating net produce. They
accepted his nine-fold soil classification but lowered the
rate of demand on all grades of soil and equalized the
revenue burden by reducing the obligations of the upris more
than those of thulwaheeks.[76] Further, they compared the

---

[73]Ibid.

[74]Henry Edward Goldsmid (1812-1855) entered the Bombay
Civil Service, 1832; Assistant to the Revenue Commissioner,
1835; devised the Revenue Survey of Western India and applied
it, 1835-1845; Private Secretary to the Governor of Bombay,
1847-1848; Secretary in the Revenue Department, 1848; Chief
Secretary in the Revenue Department, 1854.

[75]George Wingate (1812-1879) served in the Bombay
Engineers from 1829; retired as a Major; was Revenue Survey
Commissioner in Bombay, 1835-1845.

[76]Kumar, op. cit., pp. 120-121.

results of the field survey with the records of sums actually paid in tax over the preceding decade in an effort to reconcile Ricardian calculations with the old rivaj rates and to reach a fair and acceptable compromise.[77] These modifications were so successful that their formula was later adopted throughout Western and Central India.[78]

The new survey yielded a reasonable revenue for the state, but it eliminated any lingering sense of corporate responsibility for the land revenue. For tax purposes Goldsmid and Wingate treated all cultivators equally and ignored the village community as a revenue-assessing and collecting body. Their unit of assessment was the individual field; their agency of settlement was government officials; and the object of their system was the endowment of each ryot with a permanent and saleable property right.[79] The only privilege they allowed village leaders to retain was that of dividing property among their heirs at will: all other proprietors were forced to accept the law of primogeniture.[80]

---

[77]Stokes, op. cit., p. 104.

[78]Martineau, op. cit., vol I, p. 26.

[79]Goldsmid and Wingate, "Joint Report" 17 October 1840, Official Correspondence on the System of Revenue Survey and Assessment in Bombay Presidency, revised ed. 1859. p. vi.

[80]Stokes, op. cit., p. 125.

Thus did Goldsmid and Wingate complete the destruction -- begun under the unseeing eye of Elphinstone -- of the Deccan village community. As good Utilitarians they believed that the natural and historical Indian society was a state of independent ryots, not a network of villages. "Corporations, communities, municipalities, republics ... where involving a common ownership and participation of liabilities and advantages," they asserted in 1840, "appear to us in opposition to nature".[81] This was the new orthodoxy of the Company servants of the 1840's and 50's; and it was supported by a new view of Indian village history cooked up for the purpose. "Joint responsibility for the payment of revenue and joint village management were, perhaps, universal in the Deccan", Goldsmid and Wingate conceded; but they could "find no traces of joint ownership, and must believe that it never existed".[82] The notion popular among members of the Boards of Revenue in Madras and the North-West Provinces -- that the village community improved the ryots' lot by means of mutual aid in times of distress -- was dismissed by them as quixotic:

> Our views of human nature are not sufficiently favourable to permit our indulging in expecta-
> tions so fair and promising as those portrayed
> by the /‾Deccan_7 Board in their pleasing picture
> of the anticipated effect of the village system of
> the North-Western Provinces, where families will be

---

[81]Goldsmid and Wingate, op. cit., p. vii.

[82]Ibid.

> united by the closest bonds of concord and
> sympathy -- where the poor will be supported
> by the affluent, the widows and orphans
> encouraged to look for protection from their
> natural supporters.[83]

Such spontaneous community support for the poor and

unfortunate was to their understanding not only unlikely:

it was, more importantly, evil. By encouraging idleness

and sloth, it impeded useful industry.[84] Goldsmid and

Wingate were convinced that the only way to raise India's

economic prospects and to protect villagers from oppression

was to transform the ryot into an independent property owner

who was responsible for his own welfare. Their experiment

in Indapur raised these two minor officials to preachers of

the highest influence of the repression of village self-rule.

The extinguishment of village self-government, which

took forty years to achieve in Bombay and the North-West

Provinces, was accomplished with startling rapidity in Madras.

This was largely due to the direct determination of Sir Thomas

Munro, the Governor, though he was helped by the inheritance

of villages whose institutions had virtually collapsed

under the stress of 18th century warfare. Munro's anxiety

to eradicate those village governments which remained was

born of a desire to replace what he saw as unfair, undemocratic

and unhistorical with a village system which guaranteed equal

---

[83]Ibid., p. ix.

[84]Ibid.

opportunity and political rights for the ryots.   His vision
was to rescue the economic equality of the ancient "natural
state" of Indian society and marry it with the mutual
co-operation which the villages represented.   His ambitions
brought him into immediate conflict with the Madras Board of
Revenue, with whom he waged a long and heated debate on the
merit of the ryotwari over the mahalwari settlement.

It was in Madras that the ryotwari settlement was
"born": in 1792 Sir Alexander Read, Munro's mentor, devised
it as an alternative to the zemindari permanent settlement
adopted five years earlier in Bengal.   Having found no
large estates in the south, Read concluded that the individual field, not the village, was the historical unit of
assessment for tax.   Accordingly he proposed that a survey
of each ryot's holdings be made field-by-field; that a
permanent assessment be calculated for each plot of land; and
that a contract be made annually between the state and the
ryot on the basis of the exact amount of land under cultivation that year.[85]   Munro as Principal Collector enthusiastically applied Read's plan in the Ceded Districts between 1801
and 1807 and became the most outspoken exponent of the
ryotwari system in India.

Opposition to the universal adoption of Read's

[85]Misra, op. cit., p. 452.

ryotwari settlement was first voiced in 1808 by John Hodgson,
a junior member of the Board of Revenue, after he discovered
viable village communities in the Jagir district.[86]
Hodgson's advice that collectors should settle with the
village patils rather than with individual ryots expressed
the mounting misgivings of the entire Board. Alarmed
primarily at the excessive demands on manpower, expense and
time entailed in an individual field assessment (for these
were practical rather that philosophic men), they condemned
the ryotwari survey in a formal minute as

> a Herculean task, or rather a visionary project
> in the most civilised countries of Europe, of which
> every statistical information is possessed, and of
> which Government are at one with the people, viz.,
> to fix a land rent, not on each province, district,
> or country, not on each estate or farm but on every[87]
> separate field within their dominions.

Board members believed that a ryotwari settlement was not
only impractical: it was dangerous as well. They feared
that a settlement between government officials and individual
cultivators would obliterate collective practices and with
them a vital protective buffer between the ryot and the state.

> In pursuit of this supposed improvement, we find
> / a small band of foreign conquerors_/ unintention-
> ally dissolving the ancient ties, the ancient usages
> which united the republic of each Hindu village,
> and by a kind of agrarian law, newly assessing

---

[86]Timothy Beaglehole, Thomas Munro and the Development
of Administrative Policy in Madras, 1792-1818, Cambridge, 1966,
p. 85.

[87]Quoted by Dutt, op. cit., p. 149.

and parcelling out the lands which from time
immemorial had belonged to the village
community.[88]

Exposed on the one hand to the potential rapacity of ill-

advised or zealous revenue collectors and on the other to

possible over-assessment by the state, the ryot of Madras

might in their view become as destitute as the cultivators

of Bengal.

For a while the Board had their way. Between 1808 and

1818 settlements were duly made between the state and village

patils wherever ryotwari contracts had not previously been

agreed. But far from invigorating village self-rule as

Hodgson and the Board hoped, the mahalwari settlement actually

killed all remaining sense of corporate identity and mutual

responsibility. This unexpected result was caused by the

patils' systematic oppression of the ryots: annually they

over-assessed them; in good years they confiscated their

profits; in bad years they required them to cultivate the

waste as well as their regular holdings; and consistently

they forbade them access to government officials empowered

to redress such grievances. Within a decade the ryots were

bankrupted and the villages impoverished.[89]

After this calamitous experiment the Board was hard-

---

[88]Ibid.

[89]Ibid.

pressed to refuse Munro's demand, on his accession as
Governor, to substitute ryotwari settlements as soon as
the village leases expired.   They endorsed his plan with
full anticipation of the abandonment of corporate cultivation which followed. Munro was unmoved by their grief,
regarding this as the first essential step to the birth of
a flourishing village system based on individual peasant
proprietorship and a healthy market in land.   Within a
decade the Board's worst fears for traditional self-
government in Madras were realized.   A further century
was required to realize the vision of Munro.

The history of British provision for village
government must be said, between 1800 and 1850, to be a
tale of large-scale miscalculation, misjudgment and bungling.
For all their sympathy with the ancient practices of the
people they ruled, and their anxiety as conservatives to
treat Indian civilization on its own terms, the Orientalists
who constituted the majority of India's administrators were
men floundering in a totally alien culture.   Their first
aspiration was peace, and they at least may be credited with
that;   their second was prosperity, dependent upon peace,
and even the poorest Indians better off -- if only marginal-
ly -- under British rule.   But their principal objective,
as conquerers of a disrupted and war-ravaged country, was to
preserve and build upon what little stability survived.
Hence the importance of nourishing traditional modes of

government and of allowing the Indians, as best as most possible, to manage their own local affairs: in this grand plan the preservation of a vital system of self-governing villages was essential, and the correct calculation of revenue policy on the land indispensable. It is a paradox that the Utilitarians -- who did not, for the most part, reach positions of highest influence -- foresaw more accurately than the Orientalists the effects of the various policy options on the patil-dominated village and saw that once the patil, as the figurehead of the village, was destroyed, its cohesion was lost. It is a paradox because the Utilitarians took not a scrap of interest in the fine detail of Indian culture, regarding the peoples of India through philosophers' spectacles as unenlightened exhibitors of the universal principles of human nature.

Lord Colebrooke
By my Uncle Lord Metcalfe
persons & a Pimapala and
his Volume Med Papers with view preference

Lord Colebrooke

CHAPTER THREE

THE ORGANIZATION OF GOVERNMENT:

THE DEBATE ON CENTRALIZATION : 1858 - 1861

The Mutiny of 1857 demonstrated the precarious hold --
all too evident to an earlier generation -- of a small
foreign civil service over a huge and sprawling Asian
population. Concern to strengthen the bonds unifying the
three presidencies and five provinces which comprised British
India at mid-century led Parliament in London to demand an
immediate reorganization of the regime in India. The question
of how to govern India was answered by adopting a policy
of centralization -- of concentrating power in a rigid chain
of command with London at its apex, the presidency and
provincial districts at its bottom, and Calcutta as its
effective center. It was a sweeping constitutional revolution,
effected with remarkable speed, by men who were convinced
that centralized government was the only practicable and
effective means of controlling a rebellious people.

I. ADMINISTRATIVE CENTRALIZATION

Discussion on how to govern India began with the
crucial relationship between the newly-created Secretary of
State for India, with his council of twelve in London, and
the Viceroy with his council of five in India. The
Secretary's importance in the new order was unrivalled, for

he controlled the purse-strings of the Empire. In theory both the Cabinet and his own advisory group, the Council of India, could veto his orders; but in practice neither they nor Parliament, which listened annually to the Secretary's budget speech, ever seriously contested his authority[1]. Reluctance to challenge him arose largely from ignorance of Indian affairs caused by the daunting length of imperial despatches: one document of 1845 extended to no fewer than 46,000 pages -- far more than Members of Parliament could reasonably be expected to read[2]. Until the late 1880's, when the Indian National Congress began to attract attention and Irish politicians took up the cry of British misrule in India, few individuals inside the House of Commons and fewer still outside (the intrepid Florence Nightingale being an outstanding exception) took an active interest in Indian affairs.

Moving down the chain of command from London to Calcutta, the relations between the Secretary of State for India and the Viceroy were defined as much by personality

---

[1] P.J. Thomas, The Growth of Federal Finance in India, Being a Survey of India's Public Finances 1833 - 1939, London, 1939, p. 88.

[2] Ibid., p. 60

as by constitutional arrangements. Sir Charles Wood[3],
Secretary of State from 1859 through 1865, displayed a self-
assurance bordering on arrogance in his communications with
the Government of India. The expertise which he had acquired
on a wide range of subjects during his tenure as President
of the East India Company Board of Control from 1854 to
1858 ensured his continued sway over the first three Viceroys,
whose knowledge of India was less comprehensive. This
dominance was much resented: Lord Canning[4], the first
Viceroy, denounced Wood as "one of the most insensitive public
men I ever came across -- as well as one of the most
provocative"[5]; the Earl of Elgin[6], his successor, regarded
Wood's insistent, petty meddling in matters of detail as
humiliating and complained bitterly that his predecessors
had been Governors-General, but he did not have authority to

---

[3]Sir Charles Wood, 1st Viscount Halifax (1800-1885);
MP for Grimsby, 1826; for Halifax, 1832; Joint Secretary
to the Treasury, 1832; Secretary of the Admiralty, 1835;
Chancellor of the Exchequer, 1846; President of the Board
of Control, 1852, First Lord of the Admiralty, 1855;
Secretary of State for India, 1859-1865.

[4]Charles John Canning, 1st Earl (1812-1862) MP for
Warwick, 1836; Under-Secretary of State for Foreign Affairs,
1841-1845; Postmaster-General, 1853; Governor-General of
India, 1855-1858; Viceroy, 1858-1861.

[5]Quoted by Michael Maclagen, "Clemency" Canning, London
1962, p. 268 (Canning to Frere, 8 January 1861).

[6]James Bruce, 8th Earl of Elgin (1811-1863); MP for
Southampton, 1841; Governor of Jamaica, 1842; Governor-
General of Canada, 1846-1854; envoy to China, 1857;
Postmaster-General, 1859; Viceroy of India, 1861-1863.

confer a pension of £2 a month on a retired clerk[7]. Shortly before his retirement Wood repented of his excessive interference and confessed that "upon the whole, the Government of India can manage Indian matters better than the Government at home"[8]. Yet despite this belated recantation, he retained the derisive sobriquet "Maharajah Wood"[9] and, in the scathing words of one Anglo-Indian journalist, "occupied /‾in the mind of Indian officaldom_7 the place which the Pope fills in the Protestant mind of England every 5th of November"[10].

The power of the Secretary of State over the Viceroy was augmented by the construction of the overland cable in 1868, the opening of the Suez Canal in 1869, and the completion of the submarine cable in 1870. These technological advances eliminated the time lapse in correspondence incurred during the long sea voyage around the tip of Africa and considerably reduced the latitude for discretion and independent action which it had afforded Indian officials. Further, they provided the Secretary of State with instant information and enabled him to issue directives swiftly to the Government of India.

---

[7]I.T. Prichard, The Administration of India, 1859-1868, London, 1869, vol. I, p. 122.

[8]Martineau, op. cit., vol. I, p. 447 (Wood to Frere, 17 April 1865).

[9]R.B. Smith, The Life of Lord Lawrence, London, 1885, 6th ed., vol. II, p. 293.

[10]Prichard, op. cit., vol. I, p. 123

Despite these improvements in communication and transportation, the Secretary of State remained too remote from Asia to interfere in the daily administration of the Raj. And as a consequence, the effective center of Indian administration was Calcutta. Because the imperial government was a despotism, all power was ultimately concentrated in name, if not in fact, in the person of the Viceroy. As the Queen's vicegerent, he was granted the courtesy title of Viceroy by royal proclamation in 1858 (though he was still called by his traditional title, the Governor-General of India, in official documents). With the creation of Indian orders of merit like the Star of India after the Mutiny and with durbars like the Imperial Assembly of Indian princes in 1877, the ceremony surrounding the viceregal office expanded dramatically to satisfy the insatiable craving for pageantry shared by Britons and Indians alike.

An important step towards the augmentation of viceregal power was taken by Canning in 1858/59, when he attempted to assert his personal control over imperial policy. Before the Mutiny attempts of Governors-General to take the lead in policy direction were frustrated by the practice of referring all business, however trivial, to the Executive Council (the Commander-in-Chief, three civil servants of more than ten years standing, and the Law Member plus the Governor-General) for corporate decision. The consideration of wider policy was swamped by concern for bureaucratic detail; and the

Council was transformed into what Canning called "a gigantic Essay Club"[11]. In 1858 Canning resolved to disentangle himself from this cumbersome procedure and persuaded the home authorities to sanction the reorganization of the Council on the portfolio system. By making each member responsible for a particular department and by delegating all routine matters to a department secretary, he hoped that most decisions would be taken by the bureaucracy, leaving the Governor-General in Council free to attend to major problems and strategic decisions.[12] But the plan did not work. Department heads proved reluctant to act without the Viceroy's prior knowledge and approval, paperwork continued to submerge the Council, and big issues continued to receive less attention than they deserved. The Governor-General in Council remained the clumsy instrument of government it had always been. Nevertheless, its members treated the Viceroy with deference: when opinion was divided he was able to impose his will; and when the Council was united against him (which was rare) he was capable of overriding it.

The superiority of the Governor-General in Council over the presidencies and provinces grew out of traditional Asian autocracy. Its absolute theoretical control over the

---

[11]S. Gopal, British Policy in India, 1858-1905, Cambridge, 1965, p. 17.

[12]Ibid., p. 16.

local governments was laid down by the Charter Act of 1833
and reiterated in a constitutional formula which remained
unchanged until 1918:

> Every local Government shall obey the orders of
> the Governor-General in Council and keep him
> constantly and diligently informed of its
> proceedings and of all matters which ought in its
> opinion to be reported to him or as to which he
> required information and is under his superintendence,
> direction, and control in all matters relating to
> the government of its province.[13]

The Charter Act went on to affirm the supremacy of the
Governor-General in Council by stripping all of the local
governments except the presidencies of Bombay and Madras of
their legislative powers; by forbidding them to correspond
directly with the East India Company authorites in London;
and by prohibiting them from maintaining local armies. The
"non-regulation" provinces created after 1833 (the Punjab, the
Central Provinces, and Lower Burma) were even denied
executive councils.

When the charter was renewed in 1853 the Governor-
General, Lord Dalhousie[14], sought to advance the policy of
centralization by making the Governors of Madras and Bombay
deputies of the Governor-General in Council. He suggested
to the Parliamentary Select Committee drawing up the new
charter in London that the presidency executive councils be

---

[13] 5 and 6 George IV C. 61.

[14] James Andrew Broun Ramsay, 10th Earl and 1st Marquis
Dalhousie (1812-1860); MP for Haddington, 1837; Vice-
President of the Board of Trade, 1843; President of the Board
of Trade, 1845; Governor-General, 1849-1856.

abolished and that the Governors be demoted to the level of
Lieutenant-Governors[15]. This proposal was condemned by the
majority of retired Indian civil servants who gave evidence
before the Committee because it pushed centralization too
far; it was also criticized by Members of Parliament. John
Bright voiced the concern of those who regarded a highly
centralized administration as anomalous in view of the natural
divisions of the Indian subcontinent. Mooting the desirability
of abolishing the post of Governor-General and dismantling
the Empire altogether, he asked rhetorically: "what would be
thought if the whole of Europe were under one Governor who
knew only the language of the Feejee Islands?"[16] Elaborating
on this provocative question, he suggested

> that we should have Presidencies and not an
> Empire .... I would propose to have at least
> five Presidencies in India, and I would have
> the Governors of those Presidencies perfectly
> equal in rank and salary. The capitals of
> those Presidencies would probably be Calcutta,
> Madras, Bombay, Agra, and Lahore. I will take
> the Presidency of Madras as an illustration ....
> It has a Governor and a Council. I would give
> to it a Governor and Council still, but would
> confine all their duties to the Presidency of
> Madras, and I would treat it just as if Madras
> was the only portion of India connected with

[15]R.J. Moore, Sir Charles Wood's Indian Policy,
1853-1866, Manchester, 1966, pp. 46-47.

[16]Quoted by Sir John Strachey, India, Its Administration
and Progress, London, 1888, p. 46.

> this country. I would have its finances,
> its taxation, its justice, and its police
> departments, as well as its public works
> and military departments precisely the same
> as if it were a State having no connection
> with any other part of India, and recognized
> only as a dependency of this country.[17]

The opposition of Indian civil servants and British

politicians enabled Wood -- ever watchful of opportunities

to concentrate power in his own hands -- to rebuff Dalhousie's

attempt to strengthen the Governor-General's position. He

insisted that the existing distinctions among local

authorities be maintained and that the prestige of the

administrations of Madras and Bombay be raised by appoint-

ing as Governors distinguished men capable of commanding

the respect of the Governor-General's Council.[18]

In India concern to preserve the independence of the

local governments united many British officials against the

centralization of power in viceregal hands. Believing that

the Viceroy had been invested with too much power, one Anglo-

Indian journalist reckoned that "it is quite impossible that

any one man, be his physical and mental powers what they may,

can master the details of the affairs of such an Empire as

India"[19]. This was fair. The Viceroy's limited knowledge

of the territory outside Bengal led him to rely for information

---

[17] G.M. Trevelyan, The Life of John Bright, London
1925, pp. 265-266.

[18] Moore, op. cit., pp. 47-48

[19] J.B. Norton, Topics for Indian Statesmen, London
1858, p. 143.

about the South and West on his Executive Council and on the
Government of India bureaucracy in Calcutta. Had his
advisors on the Council been selected from all over India as
Parliament intended, the Governor-General would have been
constantly exposed to a broad range of regional interests;
and indeed the local governments would have been adequately
represented. But with the exception of one man from Bombay
and another from Madras, the Executive Council was drawn
exclusively from Bengal and London. The Viceroy's
bureaucratic advisors were also recruited primarily from the
imperial capital.[20] Even after the Government of India was
separated from the Government of Fort William (Bengal) in
1854, the force of tradition allied to the vested interests
of the Bengal civil service proved impossible to break; and
recruitment to Government of India departments from outside
the capital was virtually unknown.[21]

The dominance of Bengal was hotly resented by officials
in Bombay and Madras, who were jealous of the excessive money
and attention lavished on Bengal and the non-regulation
provinces. The charge of favoritism is difficult to
demonstrate statistically given the confused accounting
methods which prevailed before the reorganization of imperial
finances in 1861. Nevertheless, random evidence suggests
that in comparison to the northern provinces, Madras if not

[20]Ibid.

[21]B.B. Misra, op. cit., p. 107.

Bombay was starved of funds for public works: the neglect
of its roads was notorious throughout the Empire, and the
lack of amenities earned it the nickname of "the benighted
presidency". Charges were often made by presidency civil
servants that projects proposed by them were rejected by the
Calcutta bureaucracy, which they claimed (with good cause)
was acquainted only with the habits, tastes, and law codes
of Upper India. Further, local officials alleged that the
Bombay and Madras representatives on the Viceroy's Council
were disdained by the Bengal members as if they belonged to
an inferior caste.[22] One embittered Governor of Madras
recommended that the only way to kill the obnoxious "spirit
of Bengal" which permeated the Government of India was
to transfer the imperial capital from Calcutta to Delhi --
a suggestion often repeated and finally accepted in
1913.[23]

Partiality for Bengal and Upper India provoked
Madras and Bombay to evade central control as much as
possible. Their efforts to carve out independent spheres of
power were pursued with a niggling pettiness which

---

[22]Thomas, op. cit., pp. 64-65

[23]Humphrey Trevelyan, The India We Left: Charles
Trevelyan 1826-1865; Humphrey Trevelyan 1929-1947, London
1972, p. 76.

Sir George Campbell[24], a non-regulation civilian who later

became Lieutenant-Governor of Bengal, judged to be futile

and even counter-productive.

> Bombay and Madras are, as it were, the most
> distant horses of the coach which the
> Governor-General as coachman has under his
> command, heavily bitted, but which he has
> not a long-enough whip properly to reach;
> so that while they are prevented from going
> forward, they have every opportunity of
> jibbing and going backward.[25]

Friction between the Calcutta bureaucracy and the local

governments became incessant and increasingly irritating to

both sides after 1858 (as will be discussed in Chapter Five).

Not even the most enthusiastic supporter of

centralized government could claim that the system functioned

smoothly; for, on the one hand, it made the Governor-

General in Council ever suspicious of the administrators of

the two great presidencies; and on the other, it made the

civil servants of Bombay and Madras anxious to circumvent

and thwart Calcutta's control.

----

[24]George Campbell (1824-1892); went to India, 1842;
served in the North-West Provinces and Cis-Sutlej States,
in the Punjab, 1841; called to the Inner Temple while on
furlough, 1854; Modern India, 1852; India As It May Be
1853; Commissioner of the Cis-Sutlej States, 1855; 2nd
Civil Commissioner of Oudh after the Mutiny; Judge of the
Calcutta High Court, 1862; Head of the Orissa Famine
Commission, 1866-1867; Chief Commissioner of the Central
Provinces, 1867-1871; Lieutenant-Governor of Bengal,
1871-1874; MP for Kirkcaldy, 1875-1892.

[25]Sir George Campbell, India As It May Be, London,
1853, p. 54.

The construction of a clear chain of command from the
Queen and Secretary of State to presidency and provincial
district officers between 1858 and 1861 was thus not remarkably
successful. The constitutional provisions instituted in
1858 ensured the Secretary of State's ultimate sway over the
Government of India by granting him the right to veto
viceregal proposals, correspond directly with the presidency
Governors, and control the Indian budget. But they did not
give the Viceroy an equally unambiguous position of supremacy
over his inferiors. No significant changes were made in his
relationships to his Council, the central bureaucracy and
the local governments. As a consequence, a fairly un-
systematic approach to the formulation of imperial policy
survived; and the debilitating, century-old
power struggle between Calcutta and the local capitals
continued unabated.

II.   LEGISLATIVE CENTRALIZATION

Canning did rather better in asserting viceregal
control over legislation. Between 1858 and 1861 he introduced
reforms which enabled him to eliminate all potential
opposition within the imperial Legislative Council and to
endow the new presidency legislative councils, set up in
1861, with a minimum of power. His success in increasing
the authority of the Viceroy over policy direction was
achieved by enlisting the support of the Secretary of State,
Sir Charles Wood, whose interests for once coincided with
his own.

Shortly after the Mutiny Canning and Wood began to
discuss their strategy for destroying the Legislative
Council created by Lord Dalhousie in 1853. To their minds
the Governor-General had vested a dangerous amount of power
in non-official -- and therefore uncontrollable -- delegates:
he had appointed two judges from Calcutta to sit on the
Governor-General's Council when it sat to make laws. He
had also given the Council too much independence: he had
drawn up a code of procedure which required business to be
conducted according to parliamentary practice, meetings to
be open to the public and a record of debate to be published;
and he had granted this new body an unrestricted license to
debate and legislate on all imperial issues.[26] There is
little doubt that if Dalhousie had informed Wood (then
President of the Board of Control) of his intention to
delegate unlimited power to the Council, the proposal would
have been vetoed at once. But he cleverly refrained from
supplying London with a detailed explanation of the Council's
privileges until Wood asked to inspect them in 1864.[27] By
then it was too late to reject them. When Wood expressed
horror at the Council's independence, Dalhousie cooly

[26]Misra, op. cit., p. 22.

[27]Moore, op. cit., p. 51.

advised him:

> your power over the Legislative Council is
> limited exclusively to the right of
> disallowing any act which they may pass and
> of requiring its repeal. The Legislative
> Council is a separate body constituted by
> law and with the exception I have just named,
> wholly independent of all other authority ....
> You will find them asserting their legislative
> independence just as strongly as the 658
> English gentlemen at Westminster .... And you
> may rest assured that if any demand be made upon
> them to submit, either generally or specifically,
> their legislation for previous consideration
> in England, they will ... most decidedly refuse.[28]

The net effect of these sweeping innovations was to transform

the Council as legislature from an intimate group working

behind closed doors into a pretentious body welcoming

public scrutiny. With a free rein to operate independently

the Legislative Council was quickly set up by its non-

official delegates as a check on the executive. Its power

to impede the Governor-General's direction of imperial

policy was established in 1856, when it demanded the right

to call for witnesses and secret documents; and its scope

for opposition was enlarged in 1858, when it initiated

correspondence with the local governments without prior

reference to the Executive Council.[29] The nominated members

were certainly obstreperous, but they were also politically

inept; and their defeat in the power struggle which followed

---

[28]Dalhousie to Wood, 18 September, 1854, I.O.L. Eur. Mss. F 78/18/1.

[29]Misra, op. cit., p. 25.

Canning's decision to eliminate them from the Legislative
Council was almost a foregone conclusion.

No sooner had Canning informed Wood of his intention
to reduce the Council's independence than Wood resolved to
abolish the Legislative Council altogether.[30] His determination stemmed from a conviction that Dalhousie had duped him
into endorsing a scheme which he would never have approved
had he been fully apprised of the Governor-General's plans --
and he was not accustomed to playing the fool. As he
explained to Sir Bartle Frere,

> Whatever notions may now prevail, nobody at that
> time (1853) -- and I myself introduced the Bill --
> ever dreamt of a debating body with open doors and
> even quasi-independence. Lord Dalhousie began
> wrong, and I am afraid that everything since then
> has tended in the same direction .... It is clear
> that the Legislative Council cannot go on
> constituted as now .... We cannot stand half a
> dozen gentlemen aping the House of Commons as an
> independent representative body.[31]

The posturing of the judges was equally distasteful to
Canning, who was infuriated by their relentless opposition
to his policies. Roundly he denounced Sir Barnes Peacock,
the Chief Justice of Calcutta (the so-called "Patriot Judge")
and Sir Mordaunt Wells, the other self-appointed head of the
opposition:

> The leaders of the agitation are the Queen's
> judges Peacock and Wells; the speeches they
> have been making in the Council (those of Wells

[30]Quoted by Maclagen, op. cit., p. 270 (Canning to
Granville, 4 July 1860).

[31]Martineau, op. cit., vol. I, p. 336 (Wood to Frere,
18 February 1861).

at least) are of the coarsest claptrap.
Peacock is honest and in earnest, and very
obstinate. Wells, who has never been twenty
miles from Calcutta, is sheer bunkum.[32]

Agreeing that Peacock was a "public nuisance", Wood urged

Canning to "keep him quiet" until the Secretary of State

and his advisors in London found an acceptable way to remove

the judges from the Council.[33]

Despite the desirability of excluding all non-official

appointees from the Legislative Council -- thereby destroying

Peacock's "grand inquest of the nation"[34] -- Wood feared that

"closing the doors" would anger the English residents of

Calcutta.[35] Concerned to avoid an ugly confrontation, he

and Canning pondered the merits of replacing the imperial

Legislative Council with an American-style cabinet of

ministers and delegating all legislative power to local

Legislative Councils in the presidencies and provinces.[36]

This alluring escape route would probably have been pursued

---

[32]Wood to Canning, 24 November 1860, I.O.L. Eur. Mss.
F 78/5.

[33]Wood to Canning, 27 May 1861 I.O.L. Eur. Mss. F
78/8.

[34]Wood to Canning, 9 April 1860 I.O.L. Eur. Mss. F
78/3.

[35]Wood to Canning, 18 October 1860, I.O.L. Eur. Mss.
F 78/5.

[36]Wood to Canning, 26 July 1859, I.O.L. Eur. Mss
F 78/1.

but for an intervention by Sir Charles Trevelyan, the Governor of Madras. In the spring of 1860 he refused outright to sanction a new imperial income tax, making this his pretext to challenge the right of the central government to impose a uniform fiscal system on India. Although he was swiftly rebuked and the Government of India's predominance was asserted, his opposition reminded Canning and Wood of the overriding need to maintain a strong central government. In August 1860 Wood breathed a sigh of relief that the temptation to invest all legislative power in local bodies had been overcome in the nick of time:

> I certainly think it would not be wise at this moment to set up presidential debating societies. What a much worse state of things it would have been, if Trevelyan had been making inflammatory speeches in the Legislative Council of Madras, with the concurrence of all the members, officials, non-officials, and natives! Of course they would have asserted the pleasant doctrine that they need not be taxed ....[37]

The dangers of setting up powerful local legislatures were, Wood concluded, "almost insuperable, without a risk to the credit, and indeed the cohesion and existence, of the Indian Empire".[38] He and Canning finally agreed to retain the imperial Legislative Council to advise the executive on general policy for the whole subcontinent and to exercise the supreme right to tax; but they sharply reduced its authority by empowering presidency councils to make local laws with the advice and consent of the Viceroy.

[37] Wood to Canning, 27 August 1860, I.O.L. Eur. Mss. F 78/4.

[38] Ibid.

Once legislative power had been divided between
Calcutta and the presidency towns, Wood and Canning turned
to the knotty problem of the representation of popular
interests, which Dalhousie had attempted to solve by adding
the judges to the Council. Wood made no attempt to hide his
unshakeable belief that "the Government of India must be a
despotism": the "most merciful rule over conquered millions
is a despotism and the most tyrannical is that of the lower
members of the dominant class" (i.e. people like Peacock and
Wells) [39]. To his mind the principle of representation --
however commendable in theory -- could not be applied to any
practical advantage in India; for if it were difficult to
find fair-minded European delegates to the legislature, it
would be almost impossible to discover suitable Indians [40].
Writing to Bartle Frere in 1861, he confided that he was

> very uneasy as to the future bodies to be con-
> stituted in India. Representative bodies, in
> any real sense, you cannot have, and I do not
> think that any external element will really do
> good. It may satisfy the English at Calcutta
> to have an English merchant or English planter
> in the Council, but I am by no means sure that
> it would improve the legislation; and you
> cannot put natives in who are in any sense the
> exponents of active opinion, or who could take
> any part in the deliberations. [41]

---

[39] Wood to Laing, 26 March 1861, I.O.L. Eur. Mss.
F 78/7.

[40] Wood to Canning, 27 August 1860, I.O.L. Eur. Mss.
F 78/4.

[41] Martineau, op. cit., vol. I, p. 336 (Wood to Frere,
18 February 1861).

Canning was equally adament in opposing popular government in
India. To Stanley's[42] suggestion that the Council might be
regarded as the harbinger of representative institutions, he
replied that such bodies were so remote "that there is no
object in forming a nucleus for them now".[43]

Frere was troubled by the plan to eliminate all non-
official delegates from the Council and warned Canning and
Wood that the problem of representation could not be so
lightly dismissed. As he saw it, the Government of India
had two choices: it could either go backward and restrict
the Council to its original official composition or go forward
and develop its popular character. The digression advocated
by the Secretary of State and the Viceroy was in his view as
impossible as it was undesirable: impossible because public
opinion in England and India would prevent the government
from reducing the powers of the Council and from restricting
the publicity which had been given to its debates; and
undesirable because of the danger entailed in formulating
policy without proper constitutional channels for registering
dissatisfaction and disaffection. The very stability of the

---

[42]Edward Henry Stanley, 15th Earl of Derby (1826-1893)
MP for Kings Lynn, 1848; Under-Secretary for the Colonies,
1852; Secretary for the Colonies, 1858; President of the
Board of Control, 1858; Secretary of State for India,
1858-1859; Foreign Secretary, 1868, 1878; Secretary for
the Colonies, 1874, 1882.

[43]Quoted by Thomas Metcalf, The Aftermath of the Mutiny,
Princeton, 1964, p. 267 (Canning to Stanley, 16 May 1859).

Raj, Frere contended, rested upon the government's alacrity in desisting from "the perilous experiment of continuing to legislate for millions of people, with few means of knowing, except by rebellion, whether the laws made suit them or not".[44]

Wood and Canning identified the racial bitterness unleashed in 1857-58 as the outstanding impediment to the implementation of the representative principle as advocated by Frere. The Mutiny had, to their minds, destroyed mutual understanding between Europeans and Indians, and with it the precondition of a system of popular representation in India. Unforgettable atrocities like the slaying of British women and children and the "blowing away" of sepoy mutineers by canon had, indeed, made unemotional and unbiased assessments by victor and vanquished alike impossible. Post-Mutiny racial prejudice consumed the most unlikely members of Anglo-Indian society. Even Macaulay, who had returned to England twenty years earlier, exhibited a hatred for the mutineers and a desire for vengeance which shocked him into confessing: "I, who could not bear to see a beast or bird in pain, could look on without winking while Nana Sahib underwent all the tortures of Ravaillac"[45]. Among the just and powerful as among the ill-bred and poorly educated, racism became alarmingly explicit; and many agreed with Sir John Lawrence that the

---

[44]Martineau, op. cit., vol. I, p. 335 (minute of March 1860).

[45]G.O. Trevelyan, The Life and Letters of Lord Macaulay, London, 1876, vol. II, pp. 433-436.

Mutiny could be regarded as nothing less than a "war of race"[46]. Against the tide of racism stood a small but important minority which deplored this sudden change of attitude. Sir Charles Trevelyan deeply regretted that the "British temper towards India" had taken a decided turn for the worse since 1857;[47] while Frere lamented that "the sympathy which Englishmen, whether long resident or fresh to India, felt for the native has changed to a general feeling of repugnance if not of apathy"[48]. The most bitter racists were not, however, members of the Indian Civil Service, but European settlers. These people had never shared the government's paternal attitude towards the Indian people or its zeal for improving Indian society. Profit rather than duty had lured them to the East, and condescension bordering on contempt characterized their relations to the Indians. Before the Mutiny the largest single group of non-official Europeans were the indigo planters of Bengal; but between 1860 and 1870 their numbers were swelled by the founders of the great textile industries of Bombay and the jute factories of Bengal as well as by traders and commercial travellers attracted by the rapid extension of the railways. A strong bond among these diverse groups was forged by a common ignorance of and

---

[46]Quoted by Thomas, op. cit., p. lxiii.

[47]Ibid., p. 14

[48]Martineau, op. cit., vol. I, p. 336 (Frere to Wood 18 February 1861).

scorn for all things Indian and an equally forceful sense of racial superiority nurtured by lurid accounts of savage Indian behavior during the Mutiny.[49]

In 1860 two events took place which ignited the latent racism of the white settlers, exposed their implacable hostility to the Indians, and proved with apparent con- clusiveness to Canning and Wood that a representative system would founder in an India warped by racial intolerance. The first racial flare-up occurred in Bengal in July 1859, when the indigo cultivators banded together to extricate themselves from an hereditary land tenure system which kept them in a state of destitution. For nearly a century these ryots had ostensibly been employed by European growers as tenant farmers; but in actuality their position had often degenerated into one of perpetual servitude. Each year they were given cash advances in return for a specified quantity of indigo. When they failed to fulfill the terms of their contracts -- as had often happened -- they borrowed more money from the planters, and in so doing became liable to meet ever greater quota demands and susceptible to ever greater indebtedness.[50] Tension between cultivators and growers rose in the spring of 1859 when the indigo crop was

---

[49]E. Thompson and G. Garratt, Rise and Fulfilment of British Rule in India, Allahabad, 1966, p. 475

[50]Prichard, op. cit., vol. I, p. 64.

exceptionally bad and the rice harvest so good that many
ryots abandoned indigo cultivation altogether to grow the
more lucrative crop. Their defiance was met by prompt
retaliation from the planters, who coerced them through
violence and kidnapping into returning to their plots, and
who approached the government for assistance in making them
honor their legal commitments. Hastily, legislation was
passed enforcing the fulfillment of contracts, setting up a
network of subordinate courts throughout the distressed
area to try negligent ryots, and establishing in Calcutta a
commission of enquiry into the cultivators' grievances.
After five months of increasing violence and growing racial
hostility the commission published its report, which squarely
blamed the planters for creating wretched working conditions
and maintaining highly repressive tenurial arrangements by
force.[51] Canning voiced the opinion of many government
officials in his forthright proclamation that the emancipation
of Lower Bengal from the plantation system would be a boon
to the Empire.[52] As if viceregal condemnation were not
enough, the planters were subjected to further ridicule with
the circulation among Calcutta society of a play called
Nil Darpan, The Mirror of Indigo: a biting satire on life
in an indigo district, this drama cast the growers as
merciless bigots.[53]

---

[51]Maclagen, op. cit., pp. 275-277.

[52]Blair Kling, The Blue Mutiny, 1966, p. 190.

[53]Ibid., pp. 198-199.

Despite public humiliation the planters maintained a firm hold on their tenants through the courts. Their success in persuading the government to undertake criminal proceedings against the cultivators for breach of contract and to mete out ridiculously light punishments for their own crimes, including murder, convinced the Indians that the authorities could be provoked into condoning and even supporting the racist stance of the Anglo-Indian community if sufficient unscrupulous pressure were exerted.[54] The consequence was a withdrawal of trust in the fairness of the government and a racial backlash by those educated Indians who would soon become leaders of the nationalist movement.[55] Canning and Wood correctly perceived that racial hatred on both sides of the color bar in Bengal augured badly for the success of any system of popular representation in the presidency.

The Viceroy and Secretary of State were also alarmed by the battle fought in 1860 between the government and the settlers of Northern India after the announced renewal of a law, passed at the outset of the Mutiny, restricting the bearing and selling of arms. The European community was outraged that a government which had been powerless to protect it during the hostilities was continuing to deny it the means of self-protection. It had developed an acute

---

[54]Ibid., pp. 221-222.

[55]Ibid.

sense of victimization the year before, when the Viceroy
had refused to grant compensation for property lost during
the fighting; and it was suspicious of further attempts to
sacrifice Anglo-Indian interests on the altar of clemency.
The egalitarian terms of the Arms Bill came as an unwelcome
surprise, for the Anglo-Indians had assumed that the imperial
government would follow the precedent set by Dalhousie in the
Punjab and exempt Christians from all disarmament measures.
Fears of renewed violence were quickly unleashed, and public
protest meetings were held in every large town in Upper
India.[56] Presenting petitions signed at these gatherings to
the Legislative Council in Calcutta, Sir Barnes Peacock
proposed an amendment to the odious bill by which Europeans,
Americans and Eurasians would be exempted. The official
members of the Council united to defeat him, believing that
all Anglo-Indian bids for preferential treatment should be
refused in order to prevent a further deterioration in race
relations. As a result, the settlers were forced to accept
either total disarmament or participation in a voluntary
defence force open to all races and sects.[57]

Peacock's espousal of discriminatory legislation and
his abusive language in presenting the Anglo-Indian case
convinced Wood that representative government would

[56]Prichard, op. cit., vol. I, pp. 76-77.

[57]Ibid., vol. I, p. 79.

institutionalize racial hatred. "I have been shocked", he

admitted,

> at the language of the judges on the (Arms)
> Bill. I am afraid that the antagonistic
> feeling of race is becoming a source of
> formidable danger. I hardly see how the
> country is to be administered unless a good
> and kindly feeling towards the natives is
> entertained by our official servants. I
> should like to express my opinion of the
> language of ---- and ----, but I am afraid
> it would not be decent.[58] (The blanks refer
> to Wells and Peacock).

Wood became so upset by the judges' "spirit of discrimination"[59]

that he confided to Canning his fear that "we may have a <u>West</u>

India case over again, where the Government in England had

to protect the negro against the planter interests in the

Assemblies of the Colonies".[60]

With fair treatment of Indian interests impossible to

achieve so long as Peacock and Wells blatantly championed

the racist causes of the Anglo-Indian community, Wood

resolved to deprive the judges of their seats on the imperial

legislature and to cripple the remaining non-officials. To

this end he suggested the appointment of six to twelve

additional members to the Executive Council when it sat to

---

[58]Wood to Canning, 27 August 1860, I.O.L. Eur. Mss.
F 78/4.

[59]Ibid.

[60]Ibid.

make laws: half were to be government officials and half
non-official Indians and Europeans.[61] To inhibit discriminatory speeches, discourage "oratorial display", and
"counterbalance" Indian votes against European ones, he
recommended that equal numbers of Indian and European non-
officials be appointed, and that they be seated side-by-side
in the Council chamber.[62] In a further attempt to minimize
racial intolerance and increase viceregal control, Canning
selected as Councillors docile men who were amenable to
supporting government policy. Two of his three Indian
nominees -- the Raja of Benares and the Raja of Puttiala,
took little interest in Council proceedings, attended
meetings infrequently and made negligible contributions to
the debate; the third, the Mahratta Raja Dinker Rao,
displayed considerable public spirit and impressive
parliamentary skills, but carefully couched his criticisms
of proposed legislation in deferential language.[63] Canning's
European nominees posed no greater threat to the Viceroy's
authority than the princes; for as members of the Indian
Civil Service, they were entirely sympathetic to the
government's aims and programs. The Viceroy's decision to

---

[61]Wood to Beadon, 26 January 1860, I.O.L. Eur. Mss.
F 78/2.

[62]Ibid.

[63]Moore, op. cit., p. 62.

pack the Council with supporters did not pass unnoticed. The
vernacular press and the British Indian Association complained angrily that the non-officials could hardly be
regarded as "representative" if all but aristrocratic
Indians and European civil servants were excluded.[64] They
were especially critical of the appointment of land-owners
rather than Western-educated city dwellers -- a choice which
reflected the long standing Whiggism of the Government of
India and its policy of buttressing the "natural leaders" of
society.[65] Their rigorous denunciation of Canning's selection
was, in itself, precisely the kind of intelligent, concerted
opposition to government policy which the Viceroy and
Secretary of State were anxious to eliminate from the Council
chamber; and their publicity campaign against the princes
persuaded Canning and Wood of the prudence of their strategy.

Once Canning and Wood had recruited co-operative
delegates to the Legislative Council, they skillfully rewrote
its rules of procedure to ensure the Viceroy's control over
every phase of legislation. First, they defined his powers
over the imperial legislature: he, alone, was authorized to
nominate the additional members, to decide when the
Legislative Council would meet (thereby ending the inter-
minable sessions of the Dalhousie era), to make up the agenda
from which the Council could not deviate, and to sanction

[64]Prichard, op. cit., vol. I., 112.

[65]Ibid.

bills which the Council had approved.[66] Secondly, they
defined his authority over the presidency legislative
councils: these bodies were required to submit all bills,
even those of a purely local nature, for viceregal approval.[67]
Thirdly, they guaranteed the Viceroy's sway over imperial
affairs by granting him the exclusive right to introduce
financial legislation and by forbidding the Council to
discuss or ask questions about the annual budget, drawn up
by the Finance Member and approved by the Viceroy.[68] In
short, Canning and Wood empowered the Legislative Council
to advise the Viceroy on pending bills but not to initiate
or amend imperial legislation: they granted it the right
to debate without the power to influence government policy.

The total dependence of the truncated imperial
legislature on the Viceroy was emphasized by Wood in a note
sent to Canning immediately after the passage of the Indian
Councils Act through the House of Lords in 1861. Its
message was reiterated to successive Viceroys lest they
contemplate the revival of Dalhousie's "petty parliament":

> I have carefully avoided the words Legislative
> Council or any other expression which indicates
> a separate existence. The additional members are
> members of your Council when it sits for a
> particular purpose, to aid you and your executive

---

[66]Misra, op. cit., pp. 30-33.

[67]Ibid.

[68]24 and 25 Vict. C. 67.

> Council in making laws, and I do not mean
> that it should be acknowledged as 'doing
> anything as ... an independent body'.[69]

This admonition testified to Canning's and Wood's success in
relegating legislation to its traditional Indian place as a
branch of administration. By destroying the independence of
Dalhousie's Legislative Council and by re-incorporating the
amended body into the Executive Council, they greatly
magnified the Viceroy's power to direct imperial policy.
Their most remarkable feat, however, was the preservation of
a semblance of popular representation without the sacrifice
of one jot of viceregal control.

III. FINANCIAL CENTRALIZATION

The linch-pin of the new imperial regime was a
centralized financial bureaucracy. The policy of concentrating financial power in Calcutta had been pursued in an
attempt to enhance administrative efficiency since 1830, but
it had met with little success. It was not until after the
Mutiny, when imperial officials began to regard the centralization of power as an essential bulwark against the disintegration of the Indian Empire, that the effective
reorganization of finances became possible.

Between 1760 and 1830 the greatest obstacle to
effective financial centralization was geography: British
territories were too scattered and East India Company

---

[69]Wood to Canning, 10 August 1861, I.O.L. Eur. Mss.
F 78/3.

personnel too few to afford anything but a nominal centralization of power in the subcontinent. By 1830 British India
had been sufficiently consolidated and administrative patterns
adequately stabilized for the government at Calcutta to
assert a limited control over imperial finances. The Charter
Act of 1833 stripped the presidencies of Madras and Bombay of
financial autonomy by depriving them of the right to tax or
borrow funds without the prior consent of the Governor-General
in Council and by making them revenue-collecting agencies of
the Government of India.[70] The transfer of power from
Madras and Bombay to Calcutta necessitated the creation of an
imperial financial mechanism to supervise the collection and
distribution of revenue throughout the Empire. At the top of
the hierarcy created in 1833 stood the Accountant General of
Bengal (after 1843, when imperial and Bengal Presidency
finances were separated, the Accountant General of India),
whose job was to analyze local government accounts, report
his findings to the Governor-General in Council, and disburse
grants for projects sanctioned by the Council to the
presidencies. On the next rung stood the Accountants
General of Bombay and Madras, who scrutinized reports
submitted periodically by presidency district officials and
compiled regional returns for the benefit of the Accountant
General of India. On the bottom rung were the district
officials, who were obliged to submit regular accounts on

---

[70]Thomas, op. cit., p. 272.

district finances to the presidency Accountants-General.[71]
The institution of this new chain of command greatly increased
efficiency, for the regular receipt of detailed information
enabled the central authorities to draw up estimates more
accurately and keep a sharper eye than had ever before been
possible on presidency finances.

Despite these innovations effective centralized
financial management remained more apparent than real; for
the Governor-General in Council and the Accountant-General of
India soon learned that it was one thing to examine local
accounts and quite another to control local expenditure.
They discovered that it was virtually impossible to devise
comprehensive plans and look forward to their methodical
implementation so long as every request for money was
considered at random and in isolation by the accountants in
Calcutta. In 1856 Canning traced the root of the problem to
the time-honored local practice of submitting haphazard
financial proposals to the central authorities: ignorant of
overall costs, the Calcutta officials sanctioned excessively
large grants with alarming frequency.[72] To impose order and
restraint, Canning set up a central Department of Accounts
and charged it with two simple but vital tasks -- examining
the annual revenue returns of the local governments and
compiling a comprehensive list of funds disbursed to them by

[71]Misra, op. cit., pp. 318-319.

[72]Richard Strachey, Minute of 17 August 1867, Finance
Department Prog., Oct. 1867, Accounts No. 22.

the Government of India. To ensure fairness and efficiency
he recommended that a corps of financial experts be recruited
from the older members of the Indian Civil Service and
required to remain for the duration of their careers either
in the Department of Accounts or in the new Finance Office,
set up in 1857 to co-ordinate financial programs throughout
the Empire. The Governor-General hoped that longevity of
tenure would enable this new elite body to acquire the
experience and technical knowledge needed to supervise local
finances effectively.[73] This consolidation of power in the
hands of professional accountants would probably have yielded
impressive gains in administrative efficiency, had the Mutiny
not left Canning's neatly formulated plans in abeyance from
May 1857 to June 1858.

After the Mutiny Lord Stanley suggested to Canning
that the best way to strengthen the grip of the Government
of India on the local governments was to add a Finance
Member to the Viceroy's Council and charge him with the
management of imperial finances.[74] Puzzled why such a post
had not been created already, Disraeli observed that

---

[73]Misra, op. cit., p. 325.

[74]Moore, op. cit., p. 229.

> able as has been the administration of India,
> considerable and distinguished as have been
> the men whom that administration has produced,
> and numerous as have been the great captains,
> the clever diplomatists, and the able
> administrators of large districts with whom
> the Government has abounded, the state of
> finances has always been involved in perplexity,
> and seems never to have produced a Chancellor
> of the Exchequer.[75]

Sir Charles Wood enthusiastically endorsed the proposal to
create "a Chancellor of the Exchequer for India with similar
functions to those performed here /‾London_7 by our
minister of that denomination"[76]. But as Disraeli predicted
a financial paragon could not be located within the Indian
Civil Service, and a search was begun in London. In 1859 a
sufficiently competent financial expert was discovered in
the founder-editor of The Economist, James Wilson. His
association with Manchester economics and his contributions
to the currency debate of the 1840's had earned him the
reputation of an eminenet theorist, while his years at the
Treasury, the Board of Trade and the Board of Control had
equipped him with a broad and invaluable practical knowledge.
Wilson readily accepted Wood's challenge to produce
"economical efficiency" and confidently asserted that
"reforms become possible only when an emergency arises.
Such an emergency has now arisen and changes are now possible

---

[75]Wood to Canning, 26 July 1859, I.O.L. Eur. Mss.
F 78/1.

[76]Sir Algernon West, The Administration of Sir Charles
Wood, London 1867, p. 67.

132

that have not been before in our day"[77].

Upon arrival in Calcutta Wilson was handed a preliminary report on the Indian economy by Sir Bartle Frere, a member of the Military Finance Commission, which had been given the prodigious task of reorganizing army accounts and recommending large-scale military reductions. After a cursory perusal of the records Frere had expressed amazement at the total want of economic planning in the decades preceding the Mutiny:

> Out here there seems no-one connected with the Supreme Government who has any definite plan of finance, and nothing could be more unworthy of a great government than the haphazard way in which we have drifted in finance ....[78]

> We have no accounts at all trustworthy, and it will take two or three years' hard work to provide them. Had I not come here and seen it with my own eyes, the utter rottenness of the whole system of accounts would have been quite incredible ....[79]

Frere concluded that the concept of a budget as a means of estimating revenues and allocations and controlling spending was completely unknown to the Government of India.

Emily Barrington, The Servant of All, London, 1927, vol. II, p. 171 (Wilson to Wood, 11 July 1859).

Martineau, op. cit., vol. I, p. 299 (Frere to Seymour, February 1859).

[79]Ibid., vol. I, p. 314 (Frere to Clerk, 8 May 1861).

Wilson's immediate reaction to Frere's report was to introduce what he called a "budget system", modelled on the English pattern, under his Financial Resolution of 7 April 1860. This document succinctly announced that annual financial estimates would henceforth be tabulated, considered and sanctioned by the Government of India at the beginning of each fiscal year.[80] At a stroke it put an end to the pernicious habit of awarding government grants aimlessly and irregularly. To implement this rule Wilson established three new financial bodies in Calcutta: the Central Revenue Department, which collected information about revenue from all parts of the Empire and advised the supreme government on all fiscal matters; the Imperial Audit Department, which examined the accounts of the presidencies, provinces and departments at the end of each fiscal year and reported to the supreme government how closely the budget had been adhered to; and the Budget and Audit Committee, which analyzed how specific budgetary allocations, sanctioned by the Viceroy and his Council, could best be channelled to the subordinate governments and central government departments.[81]

Wilson's budget system effectively subordinated the presidencies to the Government of India and enabled the new

---

[80]Misra, op. cit., p. 334.

[81]Ibid., p. 335.

134

Calcutta bureaucracy to interfere with impunity in local
financial management. The presidencies having been divested
of their own accounting and auditing staffs, local officials
became dependent upon the Imperial Audit Staff and the
accounts officers of the Public Works Department for an
exact reckoning of income and expenditure. Local reliance
on Calcutta was increased by Wilson's order that all
important appointments and all new government buildings be
approved in advance of funding by the Government of India.[82]
The final blow to local autonomy in Bombay and Madras came
in 1861 with the Indian Councils Act, which restored the
power of legislation denied in 1833, but prohibited
discussion of laws and regulations affecting the public debt
of India, customs duties and taxes imposed by the supreme
government, along with currency notes and bills. Although
the presidency legislative councils were allowed to discuss
specifically local taxes (defined as any source of revenue
which would not detract from imperial taxes), these were few
in number and limited in scope because the Calcutta
authorities considered them a threat to imperial financial
stability.[83]

Remedying the inefficiencies of the financial system
was only half of Wilson's worry. The other half was relieving
the desperate state of imperial finances themselves. The

[82]Sir Verney Lovett, India, London, 1923, pp. 268-269.

[83]Thomas, op. cit., p. 270.

Mutiny had effectively bankrupted the Raj. Putting down the
sepoys and other enemies of British rule had cost nearly
£39 million in direct charges plus an annual increment of
£2 million in interest payments on the Indian public debt.[84]
No debacle could have been more disturbing in an age which
regarded the balanced budget as the prime tenet of financial
orthodoxy. Yet failure to meet costs from annual revenue
receipts was not a new condition -- only the magnitude of the
debt was novel. Between 1834-35 and 1857-58 there had been
no more than seven successful attempts to produce a surplus
compared to seventeen years of deficits.[85] Liabilities
caused by five expansionary wars and no small degree of fiscal
mis-management had been met by loans contracted on the English
money market, as well as by loans solicited from the rulers
of native states. Whereas the latter variety of security had
often been lauded as a way of making powerful Indians
creditors of the Raj and thus its supporters, the former had
been roundly condemned as a huge drain on imperial resources
which benefitted the City of London rather than India.[86]

The deficit, despite its rapid growth, would not have
upset imperial administrators quite so much had the prospect

---

[84]Ibid.

[85]James Wilson, Speech delivered before the Legislative
Council of Calcutta, 18 February 1860, London, 1860.

[86]West, op. cit., p. 64.

for economic recovery been favorable in 1858. But the outlook
was bleak. Traditional sources of income had been declining
in real value since the 1840's. The major tax source, the
land revenue, had been permanently fixed at 40% in many parts
of India -- a limitation which had won the gratitude of rich
landowners but which had netted a static, unenhanceable annual
return to the public coffers. The second most important
source of revenue, profit from the sale of opium, had proved
equally inelastic: subject to climatic fluctuations, it had
brought in roughly £5 million per annum, or approximately 15%
of the state revenue. Although hopes ran high throughout the
1860's that the China trade could be squeezed to show greater
profits, criticism of the sale of opium on humanitarian
grounds was rapidly growing in England, indicating the
eventual demise of the trade to those who appreciated the
influence of public morality on patterns of trade. There
were encouraging signs of increases in the salt tax, which had
in the past brought in approximately 10% of the state
revenue; in the excise, which had brought in about 5%; and
in customs duties, which had brought in between 5% and 9%
annually. But administrators generally agreed that these
imposts could never bridge the enormous gap between current
income and actual expenditure.[87] Further, they accepted that
imperial spending would soar in the coming decades. They
recognized that the strategic need to employ a large army of
European soldiers (each one four times the cost of a sepoy

---

[87]Prichard, op. cit., vol. I, pp. 198-199.

to maintain), the demand for improved sanitation, education, health and transport, and the general rise in wages and prices all over India would clearly place a heavy burden on imperial finances. Many concluded that balancing a budget would demand more than a temporary stop-gap to pay off past debts: it would require the creation of permanent, enhanceable sources of income to meet ever-rising adminis-trative costs.

In 1859 the Secretary of State announced his desire to discover new taxes which would cover the current deficit and show a surplus by 1862 or 1863. Believing that it was "vital to have light taxes of various sorts, which may here-after bear increase, if the necessity arises"[88], Wood advised the Indian government "to get the end of the wedge in, for as many new sources of income as possible"[89]. Significantly, he stipulated that these taxes should be provincial -- i.e. devised according to local needs and tastes, though deter-mined by the Governor-General in Council and collected by the local governments for the Government of India. "The different parts of India are so different", he reminded Wilson, "that different systems are best suited to their varying conditions. A system of taxation perfectly adapted

---

[88]Thomas, op. cit., p. 10.

[89]Wood to Trevelyan, 25 December 1859, I.O.L. Eur. Mss. F 78/2.

to the rich and large landholders of Bengal is perfectly
inapplicable to the ryots of Madras"[90]. A license tax would
thus be lucrative and acceptable in one area, while a succession
duty or a house tax would be more appropriate in another.[91]
Wood admitted that a plethora of small taxes would be highly
inconvenient to administer, but nevertheless held that
regional taxes would spread the tax burden more equitably
than one or two general taxes. Unabashedly, he confessed:
"I am for having whatever I can get, wherever I can get it"[92].

Wilson -- schooled in English rather than Indian
finance -- ignored Wood's advice to institute provincial
taxes. Instead, he proposed an imperial income/license tax
through which people on fixed incomes would be liable to the
former and those realizing variable annual amounts from
trade would be subject to the latter. He refused to consider
the warnings of administrators throughout the Empire, who
were skeptical of assessing and collecting this double tax
without arousing resentment among the Indians, whose
experience with extortionate Mughul and Maratha tax collectors
had taught them to be wary of revealing their financial
resources. He also ignored the advice offered by the Council
of India in London, who warned that payment would have to be

---

[90]Ibid.

[91]Wood to Wilson, 26 January 1860, I.O.L. Eur. Mss
F 78/2.

[92]Wood to Canning, 26 September 1859, I.O.L. Eur.
Mss. F 78/1.

enforced "by the bayonet"[93]. Having secured unqualified
support from the European community in Calcutta, the English
press and Department of Finance officials, Wilson dismissed
such fears as exaggerated. When reports reached Wood that
Wilson had silenced all criticism in India by claiming that
he had carte blanche from London to determine financial
policy, the Secretary of State felt powerless to do more
than counsel him to expect tax evasion until the Indians
became accustomed to giving detailed information about their
incomes to government officials.[94]

On 18 February 1860 Wilson instituted an income tax
at 2% on incomes of Rs 200-500 per annum and 4% on those
above Rs 500 plus a license tax at rates varying from one to
ten rupees a year on all artisans, shopkeepers, traders, and
manufacturers. Justifying this novel direct imperial tax,
he reminded the Legislative Council that "India is and will
remain the lightest taxed country in the world, in proportion
to the good government it enjoys." It was an anachronism,
he observed, that "the finances of the state are in a
condition of unparalleled disorder and deficit" while "every
class in the community is in a condition of unparalleled
prosperity"[95]. The Council, having been assured by Wilson

---

[93]Wood to Trevelyan, 26 January 1860, I.O.L. Eur.
Mss. F 78/2.

[94]Wood to Wilson, 26 March 1860, I.O.L. Eur. Mss.
F 78/2.

[95]Wilson, op. cit.

that nothing less drastic would meet the crisis, duly
sanctioned what proved to be the most contentious tax ever
imposed by the British on India.

In the spring of 1860 Wilson was aptly dubbed "the
very apostle of centralization" by one Anglo-Indian
journalist.[96] His comprehensive reform program replaced
confused lines of authority with a clearly-defined network
of financial bodies, corrected faulty methods of accounting
and auditing, and at long last achieved both the centralization of financial power in Calcutta and the prospect of a
balanced budget. The Viceroy, the Government of India
bureaucrats and Calcutta businessmen welcomed these changes,
partly because they legitimately regarded them as ingenious
answers to the question of how to strengthen the finances of
the Raj, and partly because they had a vested interest in
the concentration of fiscal power in the imperial capital.
In contrast, local officials were infuriated by them (as
will be explained in the next chapter). Many of their
reservations were shared by the Secretary of State, the ever-
cautious Sir Charles Wood. Besides warning Wilson of the
dangers of ignoring local government hostility, he implored
him not to "attempt to revolutionize the existing state of
things too fast" and "not to centralize too much"[97]. He urged
Canning to placate local officials by persuading Wilson to

---

[96]Friend of India, 2 May 1861.

[97]Wood to Wilson, 26 March 1860, I.O.L. Eur. Mss. F 78/2.

raise the floor and lower the rate of taxation, and to lessen
the interference of Calcutta in local financial administration[98]. But Canning proved remarkably inept at curbing
the zeal of his Finance Member, and Wilson delighted in
keeping Wood "completely in the dark" while he implemented
his program of radical reform.[99]

Wilson's stubborn refusal to mollify local officials
was catastrophic for the governance of India. No sooner was
his program implemented than Bombay and Madras rose in
bitter opposition to it against Calcutta, making a mockery
of centralization as a unifying force.

---

[98]Wood to Canning, 25 May 1860, I.O.L. Eur. Mss. F 78/3.

[99]Wood to Frere, 2 September 1860, I.O.L. Eur. Mss.
F 78/4.

Sir Bartle Frere -

CHAPTER FOUR

THE ORGANIZATION OF GOVERNMENT:
PRESIDENCY OPPOSITION TO CENTRALIZATION, 1859 - 1869

No sooner had Canning and Wilson imposed the policy
of centralization on India than the presidency governments
launched a campaign to resist it.   Incensed by their loss
of control over finances and administration, they fought
vigorously for the restoration of local automony from 1859
through 1869.   During the first eighteen months their protests against centralization were confined to official
memoranda and private correspondence; but when their
objections were dismissed as baseless by the Viceroy and
his advisors, their opposition became decidedly ill-natured
and their tactics unorthodox and even unconstitutional.
Their prolonged battle against the Calcutta bureaucracy was
marked by two notorious skirmishes, the so-called "Madras
Revolt"of 1860 and Bombay's struggle for independence from
the central Public Works Department from 1863 though 1865.
These exposed the full breadth of local objections to
centralization, demonstrated the presidency's capacity to
disrupt the imperial administration, and ultimately persuaded Calcutta officials to restore a limited measure of
local sovereignty.

I.   THE   PERIOD   OF   PERSUASION: JANUARY   1859   —   APRIL
      1860

Throughout the initial phase of resistance one un-
mistakable warning was repeated in the presidency
correspondence with Calcutta: centralization would not —
as the Government of India so confidently assumed —
achieve administrative efficiency.   Instead, the transfer
of power to the Calcutta bureaucracy would lead to the
imposition of a single pattern of rule and a single
program of reform from Karachi to Chittagong; and this would
result in plummeting standards of government and a slacken-
ing pace of moral and material progress.   Local officials,
exposed to India's different customs, religions, languages
and ethnic groups, believed that government and its policies
should be adapted to regional circumstance.   They dismissed
attempts to standardize administrative practices throughout
the subcontinent as futile and expectations of conformity to
grandiose all-India schemes as naive.

In 1859 Sir Charles Trevelyan of Madras commenced
the presidency attack on centralization in language which
could be neither misunderstood nor ignored.   "Progress is
impossible", he told the Government of India,

> if, besides proving that a measure is required
> for the Tamil, Telugu, Malayan, and Canarese
> people, or any of them, we have also to show that
> it is not unsuited to the Bengalis, and the count-
> less millions inhabiting the great plains which

extend from Bengal to Hindustan.[1]

Several months later Lord Elphinstone,[2] the Governor of
Bombay, informed Calcutta in equally unambiguous terms
that centralization would destroy good administration in
India.   The reduction of all policy considerations to a
model solution based on what was appropriate to Bengal --
"a sort of Procrustean bed to which men of the most
different statures must conform" -- would in his opinion
"weaken the authority of the subordinate governments and ...
deaden the energies of all who are empowered under them".[3]
In caustic tones which expressed the anger of local
officials at the arrogation of power to the Calcutta
bureaucracy, Trevelyan thundered: "this is not consolidation,
but the collection of incompatible functions into one
unmanageable heap.   The heap is conjested and the limbs
are paralysed".[4]

Such emotional denunciations attracted the attention

---

[1]Trevelyan, Minute of 13 July 1859, Parliamentary Papers
(House of Commons), 1860, vol. 49, p. 71.

[2]John Elphinstone, 1st Baron (1807-1860) entered
Horse Guards, 1826; Lord-in-Waiting, 1835-1837; Governor
of Madras, 1837-1842;   Lord-in-Waiting, 1845-1853;   Governor
of Bombay, 1853-1860.

[3]Elphinstone, Minute of 5 January 1860, Home Department Public Proceedings, 8 September 1860, no. 13.

[4]Trevelyan, Minute of 12 May 1860, Finance Department
Proceedings, December 1860, Accounts no. 2.

of the Government of India.   But the reasoned arguments
which followed failed to persuade Canning, Wilson and Wood
to reverse their policy. Three circumstances explain this
lack of success.   First, the Government of India was run
by Bengal civil servants who were naturally jealous of their
recently-won powers over the presidencies and provinces and
unsympathetic to the cause of local autonomy.   Secondly,
the presidency governments took such an uncompromising
stance against centralization that they closed the door
to negotiation, transformed the controversy from a disagreement over government reorganization to a power struggle
between Calcutta and the local capitals, and forced the
supreme government to assert its supremacy by requiring
absolute compliance with the Viceroy's plan.   Thirdly, local
officials were too overwrought at the prospect of ceding
control to construct dispassionate arguments whose logic
might have swayed the Government of India: clarity of
expression and precision of thought frequently eluded them
as they substituted emotive phrases for coherent ideas.

In a confused and lamentably ineffective fashion
Trevelyan -- the most agitated and outspoken of presidency
officials -- accused the Government of India of pursuing
centralization in defiance of the constitution of British
India by abusing the provisions of the Charter Acts of 1833
and 1853.   That these statutes strengthened the central
government at the expense of the local governments was incontrovertible, but so was their clear intention to maintain

a balance of power between them.   Equally undeniable was
the fact that the creation of a nearly omnipotent central
bureaucracy would destroy this balance.   Had Trevelyan been
content to quote the appropriate sections of the charter
statutes to demonstrate Parliament's intention to preserve
two tiers of government in equipoise, Canning and Wilson would
have found it difficult if not impossible to refute his
argument.   Instead, he seized upon two highly contentious
pieces of evidence, which considerably weakened the
presidency case against centralization.

His first argument -- moved in that cloudy realm where
intentions are deduced from consequences -- was that Parliament had always meant the Calcutta bureaucracy to administer
the Bengal presidency alone;   and that if it had ever intended the bureaucracy to manage all of the presidencies and
provinces, it would have amended the Charter Acts to provide
for its recruitment from all over the Empire.[5]   To support
this dubious proposition he indulged in a second feat of
historical imagination.   He attributed to Members of
Parliament a keen appreciation of regional differences -- an
ascription which contradicted Parliament's notorious igno- -
rance of India-- and stated that

> the south of India differs from the north as much
> as France does from Germany or England, and if it
> had been intended that the detailed administration

---

[5]Trevelyan, Minute of 13 July 1859, Parliamentary
Papers (House of Commons), 1860, vol. 49, p. 71.

> of the south of India should be conducted at
> Calcutta, provision would have been made for
> assisting the Governor-General in his secre-
> tariat and Executive Council with officers trained
> in the peculiar system of the south....

The absence of legislation instituting a supreme bureaucracy

manned by representatives from all of India's presidencies

and provinces suggested with apparent conclusiveness to

Trevelyan that centralization opposed the imperial constitu-

tion.

Secondly, Trevelyan claimed that the Calcutta bureau-

cracy had advanced centralization over the preceding thirty

years by the classic trick of using unconstitutional language

in official correspondence.   They had introduced idioms

which grossly inflated their real powers as defined in the

charter legislation.

> The terms, in common use, of 'subordinate' and 'minor'
> presidencies, show how deeply the mistaken notion
> arising from the civilian councillors, and the
> secretaries of the Governor-General, being taken
> exclusively from the Bengal Presidency has taken
> root; according to the constitution of British
> India, there is one supreme general Government
> without any local charge, and several local
> Governments; [7]but the practice has been very
> different....

Once again Trevelyan destroyed his argument by treating

historical speculation as concrete fact; for while it was

true that the Calcutta bureaucracy preferred the terms

"subordinate" and "minor" to the correct usage "local",

---

[6]Ibid.

[7]Sir Algernon West, The Administration of Sir Charles
Wood, London, 1867, p. 67.

it was equally true that presidency officials used these
words interchangeably.   Imputing malicious motives to the
Bengal civil servants under these circumstances was more
than dishonest: it was counterproductive.

Trevelyan was out on a limb with these two arguments;
but he enjoyed the total support and respect of presidency
administrators who shared his temperamental objections to
radical change.   These were men who inherited the convictions
of a previous generation of Orientalists and Paternalists
that social stability was fragile, and that it depended
on the continuity of familiar forms of government.   Such
fears were expressed implicitly rather that explicitly in
local government memoranda, but they were meaningless in
any event to the authorities in Calcutta.   These were men
whose experience of the countryside beyond the Hoogly was
limited and whose familiarity with the practical problems
of improving the manners and morals of illiterate villagers
was virtually nonexistent.   Isolated from what local
officials knew as "the real India", they misconstrued local
government pleas to narrow the scope and reduce the pace of
change as gratuitous attempts to retard progress.

More opposition was voiced by the presidency officials
against the supreme government's plan to transplant British
financial institutions to India and introduce a European
income tax without laying any foundation in advance.   They

objected that these were features of modern European
society: having been designed to operate within the
context of parliamentary democracy, they would not
function properly within an oriental despotism. Trevelyan,
once again in the forefront of the protest, reminded the
Viceroy and his advisors that in England taxes were collected successfully because they were imposed after the
taxpayers' consent had been obtained through their elected
representatives. "In India", he pointed out, "notwith-
standing a studious imitation of the forms of popular
assembly we are farther from real representation of local
interest than ever".[8] Trevelyan was certain that the
supreme government would mistake the attitudes of the
European community in Calcutta for public opinion
throughout the Empire and sanction a scheme which accom-
modated the ruling elite at the expense of the ruled.
Bluntly labelling the income tax a piece of "class legislation", he warned Wilson that it was ill-suited to the
tastes and experience of the Indian peoples outside the
presidency towns, and that it would be misunderstood,
resented and evaded.[9] It would revive memories of Mughul and
Maratha rapacity; it would bring back the extortion by
village officials which had been largely stamped out; it

---

[8]Trevelyan, Minute of 20 March 1860, Parliamentary
Papers (House of Commons), 1860, vol. 49, pp. 112-120.

[9]Ibid.

would cover India with a "swarm of ill-paid, ill-super-
intended native subordinates"; it would inevitably,
Trevelyan predicted, bring widespread evasion.[10]

Civil servants at all levels of government in Madras
shared the Governor's apprehensions about transferring the
financial practices of a civilized society to an
undeveloped one.   The idea that the Indian banya would pay
his taxes with the honesty and alacrity of the English shop-
keeper struck them as preposterous: to their minds it be-
trayed sheer ignorance of oriental history and of the
enormous gap in morals and education between the two
countries.   One member of the presidency Executive Council
pronounced it axiomatic

> that an income tax can only be carried out
> effectively in a country where the Government
> and people are on a thoroughly good under-
> standing, and have a mutual confidence and
> sympathy, in other words, where the governors
> and the governed have the same national
> feelings and interests and where education and a
> representative system give a high moral tone
> and political enlightenment.   Here the state of
> things is far different.   The people have long
> been accustomed to despotic government, and
> tradition has taught them to seek relief from
> overtaxation by concealing their means, and from
> oppression, when it becomes unbearable, by revolt.[11]

The Collector of Madura, pointing to "the very low state of
public morality" in India, declared that "it will be most
difficult, if not impossible, to ascertain the real income

---

[10]Trevelyan, Minute of 1 December 1859, Ibid., p. 56-63.

[11]Maltby, Minute of 24 March 1860, Ibid., pp. 125-128.

of contributors; and the machinery by which the tax is to
be collected will add to the difficulty, and will often be
made use of by ill-disposed and malevolent persons to
inflict disgrace and injury on their fellow countrymen".[12]
Nearly all of the district officers of the presidency agreed.
"No native has any idea of the duty of contributing to the
resources of the Government from which he received protection", observed the Collector of Canara; "he merely consi-
ders that taxes are imposed according to the pleasure and
power of the Government and that his business is to avoid
them".[13]   Faced with the prospect of tax abuse on a grand
scale, local officials expressed a weary sense of resignation:
"if it is supposed", said one of them, "that a Collector and
his subordinates will be able to check the frightful oppression, corruption, and inequality which will result from the
necessary delegation of the powers of this Act to native
revenue officers, abhikaries, menons, and others, I can only
say that the idea is most utopian".[14]

The Government of India ignored all of the presidency
constitutional arguments but one -- the charge that an
English financial plan was being imposed without a proper

---

[12]T. Clarke, Collector of Madura, Minute of 25 October
1859, Ibid., pp. 48-50,

[13]W. Fisher, Collector of Canara, Minute of 15 October
1859, Ibid., pp. 41-42.

[14]W. Holloway, Minute of 25 October 1859, Ibid., pp.
47-48.

foundation. The Viceroy deputed Sir Bartle Frere, a close personal friend, the leading member of the Military Finance Commission and for the previous thirty years a Bombay presidency official, to present the imperial case. Sharing the presidency administrators' conservative attitude towards constitutional change, Frere pointed to the reactionary aspects of Wilson's financial policy in a letter to Trevelyan. "There is no part of Mr. Wilson's plan", he insisted,

> that might not have had a place under a different name in any scheme of Akbar's -- no single tax which is not at this present moment levied by almost any independent Native State when in difficulties .... The scheme, as a whole, is, it is true, a financial revolution, and like all revolutions a thing to be avoided if possible.... But it is not a revolution from Indian to English finance, as they who object to it assert: it is rather a return to modes of taxation, once universal in India ... which we only gave up in our own provinces within the last twenty-five years, the main alteration being that the new taxes are uniform and simple in their incidence, and free from the arbitrary exemptions and anomalies of every kind, which made it difficult to reform the old taxes without abolishing them.[15]

Neither Trevelyan nor any other presidency official to whom Frere addressed this argument bothered to refute it. Perhaps they realized the futility of trying to reconcile diametrically opposing views on the relationship between Wilson's taxes and Mughul levies. Perhaps they recognized in Frere's citation of dubious precendents an example of the long-standing British habit of reinterpreting Indian history to buttress an argument. Or perhaps they remembered the

---

[15]Martineau, op. cit., vol. I, p. 306 (Frere to Trevelyan, 23 April 1860).

.consequences of an earlier "reactionary" financial revolution
and drew the obvious conclusions about the current one.
As all of them knew from their Haileybury days, in 1765
the East India Company had assumed the diwan (the right to
collect taxes under the Mughul administration) in Bengal.
Applying Western taxation principles of uniform incidence
and simple, exact assessment to Mughul levies, it had
overturned the traditional economy.   Some cultivators had
been bankrupted and others enriched by drastic changes in
the revenue demand;   and these changes in tenurial relations
had been reflected in changes in the social structure of
the region.   In 1860 any local official who assessed
Wilson's plan in the light of this revolution would have
regarded Frere's interpretation with profound suspicion.

Throughout the eighteen months during which the local
governments bombarded the Government of India with constitutional objections to centralization, they also attacked
the income tax on purely financial grounds.   Their critique
-- which was so simplistic as to invite a barrage of well-
founded criticism in response -- started from the faulty
premise that deficit was "not the normal state of Anglo-
Indian administration";[16] and it ended with the erroneous
proposition that "our financial difficulties in India have

[16]Trevelyan, Statement by Sir Charles Trevelyan on
the Circumstances Connected with His Recall from the
Government of Madras, London, 1860, p. 5.

always been connected with military affairs, and the remedy
for them is to be found in the reorganisation of our military
system".[17]   To achieve financial equilibrium through military
cut-backs Trevelyan suggested a sharp reduction in Indian
recruits to the army and the transfer of military police
charges (which had soared during the Mutiny because of the
need to protect public treasuries and stores from marauders)
to the civil lists.[18]   Voicing the almost unanimous opinion
of presidency officials, he recommended that "instead ... of
exhausting our ingenuity in devising new taxes and raising
new loans, ... we /‾should_7 apply ourselves in serious,
sober earnest to reducing expenditure, many items of which
are capable of being immediately acted upon".[19]

Trevelyan's advice sounded shallow and half-hearted
to Wilson and his team of financial experts in Calcutta.
Although they concurred that a reduction in troops and a
reorganization of the police force were essential, they
insisted that these alone were inadequate. According to
their calculations the deficit was caused by extensive and
endemic dislocations in imperial finances which local
officials blithely ignored. Addressing Trevelyan as the
head of the presidency opposition, the three leading men

---

[17]Ibid., p. 2.

[18]Ibid., pp. 6-10.

[19]Trevelyan, Minute of 10 June 1859, Parliamentary
Papers (House of Commons), 1873, vol. 12.

in the Government of India Finance Department -- James
Wilson, James Outram and Bartle Frere -- explained that it
was impossible to meet a projected deficit of £9 million
for 1859-60 and £6 million for 1860-61 without imposing new
taxes.[20] Wood agreed: "there is no use in declaiming
against new taxation. I see all the objections to it; but
to reduce £8 million requires a very different sort of
pruning-knife than that hitherto handled".[21]

Frere, sympathetic to the fight for local autonomy
yet convinced of the efficacy of Wilson's tax plan, was
distressed to find the presidencies asserting their
independence on the issue of imperial finances. To his
mind the stability of British rule in India depended upon
the financial solvency of the supreme government; and the
refusal of the local governments to co-operate in achieving
a balanced imperial budget threatened the foundations of the
Raj. "I cannot tell you what a source of sincere regret it
has been to me ever since we received your letter regarding
the financial schemes brought forward by Mr. Wilson, to find
myself in any way opposed to you", he confided to Trevelyan.

> Not only because I had hoped that occasions
> would rarely arise on which we should differ,
> but because I can't help fearing that the
> course you have taken will interfere very
> seriously with the emancipation of the
> Government of Madras and Bombay from that
> interference by the Government of India,

---

[20]Outram, Frere and Wilson to Trevelyan, 9 March 1860,
Parliamentary Papers (House of Commons), 1860, vol. 49, pp.
106-109.

[21]Wood to Trevelyan, 26 March 1860, I.O.L. Eur. Mss.
F 78/2.

156

which you, I know, think quite as mischievous
as I do. You have taken the battle on a
question of finance and army organization -- two
of the three classes of questions which, it seems
to me, must always be left to the Government of
India, external politics being the third.... I
greatly fear that whatever the Secretary of State
and people at home may think of your arguments,
they will begin to doubt how the Government of
India can be carried on while such opposition on
a financial question is possible.[22]

Frere was further distraught to discover that the presidency

officials' estimates of military expenditure for 1859-60 --

the figures which persuaded them that cut-backs would suffice

-- were far lower than actual costs. The Madras accounts,

for example, were in error by no less than £4 million.[23]

Why, he asked Sir George Clerk,[24] Governor of Bombay, did

the local administrators hold that their totals were correct

when their calculations were based on a fragment of the

information available to the central government? How could

they reject the income tax and argue for reductions on the

_____

[22]Martineau, op. cit., vol. I, pp. 305-306 (Frere to
Trevelayan, 9 April 1860).

[23]Ibid., vol. I, p. 309 (Frere to Clerk, 9 May 1860).

[24]Sir George Russell Clerk (1800-1899); entered service of the East India Company as a writer, 1817; Political
Agent at Umbala and Ludiana; Envoy at Lahore, 1842; Agent to
the Governor-General in the North-Western Frontier during the
1st Afgan War; Lieutenant-Governor of the North West
Provinces, 1843; Provisional Member of the Supreme Council,
1844; twice Governor of Bombay, 1847-1848 and 1860-1862;
Under-Secretary of the Board of Control, 1856-1858; Permanent Under-Secretary of State for India, 1858-1860; Member of
the Council of India, 1863-1876.

one hand, and sanction inadequate cut-backs on the other?[25]

With regret Frere informed the Secretary of State
in London that it would remain impossible to reduce military
spending so long as the local and supreme governments
continued to disagree over basic figures.   "The worst
feature of all", he complained,

> is the incapacity of most of the official men here
> to discover or admit that all is not perfection.
> I could not give a better instance than the one
> before you in the discussion between Sir Charles
> Trevelyan and Lord Elphinstone on the one hand,
> and Mr. Wilson on the other, as to the cost of the
> army and police for this year now ending, and the
> amount of reduction which can be relied on as in
> progress for 1860-1861.   The difference, between
> the two results is not a few thousand rupees, but
> millions sterling, and this not a question of
> calculation, but of fact....[26]

Wood was furious with the presidencies for promising cut-
backs only to deceive.   "It is absolute nonsense talking
of meeting the emergency by reduction, when none of you
reduce in practice", he wrote angrily to Trevelyan.

> The expenditure is higher now than I estimated in
> August last.   What on earth you are all after, I
> cannot conceive.   That reduction ought to be made
> and must be made, is evident to everybody.   Every-
> body says so, -- and nobody does it.   I have never
> ceased writing, publicly and privately, to every
> authority in India, ever since I came to the India
> Office, urging and preparing reduction in every
> way, and on grounds which nobody can controvert ...;
> but I can discover no reductions actually made any-
> where by the Governments.[27]

---

[25]Martineau, op. cit., vol. I, p. 309 (Frere to Clerk,
9 May 1860).

[26]Ibid., vol. I, p. 300 (Frere to Wood, 3 May 1860).

[27]Wood to Trevelyan, 9 April 1860, I.O.L. Eur. Mss.
F 78/3.

When Trevelyan replied that the Madras government would
order substantial cut-backs in military spending only if
the other local governments agreed to decrease costs by an
equivalent amount, Wood lost his temper.   He denounced the
"doctrine of <u>conditional</u> reduction" as totally unacceptable
and roared: "it is your duty to reduce as much as you can;
and it is our business to enforce reductions elsewhere".[28]
He forthrightly condemned as unrealistic the presidency
officials' demand that in light of their loyalty during
the Mutiny and their frugality thereafter, they be absolved
from paying for the disloyalty and continuing extravagence
of Bengal and the Northern provinces.[29]   "If the new taxation fell only on those whose conduct has caused the
expense", he pointed out to Trevelyan, "it might perhaps be
said that the Madras population ought not to pay.   Unfor-
tunately the innocent have to pay the cost of the exertions
rendered necessary to protect them, by the conduct of those
who probably never did pay, and certainly cannot be made to
pay, for the expense which they caused."[30]

   This seemingly irresolvable disagreement over military
spending brought the supreme and local governments to

---

[28]Wood to Trevelyan, 20 March 1860, I.O.L. Eur. Mss.
F 78/2.

[29]Humphrey Trevelyan, <u>op</u>. <u>cit</u>., p. 80.

[30]Wood to Trevelyan, 20 March 1860, I.O.L. Eur. Mss.
F 78/2.

loggerheads. Trevelyan and Clerk deprecated Wilson's tax plan in increasingly bitter and self-righteous tones. Meanwhile -- as Frere observed to his annoyance -- Wilson clung ever more tenaciously to the belief "that to treat India as containing numerous different nations is as great a mistake as to dissolve the Union or restore the Heptarchy" and "that you may do what you please in India, if you only do it with a high hand".[31]

II.   PHASE TWO: THE MADRAS REVOLT OF 1860

The deadlock was suddenly broken in April 1860 with the Viceroy's pontifical resolution to "uphold our own -- I will not say -- infallibility, but -- unquestionability to the utmost".[32]   In blatant defiance of parliamentary procedure Canning pushed Wilson's financial program through the imperial Legislative Council in a single session. Incensed at the irregularity of this maneuver, the Madras government sent an open telegram to Calcutta, demanding that the usual three months be allowed for representations and consultations.   In reply the Government of India rebuked the local government for not sending the telegram in cypher and brusquely ordered its compliance with the new legislation.

---

[31]Martineau, op. cit., vol. I, p. 311 (Frere to Ellis, 31 July 1860).

[32]Barrington, op. cit., vol. II, p. 301 (Canning to Wilson, 24 July 1860).

Trevelyan retaliated by instructing the Madras member of
the Legistative Council to table a list of objections to
Wilson's program and request that they be officially printed.
But the Finance Member countered this potential embarrassment by summoning the representative and warning him that
loyalty to the Queen required his silence on the matter.[33]
Trevelyan accused Wilson of claiming "the exclusive use of
publicity, which is the privilege of absolute despotism",
and then sought recourse through means as unconstitutional as
Canning's.[34] In May he breached the official confidential-
ity -- which had so far kept the deliberations over the
income tax out of the press -- by ordering the publication
of Madras Executive Council minutes opposing Wilson's tax
scheme. A telegram prohibiting publication of the secret
documents arrived from Calcutta only a few hours too late
to stop him from committing this gross indiscretion.

The most scandalous minute to be published was
Trevelyan's report that "nearly all who have been consulted
speak of /the income tax_7 as certain to be extremely
unpopular. They allude to 'distrust','dissatisfaction',
'discontent', 'uneasiness', 'alarm', disaffection', which
will result from it; and some of them use language which

[33]Humphrey Trevelyan, op. cit., p. 81.

[34]Trevelyan, Minute of 4 April 1860, Parliamentary
Papers (House of Commons), vol. 49, pp. 130-132.

cannot be mistaken".[35]   A survey of the official minutes
from which Trevelyan drew these quotations supports his
contention that fear of rebellion was almost universal.
"Our political safety in India depends, in no small degree,
on our taking no measures that tend to unite the now
sufficiently dislocated interests, feelings, and objects
of its various populations", warned one collector ominously.[36]
"They have naturally a common interest against conquerers,
however just.   Happily, they but partially know it, and
they have few points of union.   Why then give the mahajan
of the North Western Provinces, the pandit of Benares, the
sahakar of Bombay, and brahmin money-lender of Tanjore, and
the moplah trader of Malabar a common war cry?" asked
another.[37]   The Collector of Cuddolore remembered several
occasions when "the people have resisted by open force
what they have supposed to be innovations upon their rights",
and reported that "there is a spirit of resistance among them
ready to show itself on every occasion when a change in
taxation is attempted which they do not happen to like".[38]
One member of the Madras Executive Council, having discussed
the possibility of a second Mutiny with an English army

---

[35]Trevelyan, Minute of 1 December 1859, Ibid., p. 57.

[36]W. Robinson, Minute of 8 November 1859, Ibid., pp.
53-55.

[37]Ibid.

[38]A. Hall, Collector of Cuddalore, Minute of 29 October
1859, Ibid., pp. 51-52.

officer informed the Governor that "far from being cowed
by the suppression of the rebellion, the natives discuss
not the hopelessness of resistance, but the causes which
led to its failure.   In such a frame of mind we must be
extremely cautious about introducing unpopular taxation."[39]
Another Executive Council member suggested that the only
way to "avoid the great danger of raising a flame of
discontent throughout the whole Empire, and uniting the
entire population in a feeling of opposition to us at the
same moment" was to introduce the tax gradually, province
by province.[40]

The prophecy of a second Mutiny instantly titillated
the public in Britain as well as in India.   Sir Robert
Montgomery,[41] the Lieutenant—Governor of the Punjab,
reported that irresponsible members of the vernacular press
were taking special delight in the scandalous prognosis
and that several Punjabi newsmen were going so far as to

---

[39]W. Elliot, Minute of 8 December 1859, Ibid., pp. 63-64.

[40]E. Maltby, Minute of 24 March 1860, Ibid., pp. 125-128.

[41]Sir Robert Montgomery (1809-1887); entered Bengal
Civil Service, 1828; served in the North-West   Provinces;
Magistrate-Collector of Allahabad, 1839; Commissioner of
Lahore, 1849; Member of the Punjab Board of Administration,
1851; Judicial Commissioner, 1853; Chief Commissioner of
Oudh, 1858; Lieutenant-Governor of the Punjab, 1859-1865;
Member of the Council of India, 1868-1887.

interpret the Madras statements as a straighforward advocacy of rebellion. Fearing that these reports might incite the Indians to take up arms, he urged the Government of India to "place the native press under censorship...., and the sooner the better".[42] The readiness of the press to proclaim that "Madras has gone", employing the phrase used in 1857 for a regiment which had mutinied, demonstrated the significance contemporaries attached to the published minutes. The analogy was not spurious; for under the Mughul Empire such an exhibition of local independence would have been the prelude to armed rebellion against the central authority.[43] In the uneasy political climate of 1860 no one could be absolutely certain that the Indians would not confirm the Madras suspicions and rebel.

News of Trevelyan's attempt to embarrass the Government of India and force a reconsideration of the income tax came as no great surprise to Wood. For the past year and one half he had feared that the Governor would press his views in an unacceptable way if discreet protest failed. As early as September 1859 he had begged him not to act before consulting the Council of India in London. "I am most anxious to relieve you from all unnecessary trammels", he had written plaintively,

---

[42]Barrington, op. cit., vol. II, p. 267 (Montgomery to Wilson, 25 April 1860)

[43]Prichard, op. cit., vol. I, p. 56.

> -- I am out of all patience with the circum-
> locution of the mode of transacting business;
> and I will help you to the utmost of my power.
> All I ask and suggest -- and it is for your own
> sake and for that of your public usefulness --
> is that you should recommend the course for
> our sanction, in matters in which we must have a
> voice in a decision; and not adopt it without
> giving us an option .... Don't alarm some of my
> timid councellors by taking the case into your
> own hands.[44]

When Trevelyan ignored his counsel and attacked the Govern-

ment of India in the public press, Wood was irate. "It is

contrary to any conceivable mode of carrying on a government"

he raged,

> that the subordinate parts should publically
> declare their opposition to the determination
> of the chief authority.... I cannot under-
> stand how you can have thought for one
> moment that such a course was justifiable.
> Your minute would have made a very good speech
> for Disraeli to have delivered against Gladstone;
> or it might be a good speech for the Madras
> member of the Legislative Council to make
> against the Bill. But nobody in this world
> ever heard of publicity meaning a discussion
> between the Chief and a subordinate authority
> carried on in public. Such a practice is
> utterly subversive of all government; and, if
> any evil occurs in Madras, you will have much
> to answer for ....[45]

Bitterly disappointed that such a respected administrator

should commit such a flagrant indiscretion, Wood concluded

that Trevelyan should have resigned rather than oppose the

Government of India.[46]

---

[44]Wood to Trevelyan, 27 September 1859, I.O.L. Eur.
Mss. F. 78/1.

[45]Wood to Trevelyan, 3 May 1860, I.O.L. Eur. Mss.
F 78/3.

[46]Wood to Trevelyan, 10 May 1860, I.O.L. Eur. Mss.
F 78/3.

Canning -- who had never liked Trevelyan -- seized the opportunity to rid India of "that beggar on horseback".[47] The clemency which he had so notoriously displayed towards the mutineers two years earlier was altogether untraceable in his treatment of the Governor of Madras.   His scathing analysis of Trevelyan's motives focused on vanity as

> the bottom of his doings.   He has conceived such an overweening estimate of his own power, judgement, and capacity for rule, that he considers every way of bringing .about his own views to be allowable. This is not only the most charitable, but, I really think the true interpretation of him.   But it makes him a pestilent man to hold authority.[48]

Wilson, who shared Canning's hatred of Trevelyan, agreed that vanity had destroyed good judgment and with it the capacity to exercise power wisely:

> He has so impulsive a mind, so ill-balanced, with such an overweening confidence in himself, no matter what the subject might be, equally to command a squadron, lead an army, or regenerate the civil government of a country: with a large smattering upon everything but the most dogged obstinacy I ever saw: and with an inordinate vanity and love of notoriety to be gratified; without the slightest judgement or discretion or forethought or calculation of consequences: all these characteristics lead a man so heedlessly into danger and control him so completely as to leave him hardly a responsible being.[49]

---

[47]Quoted by Maclagen, op. cit., p. 261 (Canning to Granville, 12 June 1860).

[48]Ibid.

[49]Barrington, op. cit., vol. II, p. 252 (Wilson to Bagehot, 4 July 1860).

Wilson cleverly enlisted his son-in-law, Walter Bagehot,[50] to launch a press campaign against Trevelyan in Britain to expose his "monstrous act of misjudgement and insubordination".[51] In a series of articles appearing in the Economist in the spring of 1860, Bagehot rehearsed at length the financial quandaries of the Government of India and praised Wilson's program as the only feasible way of solving them. He ended his survey with a sharp criticism of Trevelyan's indiscretion:

> Sir Charles Trevelyan thinks there is danger in the course Mr. Wilson has taken. But is there not greater danger in his own course? He has told the natives of Madras that new taxes which are unjust and unnecessary are about to be levied upon them. He has used his authority as local Governor to spread this doctrine. He has hinted that he expects the natives will rebel. Who will be to blame if they do rebel? Surely the ruler who was entrusted with an authority over 3,000,000 of people, and who incited them to resist.[52]

Trevelyan responded in an equally vituperative manner by decrying Canning's "do-nothing" administration and by accusing Wilson of acting without religious or gentlemanly feelings -- a truly disparaging indictment from an aristocratic Evangelical.[53] He also condemned the Finance Member

---

[50]Walter Bagehot (1826-1887) economist, journalist and constitutional historian; Editor of The Economist, 1860-1877.

[51]Barrington, op. cit., vol. II, p. 247.

[52]The Economist, 12 May 1860.

[53]Humphrey Trevelyan, op. cit., p. 82.

for painting an inordinately gloomy picture of Indian finances
to win unwarranted acclaim in improving them and to advance
himself to become Chancellor of the Exchequer upon returning
to England.[54]

By all reckoning Wilson's transparent ambition and
Canning's lethargic style of adminstration were pardonable
sins in comparison to Trevelyan's rash disregard for Indian
security. Even his friends on the Madras Executive Council
denounced him for publishing their candid views on the
possiblity of a second Mutiny without their consent. Canning
petitioned for his recall from India, and on 10 May 1860
the Cabinet unanimously voted for his dismissal as Governor
of Madras.[55] This was a drastic measure. But it was the
only response deemed appropriate to Trevelyan's forceful
exposition of a cause which had already gained widespread
support and which could -- if left unchallenged -- tear the
Indian Empire apart. The home authorities and Government
of India officials believed that by disgracing the leader
of the campaign for local autonomy they had discredited the
cause itself. Their confident expectations were foiled,
however, within a matter of months.

III. PHASE THREE: BOMBAY'S STRUGGLE AGAINST THE
PUBLIC WORKS DEPARTMENT: 1863 - 1865

---

[54]Ibid.

[55]Wood to Trevelyan, 10 May 1860, I.O.L. Eur. Mss.
F 78/3.

After losing the initial battle against centralization
presidency officials embarked on a policy of sabotage against
the Public Works Department, which lasted the entire decade.
It was born out of the spontaneous fury of local administrators and was raised to the level of open warfare from 1863
through 1865 by Sir Bartle Frere, Governor of Bombay. Angered
by Calcutta's intervention in the planning and execution of
local building projects, Frere determined to reassert presidency control.

The slogan of Bombay's fight for independence was
Frere's enigmatic phrase "centralise by individuals, not by
departments".[56] Using centralize as a synonym for empower,
he meant that authority should be vested in the district
officer and not in the Calcutta bureaucrat. To his mind
the former was the better way to govern an Asian people
because it reproduced the essential features of traditional
Oriental despotism: it personified government, brought the
ruler close to the people, and allowed him to redress their
grievances by an immediate assertion of individual will.[57]
"Natives much prefer serving under a master whose wishes
and temper, once understood, are to them a law and rule of
conduct", he observed. "An Englishman asks, 'What are my

---

[56]Martineau, op. cit., vol. I, p. 101 (Frere to the
Government of Bombay, 15 January 1858).

[57]Ibid., vol. I, p. 271 (Frere to Clerk, 16 January
1859).

rights and duties?'   The Asiatic guesses what they will be
by the answer to his question, which is always, 'Who is my
master?'"[58]   To Frere's mind centralization met two important requirements of good imperial government: it harmonized
the ruling patterns of the present with those of the past
and it adapted itself to the temperament and customs of the
people. Centralization by department did neither.   It
depersonalized government, divided authority among local
department officials, removed all effective power to Calcutta,
made the ruler remote and inaccessible to the ryot, and need-
lessly complicated the problems of governing an Oriental
people.[59]   Centralization by individual achieved two other
essential goals which centralization by department could not
attain -- administrative efficiency and protection against
imperial disunity in the event of a second Mutiny.   "Both
systems aim at centralisation", Frere remarked,

> but the one attains real and efficient central-
> isation as long as there is a force at the centre;
> the other becomes deranged by the slightest trial
> or shock; and unless in seasons of difficulty
> some man is bold enough to break all rules, and
> assume at his own peril the individual local
> authority (which the other system spontaneously
> gives), the results are invariably disastrous.[60]

Frere was convinced that Calcutta's "habit of never saying

---

[58]Ibid.

[59]Sir William Worsfold, Sir Bartle Frere, London,
1923, p. 77.

[60]Martineau, op. cit., vol. I, p. 101 (Frere to the
Government of Bombay, 15 January 1858).

'though there is nothing to satisfy the forms of the
secretariat, still we will trust a Government composed of
so many old and experienced servants, at least til we have
heard them', must soon destroy the race of Indian officials
who would venture to act on their own responsibility without
previous orders".[61] He was equally certain that the consequence of shackling the local official would be administrative paralysis: "When you have extinguished that feeling of
mutual confidence between superior and subordinate authorities,
and made public men as timid here of acting without orders
as they are in England, you will have removed one great
safeguard of our Indian Empire".[62]

In no bureau of the imperial government were the
laibilities of centralization by department so obvious as
in the Public Works Department -- "a monster of centralisation
-- a mere accumulation without consolidation $\underline{/}$which$\underline{7}$ has
grown out of all control", according to Trevelyan. "It
reminds one of the picture at the commencement of Hobbes's
Leviathan of the State absorbing everything".[63] Established
in 1855, it supervized the erection of government-financed

---

[61]Ibid., vol. I, p. 438.

[62]Ibid., vol. I., p. 435 (Frere to Wood, 11 May 1864).

[63]Trevelyan, evidence submitted to the Select Committee
on Indian Finance, 25 February 1873, Parliamentary Papers
(House of Commons), 1873, vol. 12.

railways, roads, irrigations schemes and public buildings. After the Mutiny it accelerated the rate of construction in response to the cotton boom (fuelled by money which had previously enriched the American South) and the rise in overseas investment (induced by the prospect of financial stability and a high return on government bonds). This expansion enhanced its power over the local governments, which were required to submit all proposals to department officials in Calcutta for approval prior to construction. Wilson's budget system further strengthened central government control by linking the funding of works-in-progress to the sanctioning of plans submitted regularly by local administrators.

Supervision by men thousands of miles away would not have galled Bombay civil servants had the department been sensitive to local requirements and responsive to local advice. But the Calcutta bureaucrats -- led by their ambitious and energetic Secretary, Colonel Richard Strachey[64] -- were neither. Schooled in the Bengal civil service, they held the familiar if fallacious belief that the needs of the capital were an appropriate guide to those of the Empire at

[64]Richard Strachey (1817-1908); entered Bombay Engineers, 1836; transferred to Bengal; Under-Secretary to the Public Works Department, 1857; Consulting Engineer, Railway Department, 1858; Secretary to the Public Works Department, 1862; Inspector of Irrigation, 1866; Member of the Legislative Council of India, 1869; Member of the Council of India, 1875; President of the Indian Famine Commission, 1878-1879; Chairman of the East India Railway Co., 1889.

large.   In an attempt to enlighten them about conditions
in Western India, Bombay officials wrote voluminous memoranda.   Their zeal was impressive; but their efforts were
in vain.   As Frere observed several months after arriving
in Bombay from Calcutta, the central department could never
be supplied with sufficient information to mastermind public
works in Bombay, let alone throughout the subcontinent.
"Rely on it, my dear Strachey", he warned,

> you cannot be both Superintending Engineer of every
> work in India, and also Secretary in the Public
> Works Department to the Government of India.   You
> may easily ensure that not a work is commenced
> throughout India till you have been satisfied as to
> the minutest detail of plan and estimate.   But you
> will find this will end in the paralysis of the
> Public Works Department.   You wish to ensure a
> maximum of works and efficiency and a minimum of
> expense.   The means you adopt will ensure the
> reverse.   All our money will go in establishments
> and designs and writing; the work done will be
> minimum.
>   I cannot admit that for four-fifths of the
> work you have any advantage over provincial
> engineers.   There are many great engineering
> problems, in solving which you have immense
> advantage over us, and are more likely to be
> right.   But in the humdrum work of roads and
> bridges -- plain earth-work masonry -- the only
> problem is how to get as much as possible for the
> money, and the more you check and correspond, the
> less is done.   A wise imperial Public Works Depart-
> ment would do absolutely nothing in such matters,
> but give all the money it could spare to the local
> governments and judge by results whether it had
> been well spent.[65]

In making this recommendation Frere pointed out that some
local governments needed more guidance from Calcutta than

---

[65]Martineau, op. cit., vol. I, p. 421 (Frere to
Strachey, 12 October 1863).

others because of regional administrative problems; and he
advised Strachey to make a clear distinction between the
backward areas of the Empire -- like Burma and the tribal
zones of the Western and Northwestern frontiers, which
required close supervision -- and Bombay and Madras, which
needed only broad policy guidelines.[66] All of Frere's
suggestions fell on deaf ears. Strachey did not care for
the Governor's preaching tone any more than Frere enjoyed
the Secretary's dictatorial manner, and both stubbornly
refused to recognize the competence of the other in administering local public works.

In the autumn of 1863 Frere resolved to evade
Strachey's control completely. Whenever it seemed likely
that the Calcutta bureaucrats would reject local plans,
Frere sanctioned them without reference to the Public Works
Department and demanded funds from the Finance Department
after the works had been completed. To circumvent budgetary
control he allowed Bombay officials to submit local public
works estimates in a "crude and unrevised" state (according
to the Finance Member of the Viceroy's Council) several weeks
after the imperial budget had been drawn up.[67] The Finance
Member suspected that these unintelligible figures bore
little relation to actual costs,[68] and he accused Frere of

---

[66] Ibid.

[67] Trevelyan, evidence ... of 21 February 1872, Parliamentary papers (House of Commons), 1873, vol. 12.

[68] Ibid., evidence of 25 February 1873.

having "assembled a congress of collectors and officers of
the Public Works Department at Poonah, and gathered up all
the projects for public works of all sorts that had ever
been proposed, and sent the greater portion of them, as was
alleged, for our sanction at Calcutta".[69]   He also condemned the local government for granting municipal loans
without consulting the Government of India.[70]   Presidency
officials had, for example, rebuilt the fortifications of
Bombay city in breach of the rule that works exceeding
£10,000 should not be commenced without the supreme government's approval; and they had rebuilt and decorated the
Governor's summer residence at enormous cost without
informing Calcutta.[71]

Presidency officials could not have pursued such an
independent course without the invaluable if unwitting aid
of the Secretary of State, Sir Charles Wood.   The constitutional right of the Governors of Bombay and Madras to
correspond directly with the home government enabled Frere
to place his case personally before Wood and to appeal for
support from the Council of India.   This arrangement suited
Frere's mischievous purposes admirably.   He bombarded Wood
with scathing accounts of "the constant worrying interference

[69]Ibid., evidence of 21 February 1873.

[70]Ibid.

[71]Ibid.

in details, which keeps all local officials and departments
in a state of chronic irritation and rebellious feelings
towards the Government of India"[72] and persuaded him to
condemn Strachey's despatches as "impracticable"[73] and "provocative".[74]   He also cajoled Wood to sanction expenditure
which Strachey had already refused.   For example, he led
Wood to believe that Bombay city's civic improvement fund
was larger than it actually was and to approve imprudent
withdrawals from it.[75]   When the Finance Member challenged
Wood to explain his role in depleting the fund, Wood confessed:
"it did not occur to me that what we had sanctioned would
be carried so far in practice and be so objectionable".[76]

Frere's avoidance of Calcutta's control was calculated
to annoy Strachey, yet ironically it also angered Sir
Charles Trevelyan, whom Wood had sent back to India as
Finance Member of the Viceroy's Council in 1862.   The roles
of three years earlier were reversed: Trevelyan was now
responsible for balancing the imperial budget and Frere was the
spokesman for local autonomy.   Just as Frere had been
sympathetic to Trevelyan's battle against centralization but

---

[72]Martineau, op. cit., vol. I, p. 441 (Frere to Wood
8 September 1864).

[73]Wood to Trevelyan, 26 November 1863, I.O.L. Eur. Mss
F 78/15.

[74]Wood to Lawrence, 4 January 1864, I.O.L. Eur. Mss. F 78/15.

[75]John Lawrence, evidence of 1 July 1873, Parliamentary
Papers (House of Commons), 1873, vol. 12.

[76]Wood to Trevelyan, 9 December 1863, I.O.L. Eur. Mss.
F 78/15.

critical of his mode of opposition, Trevelyan was suppor-
tive of the local government's case but infuriated by its
tactics. Repeatedly, Trevelyan warned Frere that reckless
spending would throw "all financial control to the winds" and
create enormous imperial deficits,"[77] But Frere had
apparently forgotten the homily which he had addressed to
Trevelyan in 1859 on the relationship of financial solvency
to imperial stability and on the local governments'
obligation to co-operate with the Calcutta bureaucracy.
Taking not the slightest notice of Trevelyan's pleas for
restraint, he continued to submit improper accounts and
disobey Government of India regulations.

Bombay officials became increasingly obstreperous in
1864 when Lord Lawrence,[78] the new Viceroy, refused to listen
to their demands for a limited measure of autonomy in determining public works policy. Lawrence, who was physically
weak after thirty-five arduous years in the Punjab and North-
West   Provinces, had accepted the viceroyalty on the
condition that he be allowed to concentrate on foreign
affairs and delegate the supervision of domestic matters to

---

[77]Trevelyan, evidence of 21 February 1873, Parliamentary
Papers (House of Commons), 1873, vol. 12.

[78]John Lawrence, 1st Baron (1811-1879); Joined the ICS
and reached Calcutta, 1830; Assistant District Officer at Delhi,
1830-1838, 1843-1846; Commissioner of Transportation, Sutlej
Jallundhar Doab; Resident at Lahore; Member of the Punjab
Administration Board, 1849-1853; Chief Commissioner of the
Punjab, 1853; Lieutenant-Governor of the Punjab, 1859; Member
of the Council of India, 1858; Viceroy, 1864-1869.

the central government departments.[79]   Before leaving London

he had made his unwillingness to worry about public works --

or to strain imperial finances over them -- abundantly clear

to Wood.[80]   When, therefore, he was greeted in Calcutta

with a barrage of official petitions and private letters

cataloguing the egregious sins of the Public Works Department

and pleading for release from its clutches, he forwarded the

letters to department officials and gave them his unqualified

support in dealing with them.[81]   Further, he declined Frere's

repeated invitations to visit Poona and Bombay and to see for

himself what the government ought to be doing, thereby

antagonizing local officials even more.[82]

By the winter of 1864 relations between Bombay and

Calcutta had degenerated to the level of those between Madras

and Calcutta four years earlier.   This time Wood imposed a

truce and secured agreement to a compromise plan.   He pro-

posed enlarging presidency control of "minor matters" such

as ordinary roads and irrigation schemes and making Govern-

ment of India control "merely financial" i.e. we can allow

you so many lacs for them.   When I say merely financial, I

[79]Worsfold, op. cit., p. 32.

[80]Martineau, op. cit., vol. I, p. 429 (Wood to Frere, 4 January 1864).

[81]Worsfold, op. cit., p. 32.

[82]Ibid.

I mean that $\sqrt{\;}$Calcutta officials$\_7$ must not go into the mode
of execution".[83]   At the same time he insisted on maintaining strict imperial control -- entailing prior criticism of
all plans and supervision of all works-in-progress -- over
all major works like main roads and large-scale sanitation
works.[84]   Frere accepted these terms reluctantly but
loyally: he was not only less impetuous than Trevelyan;
he was also aware of the penalty for persistent intransi-
gence. But having vowed to co-operate with Calcutta, he
warned Wood that the plan was doomed to fail.   "You may
rest assured", he wrote in uncharacteristically sarcastic
tones,

> that in future we will keep within the bounds
> marked out for us, and you will not blame us if
> the Government administration stagnates while
> everything else in the Presidency is advancing...;
> and you may rest assured that, having stated my
> opinion, no exertion shall be wanting on my part to
> give the utmost effect to the system which $\sqrt{}$Lawrence$\sqrt{}$
> prefers, repressive and enfeebling as I believe it
> must prove in its results.[85]

Frere dutifully remained silent about his lingering doubts,
but other Bombay officials seethed openly with resentment
against the Public Works Department.   In 1867 Sir Seymour

---

[83]Martineau, op. cit., vol. I, p. 429 (Wood to Frere,
4 January 1864).

[84]Ibid.

[85]Ibid., vol. I, pp. 441-442 (Frere to Wood, 8 September
1864).

Fitzgerald, [86] Frere's successor, complained bitterly about
"the vexatious interference with this Government by the
Government of India" and accused the central authorities
of trying to pick yet another fight by supervising activities
too closely. [87]   In a fit of exasperation he informed Frere
in England that any semblance of cordiality between Bombay
and Calcutta had withered away as the Government of India
had become "more encroaching and uncourteous every day". [88]
Sparring continued unabated until 1870, when the relationship
between the central and local governments was redefined
and presidency control over public works restored.

The "Madras revolt" and the Bombay struggle against
the Public Works Department demonstrated the power of the
supreme government to enforce centralization against implacable opposition; but they also exposed the difference between
outward obedience and real co-operation.   It must be
concluded that the Government of India's refusal to accom-
modate reasonable presidency demands for limited financial
and administrative autonomy was short-sighted.   On the one

---

[86]Sir William Robert Seymour Vesey Fitzgerald (1818-
1885);   3rd Baron; MP for Horsham, 1852-1865; Under-Secretary
for Foreign Affairs, 1858-1859; Governor of Bombay, 1866-
1872; Privy Councillor, 1866;   MP for Horsham, 1874-1875.

[87]Martineau, op. cit., vol. I, p. 442 (Fitzgerald to
Frere, 8 July 1867).

[88]Ibid., vol. I, p. 442 (Fitzgerald to Frere, 8 August
1867).

hand, it reduced government efficiency by provoking local officials to resent Calcutta's interference and resist its authority. On the other hand -- and no less significantly -- it created widespread local support for the constitutional plan known as "decentralization".

CHAPTER FIVE

THE   ORGANIZATION   OF   GOVERNMENT :

THE   DEBATE   ON   DECENTRALIZATION,   1860 - 1870

From 1860 to 1870 it became increasingly apparent to
even the most dedicated advocates of centralization that
India could not be ruled from Calcutta. It was virtually
impossible for central government bureaucrats to govern
without the co-operation of the presidency and provincial
governments and the district officers who carried out the
day-by-day administration of the Empire. Between 1833 and
1860 the men in the field had been systematically stripped
of the power and motivation to implement Calcutta's orders
efficiently and economically. As a result standards of administration declined as outlined in the previous chapter, and
the imperial budget lurched into deficit no fewer than seven
times in the decade. To alleviate these unforeseen and
alarming consequences of centralization, Finance Members
throughout the 1860's put forward schemes to "decentralize"
administration and finance -- i.e. to devolve power back to
the local governments. Their aim was threefold: to restore
sufficient local autonomy to awaken presidency and provincial
self-interest in thrift and careful planning; to eliminate
the most irritating aspects of Calcutta's interference in

local affairs while maintaining an effective degree of central
supervision; and to develop local (provincial and municipal)
taxes to supplement waning imperial revenues.

It was not their immediate goal to institute local
self-government. Most officials in Calcutta and many in the
presidencies and provinces perceived decentralization and
local self-government as two separate and completely un-
related issues. While they supported the former as a convenient means of redistributing power among British civil
servants to improve bureaucratic morale and strengthen
imperial finances, they abhorred the latter as undesirable,
unnecessary and inimical to good government. Theirs was
the majority opinion, but it was not uncontested. Several
highly influential officials in Calcutta and the local
capitals saw an inextricable link between decentralization
and Indian self-rule. They believed that new taxes should
not be imposed without enlisting the Indians' advice and
consent and hinted that taxation without representation was
as tyrannous -- and every bit as dangerous -- in contemporary India as in North America a century earlier. Fearful of
a second Mutiny, they advised the Government of India to set
up representative councils to guide British officials in the
collection and distribution of the new provincial and
municipal taxes. To their minds federalism was a better form
of government for India than centralized despotism because it
united British officials and Indian representatives in town,
district, presidency and provincial, and imperial councils to

discuss how revenue should be raised and the administration
carried on.

The focus of the debate on decentralization was the
Public Works Department, the most centralized branch of the
imperial government. Local officials regarded it as a
monument to bureaucratic mismanagement because it lacked
personnel competent to supervize presidency and provincial
public works but nevertheless meddled in the pettiest of
projects. Further, it lacked funds to expand building to
meet reformers' growing demands yet squandered existing
resources. With Frere they recommended that district
officers be given far greater latitude in deploying men and
money to suit local requirements. Government of India
officials were also critical of the Public Works Department.
They viewed it as a huge drain on imperial revenues which
the Raj could ill-afford so long as deficits were incurred
in meeting basic operating costs. They pointed out that
improved sanitation, irrigation, communication and transportation were desirable but not essential; and they argued
that if the supreme government could not pay for these
improvements, local (provincial and municipal) resources
should be exploited.

It is ironic that "Maharajah Wood", the prime mover
behind centralization in the post-Mutiny years, should have
been the first to propose the decentralization of the Public
Works Department. Despite his desire to set up a clear chain

of command from his office in London to the district kutcherry,
he was nevertheless alarmed at Wilson's determination "to
centralise too much"[1]; and he was convinced that the new
financial structure would concentrate so much power in
Calcutta that local initiative would be stifled. Complaining that the supreme government would be "overloaded and the
local governments too much crippled"[2], he warned Wilson that

> financial control ... should not be exercised
> in detail. It is nonsense that the Supreme
> Government should attempt to regulate petty
> salaries and expenses. If Trevelyan and
> Elphinstone with their governments and
> officers cannot do that, they are good for
> nothing; and I am quite sure that you can
> be far better employed in greater things.[3]

To reconcile central financial control with local autonomy he
recommended that the Public Works Department be "decentralised
in detail": that the Government of India allow each local
government to spend one-sixth of its annual grant on small-
scale projects without reference to Calcutta[4]. He reassured
Wilson that decentralization would not entail a loss of
central control over the presidencies and provinces:

> I do not mean to relieve the Minor Governments
> at all from your control as to the sums to be
> spent by them. I do want to relieve them from
> control in the detail of the works, and as to

---

[1]Wood to Wilson, 26 March 1860, I.O.L. Eur. Mss.
F 78/2.

[2]Wood to Trevelyan, 25 August 1859, I.O.L. Eur. Mss.
F 78/1.

[3]Wood to Wilson, 26 March 1860, I.O.L. Eur. Mss.
F 78/2.

[4]Wood to Wilson, 10 March 1860, I.O.L. Eur. Mss.
F 78/2.

> all minor matters <u>from</u> <u>any</u> <u>control</u> in respect
> of them. I believe the Madras Engineers to be
> more likely to know how to contract a work at
> Madras than the Bengal Engineers, and the
> Madras Government to know better than you what
> works will be useful in Madras. As regards
> <u>works</u>, therefore, I want to liberate them from
> over-meddling.[5]

Persuaded that Calcutta's authority would not be diminished,

Wilson endorsed Wood's plan and suggested that one-quarter of

the income tax be channeled back to the local governments.

In addition he speculated that it might eventually be

possible to extend decentralization and erect a federal tax

structure on the American model.[6]

Wilson's and Wood's enthusiasm for decentralization

was short-lived. In April 1860, when Sir Charles Trevelyan

refused to collect the new income tax for essential imperial

charges, they decided that the possibility of dividing tax

proceeds for non-essential public works was remote.

Predicting that renewed financial chaos would occur if the

local governments were reinvested with any appreciable degree

of autonomy, they hastily dropped plans for decentralizing

the Public Works Department and resolved that centralization

was the key to good government in India.

---

[5]Wood to Wilson, 27 February 1860, I.O.L. Eur. Mss.
F 78/2.

[6]Thomas, <u>op</u>. <u>cit</u>., p. 153.

In 1861 a public debate on decentralization was
kindled when Samuel Laing[7], Wilson's successor, discovered a
deficit of £400,000 for the previous fiscal year. In a
desperate attempt to balance the budget he proposed reducing
the presidency and provincial public works grants and empowering the local governments to make up the difference through
local (provincial and municipal) taxation. Petty transit
levies, succession duties, house taxes and land revenue cesses
had been raised to fund municipal roads, bridges and public
buildings for centuries; but they had never before been
collected by the provincial or imperial governments or used
outside the towns in which they were collected. Laing
believed that the financial stability of the Raj could be
secured by exploiting these traditional sources of revenue
and diverting the proceeds from the town of origin to other
parts of the presidency or province.[8] Local officials were
quick to disabuse the Finance Member of his fantacies. They
conceded that the Indians would more readily pay familiar
taxes which had long been exacted from their ancestors than

---

[7]Samuel Laing (1812-1897); called to the bar at
Lincoln's Inn, 1837; Secretary to the Railway Department of
the Board of Trade, 1842-1846; Member of Lord Dalhousie's
Railway Commission, 1845; Financial Secretary to the
Treasury, 1859-1860; Finance Member of the Supreme Council
of India, 1861-1862; MP 1852-1857, 1859, 1865-1885.

[8]Laing, Budget Speech, 16 April 1862, Proceedings of
the Legislative Council of India, Jan. - Nov. 1862, vol. I.

foreign ones like the income tax which they did not understand. But they emphasized that municipal taxes were far
less lucrative than Laing assumed and that they were
altogether insufficient to cover rising public works costs.[9]

Local officials suggested three alternative tax
arrangements to put imperial finances on a firmer footing
while devolving control of public works to the presidencies
and provinces. First, they proposed that the imperial public
works grants be reduced as planned but that the scope of
local taxation be extended to include sources of revenue
traditionally reserved for the Government of India (like the
land revenue); secondly, that the grants be cut but local
taxes ignored altogether and public works be financed
entirely from imperial heads of revenue transferred to the
local governments; thirdly -- and most desirably -- that
the entire funding process be reversed and all sources of
revenue be surrendered to the local governments, which would
be required to subscribe to an annual maintenance grant for
the Government of India. The last option embodied the
ultimate hope of many local officials for years to come. As
one member of the Madras Executive Council put it: "if
/‾the local governments_7 are to enjoy real liberty of action
and self-management, it seems to me that the Acts of

---

[9]   P. Banerjea, _Provincial Finance in India_,
London, 1929, p. 27.

Parliament affecting India must be altered so as to give them a control over the general tax and expenditure within their range, subject to the condition of supplying a fixed contribution to the Imperial Treasury"[10].

None of these suggestions -- least of all the last -- was acceptable to Laing, who accused the local governments of misunderstanding the function of decentralization within an imperial despotism. Methodically, he attacked each of their ideas. He condemned their proposal to expand local taxes as undesirable, pointing out that these duties and cesses were meant to supplement imperial taxes, not replace them: like English local rates they were designed to raise money for local projects from residents who would benefit directly from them.[11] He next dismissed the proposal to cede assets equivalent to transferred heads of expenditure as objectionable because it would deplete imperial financial resources and increase rather than diminish the problems of balancing the Calcutta budget. Finally, he criticized the proposal to fund the Government of India from local grants because "the great branches of expenditure, such as the Army and National Debt, are Imperial; and while this is the case, the great branches of Revenue must remain Imperial".[12]

---

[10]Ibid.

[11]Laing, Budget Speech, 16 April 1862, Proceedings of the Legislative Council of India, Jan. - Nov. 1862, vol. I.

[12]Ibid.

The controversy over local taxation was halted in the
spring of 1862 by the news that the anticipated deficit of
£500,000 for the fiscal year 1861-1862 had been averted. "If
the feeling here is one of astonishment", Laing told the
imperial Legislative Council, "in England it amounted almost
to incredulity" to discover "the Budget in Equilibrium".[13]
The Finance Member was anxious to introduce decentralization
despite the improved state of the economy, and he reiterated
its numerous advantages over centralization in his annual
financial statement to the Government of India.[14] But the
sense of urgency was gone, and the surplus of £1.8 million
in 1861-63 and a somewhat smaller surplus in 1863-64
removed the imperial government's primary motive for discuss-
ing both local taxation and administrative and financial
devolution.[15]

Shortly before returning to England in 1861 Laing
marvelled that "the Revenue of India is really buoyant and
elastic in an extraordinary degree" -- an assessment which
was soon proved to be totally ill-founded.[16] With the

---

[13]Ibid.

[14]Ibid.

[15]Ibid.

[16]Ibid.

winter of 1864-65 came a widespread drought, a general rise
in salaries, a necessary investment of £10 million in
military works, and an increase in costs throughout every
branch of government.[17] Feeling "cabined, cribbed, and
confined" by the unfortunate combination of circumstances,
the Viceroy, Lord Lawrence, implored the Calcutta bureaucracy
and the local governments to reduce spending. But his
entreaties were ignored, and he was soon complaining -- like
Wood in 1860 -- that everyone paid lip service to economy and
no one practised it.[18] His annoyance was heightened by his
conviction that balancing the budget by raising taxes would
create dire "complications". Observing that "the minds of
the natives are unsettled", he concluded that the problems
of reducing government spending paled to insignificance in
comparison to those of extracting more money from the
Indians.[19]

Lawrence's apprehensions were not shared by the
Finance Member of his Council, Sir Charles Trevelyan, who
viewed Calcutta's embarrassing financial predicament as a
splendid opportunity to introduce local self-government.
He believed that the best form of imperial rule was

---

[17]Smith, op. cit., vol. II, p. 338.

[18]Ibid.

[19]Lawrence to Wood, 29 May 1864, I.O.L. Eur. Mss.
F 78/20.

Indian self-government below and British paternal despotism above -- an arrangement which demanded more than the devolution of power from Calcutta to the local capitals outlined by Laing. It necessitated the establishment of representative municipal committees to manage town and village affairs. It also required the use of municipal taxes in the towns and villages where they were collected -- not at the other end of the district or province, as intended by Laing. "Great public benefit is to be expected from the firm establishment of a system of municipal administration in India", Trevelyan asserted.

> Neither the Central nor the Local Governments are capable of providing either the funds or the executive agency for making the improvements of various kinds, in all the cities and towns of India, which are demanded by the rapidly developing wealth of the country. The imperial revenue barely suffices for the increasing demands upon it for objects of general interest; and the practical alternative is a large addition to imperial taxation, in order to meet the wants of the town populations under a centralised system, or a transfer both of the duty and the charge to the populations. Not only will the local requirements be more promptly and fully provided for under the municipal system than they could be under any Government agency, but, when the people see that they have the management of their own affairs in their own hands, they will feel confidence to do things which they would not have accepted from Government.[20]

In 1864 Trevelyan translated these general propositions into concrete policy by transferring charges for town police from

---

[20]Trevelyan, Budget Speech, April 1864, Proceedings of the Legislative Council of India, Jan. - June 1864.

debits against the imperial income tax to ones against municipal funds drawn from town duties and taxes on houses, licenses, horses and carriages.[21] His desire to finance town government from these taxes was shared by Sir Charles Wood, who declared in 1863 that municipal "self-assessment" was the only feasible means of providing for primary and vernacular education[22], and by the Royal Sanitary Commission, which reported in 1864 that municipal funds were the only available source of revenue for ridding Indian cities of "offensive and objectionable" "abominations".[23] In response to this encouragement the local governments duly established municipalities throughout British India between 1864 and the end of the decade: they set up municipal funds and appointed committees to advise district officers on their expenditure.[24] These events were significant to the growth of local self-government; but neither the sums of money raised by the municipalities, nor the powers granted them by government, were large. This explains Lawrence's willingness to condone these measures despite his opposition to increased taxation.

---

[21] Gazette of India Extraordinary, 14 September 1864, Resolution of the Government of India in Finance Department no. 2245, 31 August 1864.

[22] Ibid,

[23] Report of the Royal Sanitary Commission, Parliamentary Papers (House of Commons) 1865, vol. 40, p. 539.

[24] See Appendix A.

In 1865 Trevelyan complicated the Government of
India's financial problems and incurred Lawrence's fury by
repealing the income tax, which he had abhorred since its
inception in 1860. In its place he proposed floating a
loan of £1.2 million for public works and raising export
duties. Neither of these was acceptable to the Viceroy or
Secretary of State. Wood, who was prepared to resort to
loans only in emergencies and altogether unwilling to
antagonize Lancashire manufacturers by increasing the duty on
textiles, vetoed the budget.[25] "It is as bad as it can be"
he wrote to Frere in Bombay; "the export duties are as
foolish as anything can be, and the loan is worse. Heaven
help us from such selfish and shortsighted statesmanship".[26]
Trevelyan -- disgraced by his financial views once again --
resigned in a pique and sailed at once for England, leaving
a yawning gap between the Government of India's annual
income and expenditure.

As the deficit mounted by £2.5 million in 1866-67,
£1.6 million in 1867-68 and £4.4 million in 1868-69, imperial
and local administrators reconsidered Laing's decentralization
scheme as the only practicable means of balancing the imperial

---

[25]Banerjea, op. cit., p. 191.

[26]Wood to Frere, 17 May 1865, I.O.L. Eur. Mss.
F 78/21.

budget without sacrificing public works.[27] Their deliberations were guided by Trevelyan's successor as Finance Member,
William Massey.[28] In a demi-official circular letter sent
to the local governments in February 1866, he repeated
Laing's statement of faith in a localized and diversified
tax system, broadened the scope of devolved responsibilities
(to include education, police, and district jails, as well
as road maintenance and repair), and entirely replaced the
imperial public works grants with local taxes. To aid the
presidencies and provinces in choosing lucrative and
enhanceable sources of revenue, he appended a list of
suggestions, including a license tax on trades and professions
(Wilson's tax never having been imposed), a house tax, an
octroi duty[29] in towns and an inheritance duty on land.[30]

---

[27]S. Bhattacharyya, Financial Foundations of the
British Raj, Simla, 1971, p. 62.

[28]William Nathaniel Massey (1809-1881); called to
the bar from the Inner Temple, 1844; Recorder of Portsmouth
and Plymouth; MP, 1855-1865; Under-Secretary in the Home
Department; Finance Member of the Legislative Council of
India, 1865-1868; Privy Councillor and MP, 1872-1881.

[29]octroi: transit duty on goods being transported
through towns in the moffusil (countryside).

[30]Massey, Minute of 21 February 1866, "Proposed
Transfer to the Local Accounts of a Portion of the Charges
Now Falling upon the Revenues of India", Finance Department
Proceedings, October 1867, Accounts no. 22.

In response to this circular all of the local governments except the Central Provinces and the Punjab flatly refused to finance the broad range of new projects on the meagre reserves afforded by local taxation. They rehearsed the three criticisms levelled against Laing's plan in 1861-62, and they reiterated Trevelyan's advice that municipal taxes be spent at source rather than diverted elsewhere in the presidency or province.[31] They emphasized that whereas the Indians would readily pay municipal taxes for projects which benefitted them directly like village roads, schools and sanitation, they would grudgingly contribute to district or provincial programs like trunk roads and irrigation works which were constructed so far away from their homes to be of no immediate interest or use. According to Cecil Beadon, Lieutenant-Governor of Bengal, "the mere provincialisation of the taxes would not, in the least, remove their unwillingness to pay it". "To the native of Bengal", he explained,

> a system of Provincial Taxation would not differ in appearance from one of Imperial Taxation. There is little sympathy between the inhabitants even of adjoining Districts, and none at all between those which lie at opposite extremities of the Province. For instance, it does not in the least signify to the tax-payers of Chittagong or Cachar whether their taxes are spent for the benefit of all Bengal, or for that of all India. In either case they cannot perceive that any given tax is imposed for their benefit ....[32]

---

[31] Finance Department Proceedings, October 1867, Accounts no. 22.

[32] Cecil Beadon, Minute of 8 March 1867, Ibid.

Sir Bartle Frere believed that the Indians could not be tricked into paying town duties for provincial public works without jeopardizing the credibility of the British Raj. "I need not point out", he admonished Massey,

> how wide-spread will be the dissatisfaction, and how general the distrust of Government's fair dealing which will be created if the local tax-payer now finds that the tax which he asked should be imposed upon him to support a school for his children, or to furnish water for his household, is swept into the Government treasury to pay for police, or to build a district jail, or a bridge, in some neighbour-ing town in which the tax-payer has no interest.
>
> No rules that I can think of can prevent this kind of thing happening under the scheme before us to an extent quite sufficient to disgust with the very name of local taxation not only the tax-payers, but the zealous and meritorious public officers who have heretofore exerted themselves to impose local taxes, and who will naturally feel dishonored and degraded if the promises under which they induce the local community to tax itself are not rigidly and honorably observed.[33]

This was a compelling argument against decentralization as conceived by Laing and Massey, who confused local (provincial) and local (municipal) taxes and regarded them as inter-changeable. It was also a good reason for linking decentral-ization to local self-government -- as local administrators increasingly realized -- because the latter was based on the premise that the government closest to the people could not only govern it best, but could exact the greatest revenue with

---

[33]Frere, Minute of 15 November 1866, Ibid.

the least resistance. In the final analysis, however, the predilictions of the Indian taxpayer were less important to presidency and provincial administrators than the restoration of local autonomy; and when in 1868 they were offered a decentralization plan which granted the second at the expense of the first, the majority accepted it without hesitation.

Massey's plan was vigorously attacked from a completely different angle by two of the most influential men in India, W. T. Denison[34], Governor of Madras, and E. Drummond[35], Lieutenant-Governor of the North-West   Provinces. These men disapproved of decentralization on principle. Employing the arguments put forward by presidency administrators against the income tax in 1860, they alleged that local (provincial and municipal) taxes were inadequate solutions to the imperial financial crisis -- "mere palliatives when applied to remedy an evil which has its origin so deeply

---

[34]Sir William Thomas Denison (1804-1871): joined the Royal Engineers, 1826; Lieutenant-Governor of Van Deemen's Land, 1847; Governor of New South Wales and titular Governor-General of Australia, 1854-1861; Governor of Madras, 1861-1863; Acting Viceroy, Dec. 1863-Jan. 1864.

[35]The Hon. Sir Edward Drummond (1813-1895): ICS; went to Bengal, 1833; Accountant-General, 1856; Auditor-General, 1860; Financial Secretary to the Government of India, 1862; Lieutenant-Governor of the North-West Provinces, 1863-1868; Member of the Council of India, 1875-1885.

seated" (Denison) [36] -- and that the only effective cure was "to face the difficulties boldly" and raise imperial taxes drastically (Drummond). [37] They also contended that local taxes were inappropriate English antidotes to a peculiarly Indian ill. Drummond observed, in terms reminiscent of Trevelyan as Governor of Madras, that

> ... the circumstances of the two countries, their systems of revenue are radically different, and the duties and responsibilities which attach to the land, and, in England, fall chiefly on the landlord, in India devolve necessarily upon the Government.
>
> It is perfectly true that the proportion of local to Imperial expenditure is very much less in India than it is in England, but repeated experience has shown that nothing can be more fallacious, or so likely to lead to fatal mistakes, than attempts to apply rules, deducted from the experience of one country to the state of another country: and in India especially, where society has been so long and is still in a state of stagnation, any change is looked upon with suspicion, and changes in the forms of the monetary burthens imposed upon the people, with more suspicion than any other. [38]

These arguments are important not because they were valid criticisms of decentralization, but because they were the standard responses of conservative local administrators to new taxes allied to government reorganization throughout the 1860's: they expressed their fear that sudden change

---

[36] Drummond, Minute of 8 March 1866, Finance Department Proceedings, October 1867, Accounts no. 22.

[37] Denison, Minute of 20 March 1866, Ibid.

[38] Drummond, Minute of 8 March 1866, Ibid.

would lead to mutiny and their conviction that a massive
reduction in government services -- whatever the restraint
on India's social and material progress -- was preferable to
constitutional or financial innovation. Tactically, these
arguments are important because they enabled Lawrence to
report "an almost universal hesitation, to use no stronger
word" about decentralization to Sir Charles Wood and persuade the Council of India in London as well as the Imperial
Executive Council in Calcutta to drop the plan from their
agendas for 1866.[39]

Lack of enthusiasm for his initial scheme led Massey
to explore new ways of distributing the financial burden in
order to balance the imperial budget. In this study he
received the invaluable aid of Colonel Richard Strachey, the
Secretary of the Public Works Department -- the most unlikely
but important convert to decentralization in the 1860's.
Faced on the one hand with the imperial government's
reluctance to increase the deficit by devoting its limited
funds to public works and on the other with the local
governments' implacable resistance to financial and administrative supervision from Calcutta, he embraced decentralization
as the only reasonable way to pay for and execute the many

---

[39]Lawrence, Minute to the Secretary of State, _Ibid_.

projects which he deemed essential to the material development of the subcontinent.[40] In the summer of 1867 he
presented Massey with a totally new plan which took local
objections to previous proposals into account and represented what Massey called an "organic change" in concept.[41]
Its most significant innovation was its stipulation that
"when any specific charge is made over to the local administrations, sufficient revenue should at the same time be
provided to meet the actual charge".[42] The transfers of
imperial heads of revenue and expenditure would be "made by
degrees so as to avoid all risk of confusion in public
accounts and to educate the local officers in matters of
financial administration ...." The short-range goal of the
plan was "to divest the Central Government of all detailed
concern of those items of expenditure which pertain to the
branches of administration, the details of which it cannot
in fact control" (a tacit admission of defeat to Frere and
the Bombay officials, who were delighted by Strachey's change
of heart). Its long-range goal was to develop a federal
financial system like the one proposed by Wilson in 1860.
"The financial position of the central authority might by

[40]John and Richard Strachey, Finance and the Public
Works of India from 1869-1881, London, 1882, "introduction".

[41]Massey, Memorandum of 17 August 1867, Finance
Department Proceedings, October 1867, Accounts no. 22.

[42]R. Strachey, "Note on the Transfer to the Local
Governments of the Control over Certain Portions of Public
Expenditure", 17 August 1867, Ibid., no. 23.

degrees be brought to assimilate generally to that of the
United States central government", Strachey predicted. But
like Wilson he acknowledged that the American system could
not be adopted in India without considerable modification,
for "a power of supervision and control of a general nature
must continue to be exercised over the finances of the separate local administrations under a despotic government like
that of India, which has no existence in the case of
democratic America". As proof of the supreme government's
commitment to decentralization as the first step towards
federalism, Strachey advised Massey to draw up a list of
local taxes "least susceptible to control by the Government
of India" yet "of sufficient importance to indicate that the
measure is intended to be a reality, and a step towards a
more complete transfer of the financial administrations to
the Local Governments".[43]

Local officials throughout the Empire lauded Strachey's
"sound and liberal views", confirming that "control to be
effectual must be localised"[44] and that "self-taxation
means difficult taxation, and therein lies its only true
strength as a cause of economy".[45] Strachey's concession of

---

[43]Ibid.

[44]Minute by the Government of the North-West
Provinces, Finance Department Proceedings, April 1868, no.
39.

[45]Minute by the Government of Oudh, Ibid, no. 40.

complete local (presidency and provincial) control over specified categories of public works, his extension of municipal taxes, and his transfer of imperial sources of revenue to the local governments satisfied the supporters of decentralization who had criticized details of the two earlier plans. However, it provoked the opponents of administrative and financial devolution to launch a decisive fresh attack on the new scheme. Lord Napier[46], Governor of Madras, began by arguing that none of the local governments except Bombay and Madras was capable of administering public works without close guidance from Calcutta -- an opinion which Frere had aired to Strachey in 1863 and which for obvious reasons never won support outside the two presidencies.[47] Next, he pointed out that centralization had been the established pattern of government for the past eight years and suggested that it would be far more prudent to eliminate the inconveniences and frictions which hampered it than to turn the pyramid of power on its head and make the Government of India a "pensioner of the provincial governments".[48] This clever appeal to the inbred conservatism

---

[46]Francis Napier of Merchistoun, 9th Baron, 1st Baron Ettrick of Ettrick (1819-1898): entered the Diplomatic Service, 1840; Ambassador at St. Petersburg, 1860-1864; at Berlin, 1864-1866; Governor of Madras, 1866-1872.

[47]Minute by the Government of Madras, Finance Department Proceedings, April 1868, no. 48.

[48]Ibid.

of local administrators on constitutional issues prompted
Sir Henry Durand[49], the Military Member of the Viceroy's
Council, to remark that any kind of control would be "much
more irksome than agreeable" and that any curb on spending
would create resentment: "the existence of such a tradi-
tional sentiment $\underline{/}$of opposition to the supreme government$\underline{/}$
may be regretted, but can hardly be soberly admitted as a
sufficient reason for hasty subversion of a carefully
elaborated financial scheme .... Radical change under such
circumstances is pernicious and most inexpedient when wholly
unnecessary".[50] Finally, Napier postulated that a frag-
mented fiscal system would appear to diminish the financial
resources of the Raj and that the illusion of insolvency
thus created would discourage essential overseas investment.[51]
Napier and Durand sincerely deplored any devolution of power
from Calcutta. Nevertheless, they recognized the force of
scare tactics in political debate and described the possible
consequences of decentralization in terms calculated to

---

[49]Sir Henry Marion Durand (1812-1871); entered
Bengal Engineers, 1828; Political Agent at Gwalior and
Bhopal; Member of the Council of India, 1859-1861; Foreign
Secretary to the Government of India, 1861-1865; Military
Member of the Supreme Council, 1865-1870; Lieutenant-
Governor of the Punjab, 1870-1871.

[50]Durand, Memorandum of 7 October 1867, Finance
Department Proceedings, October 1867, Accounts no. 73.

[51]Minute by the Government of Madras, Finance
Department Proceedings, April 1868, Accounts no. 48.

frighten the Viceroy's Council in Calcutta and the Council of India in London from sanctioning what they regarded as the first step towards bad government in India. They ignored the limited constitutional and financial changes actually proposed by Strachey and failed -- for argument's sake -- to mention that most important government programs would remain firmly under imperial control and that the local governments would remain almost totally dependent on the Government of India.

It was not difficult for Napier and Durand to persuade the Viceroy that decentralization was undesirable, for Lawrence had already made his aversion to increased taxation abundantly clear. He had also displayed a resistance to constitutional change stemming from fear of a second Mutiny. His decision to oppose Strachey's plan was based on two calculations: first, that decentralization would separate local from imperial financial records, doubling accounting costs and making the preparation of the budget a nightmare; and secondly, that the division of power among the presidencies and provinces would impede the speedy co-ordination of men and armaments required to save the Empire from Indian rebels. Reiterating that "a general spirit of wise economy" and "careful attention to the expenditure of the public revenues" would balance the imperial budget, he declared that any improvement of the existing system of government was impossible and concluded that centralization guaranteed "a moderate, reasonable, and indeed, desirable" measure of control over the presidencies and provinces.[52]

Such complacency appalled Sir Henry Maine, the Law
Member of the Council and the most eloquent champion of
decentralization (divorced from Indian self-rule) in the
Government of India. "I do not think that anybody can
have observed the recent workings of our system of
financial control without coming to the conclusion that,
if it be not on the point of an inevitable collapse, it
is at all events in great danger of going to pieces unless
the strain be lightened somewhere", he told the Viceroy's
Council in September, 1867.[53] Charging Lawrence with a
misplaced faith in expenditure cuts as a universal panacea,
he stated that reductions had never balanced the budget in
the past and never would in the future. To justify this bold
assertion he argued that viceregal prodigality -- not local
government overspending -- had wrecked havoc to previous
imperial balance sheets and that this could never be curbed
in a despotism like the British Indian Empire. Decentralization
alone could deprive the Viceroy of the power to disrupt the
financial stability of the Raj and at the same time prevent
the presidencies and provinces from recklessness, should
they ever abandon their tradition of commendable restraint.

---

[52]Lawrence, Minute of 27 September 1867, Finance
Department Proceedings, October 1867, Accounts no. 73.

[53]Maine, Minute of 13 September 1867, Ibid., no. 24.

Under existing arrangements Calcutta could not enforce
frugality at any level of government:

> The rules imposed on the local Government depend
> for their force, like all laws, on the efficacy
> of the penalty which they threaten in the event
> of disobedience. The penalty is, in the present
> case, a reproof from the Government of India.
> But if any local Government has become -- what
> any local Government might become at any day --
> entirely callous to the rebukes of the Government
> of India, through discovering -- what any local
> Government may at any time discover -- that these
> rebukes lead to no ulterior consequences, what
> impediment remains to the employment of one or more
> among the hundred expedients by which the Central
> Government may be morally compelled to condone
> infractions of its rules and to allow the share of
> its revenues which it has allotted to a particular
> province to be exceeded...? Your system... goes
> to undue lengths in what it attempts, and miscarries
> miserably to the extent of the excess. [54]

Maine concluded that whereas centralization had been built
on a sham paper authority, decentralization would be erected
on a reasonable and enforceable division of power. He
dismissed as fatuous the notions that local autonomy and
local taxes were peculiarly English or especially radical
and reminded the Council that the presidencies had only
recently lost their financial and administrative independence
and that municipal cesses for roads, schools, and village
institutions had long been collected throughout the subcontinent. To his mind "local watchfulness even by a
defectively organised body" like the municipal committees set
up in the 1860's would oversee the collection and expenditure
of municipal taxes more effectively than the local government;
and in the distant future a federal system modelled on the

---

[54]Ibid.

American plan would ensure popular supervision of the imperial

bureaucracy at all levels of government. Anxious to avert

imminent financial disaster, Maine pleaded with the

Executive Council to end the "paper discussion" of decen-

tralization and instruct him to draw up the appropriate

legislation.[55]

The majority of officials on the Viceroy's Council

and in the presidencies and provinces shared Maine's

impatience to implement decentralization, but Lawrence

remained stubbornly opposed to it. Realizing that an out-

right veto would be unpopular, he referred Strachey's plan

to London in the hope of burying it in administrative red

tape for the duration of his viceregal tenure. His ploy

was successful. Although Sir Stafford Northcote[56], the

Secretary of State for India, had publically endorsed the

principle of decentralization, he was swayed by the

opposition's scare tactics to advise the House of Commons

to delay approval for a year or two. Even then he insisted

that the scheme be instituted gradually to minimize the

---

[55]Ibid.

[56]Sir Stafford Henry Northcote, 1st Earl of Iddesleigh,
(1846-1911); called to the bar at the Inner Temple, 1840;
Private Secretary to Gladstone, 1842-1851; Report on the
Civil Service with Sir Charles Trevelyan, 1854; MP 1855-1885;
President of the Board of Trade, 1866; Secretary of State
for India, 1866-1868; Chancellor of the Exchequer, 1874-1880;
First Lord of the Treasury, 1885; Foreign Secretary, 1886-1887.

threat to imperial investments and internal security.[57]
Unwittingly, he aided Lawrence's cause and destroyed any
lingering chance of reorganizing the Indian government in
the 1860's.

Upon succeeding Lawrence as Viceroy in 1869 Lord Mayo
was distressed to learn that in addition to an accumulated
deficit of £5¾ million for the past three years, a decrease
of £1½ million in imperial revenue was expected in the first
quarter of 1869-1870.[58] "I am determined not to have another
deficit", he trumpeted, "even if it leads to the diminution
of the Army, the reduction of Civil Establishments, and the
stoppage of Public Works".[59] His first attempt to cover the
widening gap between income and expenditure consisted of
reduced spending (£800,000 deducted from public works and
£350,000 from other departments) and increased taxation (the
income tax raised from 1% to 2½% and enhancements of the
salt duty in Bombay and Madras). These drastic measures
were insufficient because the debt proved to be substantially
larger than anticipated: the local governments and Calcutta
departments had -- as usual -- grossly underestimated their
expenses and made a mockery of budget projections.[60] "We

[57]Banerjea, op. cit., p. 53.

[58]Sir William Wilson Hunter, A Life of the Earl of
Mayo, 4th Viceroy of India, London, 1875, p. 139.

[59]Ibid., p. 143.

[60]Ibid., p. 145.

209

have played our last card", Mayo confessed despondently to a
friend, "and we have nothing left in our hands to fall back
upon, except to devise measures which will prevent the
recurrence of a similar crisis hereafter".[61] The moment to
institute decentralization had come.

Within eighteen months Mayo and Sir John Strachey
(Colonel Richard Strachey's brother) hammered out a plan
which enabled the Government of India to balance its budget
at long last.[62] It transferred departments labelled
"provincial services" (jails, registration, police, education,
medical services, printing, roads, and civil buildings) from
the imperial to the local governments; meeted out a
"provincial grant" of £4½ million -- £1 million less than
that disbursed in 1870-1871 -- to the local governments in
proportion to their previous contributions to these
services; and required the presidencies and provinces to
finance the discrepancy between the truncated grants and
expenditure on the transferred services by reducing administrative costs and imposing local (municipal) taxation.
This plan, which closely resembled the one put forward by
Laing in 1861, achieved financial stability by forcing the
local governments to marshall their resources prudently,
by relieving the central treasury of the responsbility of

[61]Ibid., p. 147.

[62]"Enlargement of the Power and Responsibilities of
the Local Governments", Finance Department Proceedings,
January 1871.

financing public works, and by drawing on new sources of revenue. It also promoted administrative efficiency by restoring local autonomy and by reducing, if not eliminating, the power struggle between Calcutta and the presidency and provincial capitals.

For the purposes of this discussion what it did not attain is equally important. It did not transfer authority from British officials to Indian representatives; neither did it expand municipal taxes as the basis of municipal government. In short, it failed to devolve financial and administrative power to the lowest rung of the hierarchy -- the town and village -- and left the Government of India vulnerable to attack from those who believed that good imperial government depended upon a union of decentralization and local self-government.

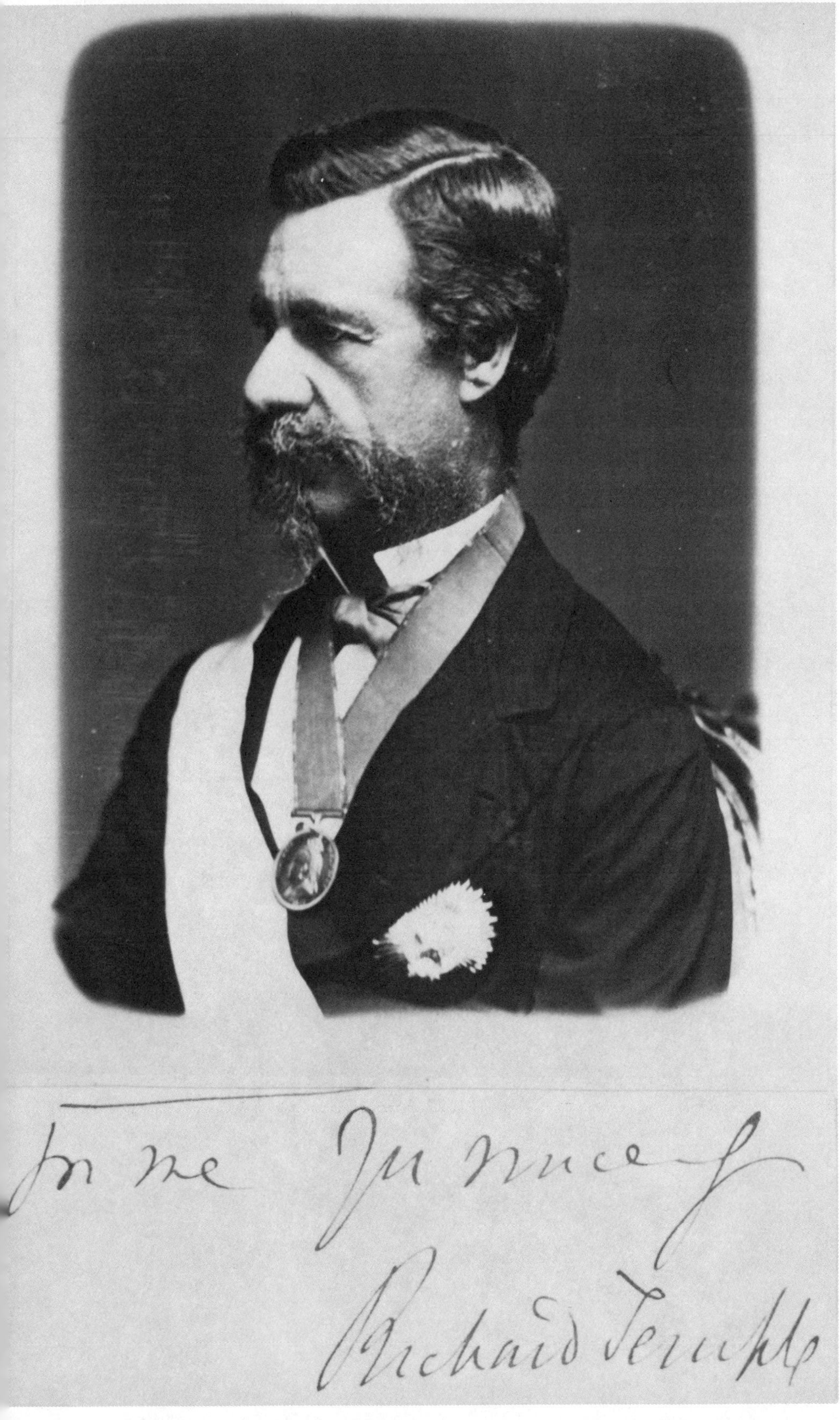
Richard Temple

CHAPTER SIX

INDIAN FITNESS FOR SELF-RULE:

BRITISH VIEWS, 1840 - 1870

In the years after 1840, arrogant detachment from
Indian life became the rule among British officials. Gone
were the Orientalist governors who strove to preserve
Indian self-rule in the villages, who agonized over Western
reforms in an alien culture, who fretted at the pace of
change. Gone were their philosophic district officers who
considered the ancient mechanism of village self-government
to be as inviolable as the workings of a clock. In their
place arrived a new generation of public school men, un-
curious about India, their knowledge solely derived from
Mill, many heavily influenced by Arnold towards "muscular
Christianity", imbued -- with few exceptions -- with a generalized contempt of the Indians' capacity for self-rule.[1]

There are several reasons why, after the unplanned
collapse of village institutions, no attempt was made by the

---

[1]For Mill's deleterious influence on "our young men
going out to India", see the introduction by H.H. Wilson,
his unsympathetic second edition editor, in History of
British India, London, 1840, p. viii-ix.

British in this period to devise a new system of local self-rule. Prime among them was the fear of upsetting India's fragile stability by dangerous experiments. Next was the fact that few villages remained whose patils had not been dislodged and whose landowning hierarchies had not been undermined: the old system appeared to have collapsed so completely that nothing could be built upon it. Third, the belief of John Strachey -- that the old villages had outlived their usefulness -- was now the voice of the land and was more than the conviction of aging Utilitarians. Fourthly, the years 1840-70 saw an increasing trend towards centralized British government from Calcutta, a trend reinforced by a new imperial confidence that what was British was better when constitutional affairs were at issue. And finally, the scale of the task of making enlightened self-governing men of illiterate ryots was now evident; and the one political philosophy that aspired to this was now discredited. Utilitarians were forced to concede that self-rule would not, after all, bring about the unfettered pursuit of self-interest, and that the drive for improvement must now come from the British.

The 1840's displayed new forms of British patronage of the Indians. There were no "Orientalists" left after the abject failure of their central policy; and the diluted Utilitarianism of J.S. Mill was of largely academic interest in India. Two new groups took the stage. One, building on the charisma of Macaulay and Bentinck, sought from 1830 the displacement of Sanskrit by English as a lingua franca and the abolition of the wilder practices of the Hindus and Moslems (like thugee and female infanticide). The second, the "paternalists", were more socially conservative and protective of Indian customs, but -- blessed with the civilized visions of Dr. Arnold and the Evangelicals -- treated the Indians as helpless children. Many of the dying breed of Orientalists were transmuted into paternalists in the 40's, their ambitions for local self-government abandoned for thirty years ahead. What was new among them was a disdain of Indian civilization and capacity for self-rule where previously a Burkean respect for village society had obtained. It was disdain directly born of the Evangelicalism and muscular Christianity whose influence was spreading in England. It met no counter in India; for the flourishing self-governing communities which might have made nonsense of it had been largely destroyed under Orientalist rule.

Typical of the paternalists of this period, and also one of the few men to articulate his views on Indian self-government, was Sir Richard Temple. From 1867 to 1880 he was successively Finance Member of the Viceroy's Council, Lieutenant-Governor of Bengal and Governor of Bombay. He wrote books to inflate British achievement in India in the eyes of the audience at home; and both here and in his correspondence he sets out the contempt of the British majority at this time for Indian civilization and Indian potential for self-rule. In such articulation he was almost unique. From 1840 to 1870 there was no "debate" on local self-government in the sense of opposing views being publicly exchanged and challenged. Consciously superior British career servants did not care for Indian self-rule and did not talk about it. Temple, therefore, is indispensable to the historian who is forced to burrow in this period (chiefly into complacent career memoirs) to find any written definition of the British majority's attitude to local self-government.

Temple, as will emerge below, spoke for his age; Sir George Campbell, his contemporary and a lone opponent, spoke perhaps for the next. From 1850 until his return to England in 1875 he was regarded by colleagues as a troublemaker. They resented his repeated calls for total self-government in all towns and villages; they resented his attempts to appeal directly to Parliament at home, often from junior positions in India; they did not like his two books, Modern India (1853) and India As It May Be (1854) and consigned him to the role of a voice crying in the wilderness. In the 1860's he seemed to them a near-subversive in his respect for the Indians during the racial backlash following the Mutiny. That Campbell, a lifelong radical, was able to make his way into the Lieutenant-Governorship of Bengal in 1871 (preceding Temple) was due to the personal admiration of the Earl of Mayo as Viceroy; but it reflected the fact that by this time his appeals were beginning to find a wider parish, not least among the Indians. Campbell was not of course alone in challenging the self-satisfaction of the British -- in India as at home -- in the mid-century; in his championship of local self-rule he was, however, the only public opponent of prevailing British policy. No one publicly replied to him. Nevertheless, he had his silent support. This was difficult to identify while Campbell was an isolated figure in the 1840's, 50's and 60's. But in the more congenial climate of the 1870's, when Mayo's decentralization plan forced fresh discussion of local self-government, they emerged from the woodwork. (Their ideas are discussed in Chapter Eight).

I.   ARE THE INDIANS CIVILIZED?

Discussion of the Indians' potential for local self-government started from the important question: are the Indians civilized? Temple and Campbell approached it with sharply opposed criteria of civilization, their ideas differing with their educational skills (Temple was a classical product of Rugby, Campbell went to Edinburgh New Academy and Madras College, St. Andrews University), their backgrounds and their cultural notions.

Temple's Rugby schooling under Arnold implanted an image of civilized man into which the Indians did not fit. For Temple, Arnold himself -- with his "granite character, his clarion voice, his joyousness in physical exercise, and his sternness against evil" -- was the terrifying model of the truly civilized person.[2] One doubts indeed whether Arnold had ever met an Indian, let alone considered the problems of cultural relativism such a figure might raise; and Temple, armed with his rigid code of muscular Christianity, was little better equipped to face such difficulties. Muscular Christianity was a narrow rod by which to measure the Indians, but Temple lacked the skills to apply any other. Science and non-classical languages were ignored at Rugby in the 1830's and 40's, and very little attention was paid to history. As a consequence Temple viewed Indian society from the limited perspectives of classical Greece and Rome and upper-middle class Victorian England. He judged the Indians by their "thoroughness and manliness"; by their ability to balance the life of action with the life of the mind; by their delight in physical exercise; and by their ability "to keep /_their_7 temper in contests, to be good-humoured in disputes, to receive hard knocks with a smiling face and if needful to hit back in return".[3]

Evaluating the Indians by ideals which were totally irrelevant to their own culture, Temple concluded (in all but these precise words) that they were totally uncivilized. He conceded to them a good eye for beauty and an appreciation

---

[2]Sir Richard Temple, The Story of My Life, London, 1896, vol. I, p.3.

[3]Ibid., pp. 7-8.

of the domestic virtues;   he commended further their capacity
to endure hardship and their enterprise in rebuilding homes
and farms after famines, droughts and wars.[4]   Nevertheless,
he rated these attributes low in comparison to the weaknesses
of the Indian character.   He condemned the complete absence
of public or private morality: he found the Indians dishonest
and quite unfitted, in consequence, to exercise political
power.   He ascribed their deviousness not so much to an
incapacity to distinguish right from wrong as to their lack
of courage to do what was right.   "Born actors, with innate
eloquence and endowed by nature with the faculty of expression
by gesture," he observed, "they had consummate plausibility
in telling a made-up tale" and stated the truth only when
taken unawares "before the breath of any motive had sullied
the mirror of their minds".[5]   Temple watched with horror as
the Indians manipulated gullible Europeans by "poisonous
insinuation" and flattery "conveyed with discrimination".[6]
Speculating that Indian depravity might have provided the
inspiration for Shakespeare's Iago, he declared that moral

---

[4]Sir Richard Temple, India in 1880, 3rd ed., London,
1881, p. 109.

[5]Temple, My Life, vol. II, p. 57.

[6]Ibid.

cowardice disqualified the Indians from self-rule of any sort.[7]

Temple blamed Hinduism and Islam for the Indians' failure of moral strength, "nerve" and physical courage. Hinduism, he contended, destroyed moral responsibility in the individual by the promise of endless reincarnations. Islam likewise discouraged civilized behavior by guaranteeing redemption to the most debauched fellow who made a death-bed profession of faith in the Prophet.[8] "Without a concept of the last judgment and the Supreme Judge, can there be bravery" -- let alone morality?[9] So long as the indigenous religions tolerated a gross moral laxity, he concluded, the Indians could never build the strength of character needed for self-government.

Campbell, writing to attack James Mill rather than Temple, was far more magnanimous. In 1852 he explained why he regarded the Indians as civilized in Modern India, a short account of Indian history and society written to prepare the British reading public and MPs for the charter renewal debate of 1853. Its specific purpose was to refute James Mill's definition of Indian society as "barbarous and semi-civilized" and to substitute a picture of an honorable people, heirs to a great culture, depressed only by slavery and war.

---

[7] Ibid., p. 58.

[8] Ibid., p. 61.

[9] Ibid., p. 64.

It did not succeed; but then Mill's History of British India (1817) had stood unchallenged for a generation, the only available work, vastly influential in its prejudices and generalized contempt for the Indians -- not least upon the career servants leaving for the East in the 40's and 50's.[10] Campbell at least aspired to counter it; Mill's second editor, H.H. Wilson, had despaired of scholars ever succeeding.[11]

Taking a far narrower range of evidence than Mill, Campbell offered two simple criteria for his high estimate of Indian civilization. His first (drawn from the Scottish tradition and Adam Ferguson in particular) was that a civilized society was one which had achieved a complex divison of labor. By this standard ancient India was truly a precocious society; for "this minuteness of apportionment is generally the result of a very advanced stage of society, but seems to have obtained among the Hindoos from early times".[12] "Great advances in the sciences and in the arts of living" had in Campbell's opinion made possible that intricate differentiation of jobs among agriculturalists, traders and craftsmen which maintained civilization.[13]

---

[10]H.H. Wilson, Introduction to James Mill, History of British India, London, 1840, vol. I, pp. viii - ix.

[11]Ibid., p. 8-9.

[12]Sir George Campbell, Modern India, London, 1852, p. 7.

[13]Ibid., p. 6.

Secondly, Campbell defined as civilized (in the manner of a
Whig historian) those societies where political power was
invested in representative bodies. He argued that the
political institutions of the Rajputs (his name for the
conquerors of Northern India in the first centuries AD) had
been republican and democratic: as free and equal citizens,
the Rajputs assembled regularly to select a panchayet and
elect a patil.[14] Campbell was forced to concede that this
pure form of popular representation had been sustained to
the 19th century only on the village level; for as the
Rajputs had extended their domain, their rule had become
increasingly feudal at the upper levels of government.[15]
But he dismissed this distortion as "a necessary organization
when freemen become conquerors and hold an area militarily".[16]
The Rajputs had civilized India and given an early parliamentary democracy to her peoples, so that the Indians "were,
as we found them,

> the most self-governing people in the world --
> that is to say, they had a faculty of manag-
> ing their own affairs in their own villages
> and caste and trade guilds quite indepen-
> dently of the government of the day, and
> could carry on wonderfully when there was no
> government at all. That is what was done by
> the village communities which survived the

---

[14]Ibid., p. 9.

[15]Ibid., p. 12.

[16]Ibid., p. 9.

crash of Empire and kept society together
the one hundred years of anarchy which
preceded the establishment of our rule.[17]

The vitality of the surviving village communities so
impressed Campbell that years later he claimed that "far
from imposing my ideas on these people, it was from them
that I learnt ideas of local self-government which I retain
to this day, and which I have brought back with me to my
native country."[18]

In both his early books Campbell drew an inordinately
complimentary picture of the Indians, past and present. He
praised their "industrial energy" -- or desire for self-
advancement -- as an uplifting virtue which distinguished
them from the notoriously complacent Celts and Negroes, and
allied them in disposition to the ambitious and energetic
Anglo-Saxons.[19] He declared that they could be quickly
educated in Christian morals and politics through their
"excellent natural intellect", their acuity in mathematics
and science (which in his opinion exceeded that of
Europeans)[20] and their receptive state of mind, "which

---

[17]Sir George Campbell, The British Empire, London,
1887, pp. 43-44.

[18]Sir George Campbell, Memoirs of My Indian Career,
ed., by Sir Charles E. Bernard, London, 1893, vol. I, p. 35.

[19]Campbell, Modern India, p. 59.

[20]Ibid., p. 62.

tends very much to rationalism".[21] Greece and Rome had
developed from older, less sophisticated cultures of the
East; "why," Campbell asked, "commencing from a similar
level, should /‾India‾7 not be raised as the West has been
raised? After all we are but Orientals among whom the old
leaven of Greek and Roman civilization has fermented into
progress, and I see no reason why we should not introduce in
the East a similar progress. I believe", he concluded, "that
we might and should do so; that India is fully capable of
the highest civilization; and that Heaven has imposed on us
a task which we may not neglect."[22] In time, he asserted
confidently, the Indians would be capable of governing themselves independently from Britain; even now they were
sufficiently civilized to rule themselves on the village and
town level.

His attempt to explain away the vices of the Indians
as seen by Mill and Temple was as flagrant an example of the
use of "comparative history" for propaganda purposes as was
the History of Mill. Exposure to science and history in his
Scottish schools had led Campbell to take up amateur
ethnology and comparative history as hobbies; and these
studies -- which he pursued with enthusiasm throughout his
adult life[23] -- enabled him to examine the Indians from a

---

[21]Sir George Campbell, India As It May Be, London,
1853, p. 396.

[22]Ibid., p. xii.

[23]Campbell, Memoirs, vol. II, pp. 127-128.

broader perspective than Temple's and with far greater genorosity. He felt obliged to concede the dishonesty and moral weakness of the stereotype Indian portrayed by Mill, straighforwardly admitting that most Indians seemed incapable of discerning the truth. He confessed also that he could offer no explanation for their insipid fatalism and their lack of discipline and resolution which Europeans found so irritating.[24] But here he stopped. Indian character weaknesses could be shown to be transitory and eradicable, he argued, if seen in the correct historical perspective. If the right historical and ethnological comparisons were made with the Anglo-Saxon countries of Western Europe and other subject nations, India could be seen to stand as high on the ladder of civilization as Mill had placed her low.

Campbell's basic technique was to explain the vices which Mill and Temple regarded as racial peculiarity as the product of historical circumstance -- and to emphasize that if correct historical comparisons were made, then the Indians were far from an uncivilized people. Typical of his mode of procedure was his attack, in India As It May Be (1853), on the idea that superstition and idolatry had been endemic to the Indians from earliest times. In fact, he showed, they were no more widespread in "barbarous and semi-civilized"

---

[24]Campbell, Modern India, p. 59.

19th century India than they had been in Greece and Rome 2000 years earlier. The Indians shared with the Romans a "nominal belief in effete mythology" and the "same tendency to overstrained systems of philosophy and natural religion"; but, unlike their classical counterparts, they were "good and ripe for Christianity" (undoubtedly of a sober and rational Protestant variety).[25] In the same way Campbell claimed that the widespread illiteracy of the Indian ryot was not, as Mill had it, the inherent state of a race naturally slothful and blind to the world of ideas, but the historical consequence of the breakdown of the educational system in the wars of the 18th century.[26] Similarly, environment rather than heredity explained "the litigious lying character commonly ascribed to the natives", which, although seeming to Campbell's embarrassment "to be more or less prominent as the blood is more or less purely Hindoo", was most properly traced to the anarchy preceding British rule.[27] "It is not unlikely", he pleaded, "that the cunning and untruthful character of the natives may be the result of a continued and repeated political slavery, leading the vanquished to have recourse to the cunning arts."[28] In addition, war was -- in

---

[25]Campbell, India As It May Be, p. 396.

[26]Campbell, Modern India, p. 61.

[27]Ibid.

[28]Ibid., p. 62.

this simplictic view -- the cause of the peculiar lack of patriotism and political unity among the Indians, and of their "extreme selfishness which looks only to a man's own case, and cares not what may befall his neighbour".[29]

Ethnology and selective comparison were also used by Campbell to rehabilitate the reputation of India as a nation, as well as the Indians as individuals. Addressing, in Modern India, Mill's contempt for the great Hindu civilization of the pre-Christian era, he argued that the Brahmins who controlled the earliest Hindu settlements were hardly unique in their repression and superstition. The Middle East offered two conspicuous examples of omnipotent priestly cliques: one of them, the pharoahs of ancient Egypt, resembled the Brahmins in status -- a dominant military tribe which gradually assumed a priestly role -- social functions manners and appearance.[30] The theocrats of ancient Israel were another priestly oligarchy whose shared institutions and manners were so close to the Brahmins that Campbell called the latter "a great Levitical tribe".[31]

---

[29]Ibid.

[30]Ibid., p. 3.

[31]Ibid., p. 4.

Campbell was far from convincing with these two
analogies to his contemporaries or to later generations of
historians and ethnologists; but he was authoritative in his
discernment of a physical relationship between the Rajputs
of the 1st century AD and the Anglo-Saxons of Western Europe.
The Rajputs, "a robust, hard-headed, strong-featured race",
were in his opinion "absolutely identical with Europeans
except in colour"; and to sceptics he pointed out that
"colour is more easily changed than any other feature".[32]
Campbell classified the Rajputs as Aryans after his collab-
oration with Sir Henry Maine on Village Communities East and
West (1871).[33] But his first work -- which must be credited as
important original research -- dates from 1852, seven years
before Max Müller[34] explained the theory of an Aryan "race"
in the introduction to his History of Ancient Sanskritic
Literature, and nine years before Maine first published on
oriental and occidental institutions. It was a discovery of
more than academic interest: it influentially rescued the

---

[32]Ibid., p. 10.

[33]See extracts from "Speeches and Letters regarding
the Bengal Municipalities Bill", Calcutta, 1873, in Campbell,
"Local Self-Government in India", Westminster Review, CXXXI,
1884, pp. 63-83.

[34]Frederick Max Müller (1823-1900): commissioned by
the East India Company to edit the Rigveda; Taylorian
Professor of European Languages at Oxford, 1854-1856;
Curator of the Bodlein, 1856; Fellow of All Souls, 1858;
History of Ancient Sanskritic Literature, 1859; Professor
of Comparative Philology, 1868.

ancient Indians from the cultural backwater to which Mill and others had condemned them and placed them side by side with familiar ancestors of the western world.

These themes -- with special concentration on the tractable and changeable nature of the Indian character -- were developed in Campbell's second book, India As It May Be (1853). In it he declared that the virtue and civilization of the Indians, so apparent to the comparative historian, could be revived if a correct and positive approach were adopted by the British. He rejected the judgments of Oriental scholars like Sir William Jones[35] and William Robertson[36] that Indian civilization had reached a spectacular but ephemeral cultural zenith in the 3rd millennium BC, but had since declined, as well as Mill's balder assertion that the only change seen in India since early Christian times was that of abject degeneration.[37] Campbell argued forcefully that Indian society was in some sense frozen in the contours shaped by the Rajputs.

---

[35]Sir William Jones (1746-1794): Fellow of University College, Oxford, 1766; called to the bar from the Middle Temple, 1774; Judge of the Supreme Court at Calcutta, 1783; founded the Asiatic Society of Bengal, 1784; first English scholar to know Sanskrit.

[36]William Robertson, D.D. (1721-1793): wrote An historical disquisition concerning the knowledge which the ancients had of India, and the progress of trade with that country, London, 1791.

[37]James Mill, "Malcolm's Sketch of the Sikhs", Edinburgh Review, XXI, 1813, p. 433.

It had not climbed to the heights of sophistication seen in Western Europe, but neither had it declined like the Middle Eastern civilizations under the weight of invasions; it was curiously static. The reason, he wrote, was that "there was wanting in ⎡Indian⎤ civilisation that general inter-communication which marks the civilisations of the West, and makes it progressive -- which enables one generation to commence where another has left off, and so build continually upwards".[38]

II. HOW CAN THE INDIANS BE PREPARED FOR SELF-RULE ?

Under the pressure of events in the 1870's (when wide-spread demands for self-rule were stimulated by Mayo's decentralization plan) Temple, and many like him, came to accept that the Indians would eventually govern themselves. Inevitably he disagreed with Campbell, by now an influential contemporary in the senior levels of government, over how they should be prepared for the distant day. Temple looked to the imperial government as the sole agency of progress among the Indians, whom he regarded as childlike in their backwardness and whom he cast in the passive role of trac-table subjects, responsive to the reforming initiative of the British administration. In contrast Campbell conceived of progress as the fruit of a partnership between Indians who lacked skills and needed guidance but who nonetheless

---

[38]Campbell, Modern India, p. 6.

possessed the "manly virtues", and British officials who
merely instructed and encouraged.

Temple's first proposal was to vest village leaders
with authority to deal with the broad range of petty matters
for which the civil service lacked the time and personnel.
He called next for the integration of the panchayets into
the civil administration, as a cheap and time-saving device
for handling local affairs; and he recommended reactivating
these ancient bodies wherever they had fallen into decay.
He discovered on tour in the Sind in 1878 that village
leaders held nominal titles for which the corresponding
duties had long since been forgotten; but this could quickly
be changed. "It would be quite practicable", he advised,
"during the settlement proceedings and operations to assign
certain lands or certain dues to the village policeman, and
to the village headman in every village; and in many or
most villages the proper persons to fill these offices would
immediately present themselves".[39] It was likewise desirable
in both mahalwari and ryotwari areas for the village community to elect a headman from those families who had traditionally held the title, and in permanently settled areas
for the zemindars to assume the post themselves or appoint
substitutes. "The importance of the office for the repression

---

[39]Sir Richard Temple, "Village Officers and Village
Institutions in Sind", Minute of 21 August 1878, I.O.L.
Eur. Mss. F 86:193.

of crime and for the supervision of bad characters is well known", he declared, "but what is equally important, the office is essential for all measures of administrative improvement, sanitation, registration, and the like".[40] Temple looked forward to village leaders providing invaluable aid to district officials during famines by searching for emaciated people, bringing them to the attention of relief officers, and arranging for food to be taken to the bedridden -- all under the eye of government authorities.[41] He similarly proposed using them as a channel of information between the district magistrate and distressed ryots whose land the civil courts had ordered to be sold to discharge outstanding debts.[42] He also suggested that the patils be empowered to adjudicate in petty cases summarily and without appeal and thereby relieve the overcrowded civil courts of at least one-sixth of their cases.[43]

Requiring village officers to operate according to British ethical standards would significantly improve the Indian character, according to Temple. "The vesting in them with this limited degree of judicial responsibility will

---

[40]Ibid.

[41]Sir Richard Temple, "Special Inspection of Operations for Relief of Famine in Kaladgi District", Minute of 7 September 1877, I.O.L. Eur. Mss. F 86: 194.

[42]Sir Richard Temple, "Further Proposals for Legislation Regarding the Indebted Ryots of the Deccan", Minute of 14 April 1879, I.O.L. Eur. Mss. F86: 193.

[43]Ibid.

have an elevating effect on these men" he predicted, "and will tend to make them trustworthy".[44] He reported to Florence Nightingale (who periodically interrogated him by post from London about famine relief, sanitation, ryot indebtedness and the moral state of the Indians) that the headmen would be "corrupt and inefficient, in some degree, if not supervised". Nevertheless, he assured her, exposure to upright British behavior would "greatly diminish" a "low moral tone" and decrease corruption.[45]

All this delegation was, of course, to take place under the stern gaze of British officials, who would maintain a tight grip on the panchayet's activities. Temple's refusal to allow the Indians scope for trial and error in administering their own local affairs reflected the belief popular in the Indian Civil Service in the 1860's and 70's that the Indian ryot was a perennial child wholly dependent upon his imperial guardians. In typical authoritarian manner, he laid down that education by example was the only effective method of teaching the Indians the art of self-government. He was convinced that just as schoolboys at Rugby learned from their masters how to shoulder responsibility and how to live in a group, so the Indians would acquire self-control, sense of

---

[44]Sir Richard Temple to Florence Nightingale, 3 July 1879, I.O.L. Eur. Mss. F 86: 191.

[45]Temple, My Life, vol. I, p. 3.

justice and public spirit from the example of British officials. Seeing himself and his colleagues in the role of Arnoldian master-officials, charged with realizing Rugbeian refinements of character among the Indians, Temple strove to set a standard of civilized behavior. His zeal in founding schools, hospitals and the like soon attracted attention; and his industry passed from fame almost to notoriety. One verse writer, chronicling his achievements in a clumsy but amusing fashion, chided the astonishing energy which enabled

> Dick /¯to_7 ride in one revolving moon
> On horse, cart, camel, railway and balloon.[46]

Alfred Lyall,[47] a distinguished co-worker in the Central Provinces, expressed admiration and similar amusement at Temple's commitment to work. "The country is backward", he observed, "and he is determined to shove it forward; the country resists inertly as long as it can, tumbles back as often as Temple props it up, and when forcibly driven forward runs the wrong way, like a pig going to Cork Market".[48] When Temple returned to England after retiring from Indian

---

[46]Philip Woodruff, The Men Who Ruled India: The Guardians, London, 1954, p. 61.

[47]Alfred Lyall (1835-1911) ICS; entered the Bengal Civil Service, 1855; Commissioner of Berar, 1867; Secretary to the Government of India in the Home Department, 1873-1874; in the Foreign Department, 1878-1882; Lieutenant-Governor of the North-West Provinces, 1882-1887; Member of the Council of India, 1888-1903.

[48]Woodruff, op. cit., p. 63.

service in 1880 and was elected Conservative Member of
Parliament for Evesham, he vowed to demonstrate his party
loyalty by voting in every division and never seeking to be
paired with a Liberal in order to enjoy a free evening.[49]
Haunting the back benches whenever Parliament was in session,
he must have appeared as comic in his dedication to perfect
attendance as he had seemed in his posturing as the tireless
paragon of virtue during his Indian years. Such fastidious
attention to duty was regarded as slightly ridiculous even
in late Victorian England.

Temple advised that the best exposure the Indians
could get to the rigid morality of British officialdom was
through direct employment in the imperial administration.
If culture could be diffused in the schoolroom, so it could
in the office. The British would set an example for Indian
clerks and civil servants to follow, thereby "elevating and
strengthening their character, mentally and morally".[50] A
small group of prominent Indians were promoted to high
positions in the judiciary in the late 1860's, but Temple
did not regard this as adequate. One or two Indians should
be immediately be posted as Magistrates to small, easily-run

---

[49]Temple, My Life, vol. I, p. 234.

[50]C.E. Buckland, Bengal under the Lieutenant-
Governors, Calcutta, 1901, vol. II, p. 667 (Quoted from a
Minute of 5 June 1876).

districts; eventually, he advised, many more should be
placed in the key offices of District Magistrate, District
Superintendent of Police, and Civil Surgeon, as well as in
subordinate positions usually held by Europeans.[51] "The
moral effect upon the Natives of the higher kinds of
executive employment would be greater even than that of the
higher kinds of judicial employment", he asserted in 1876.

> When recommendations are made for restricting
> /¯advancement_7 to the judicial branch, there
> seems to be some idea underlying this view,
> to the effect that the judicial branch chiefly
> demands those intellectual qualities in which
> natives excel, whereas the executive branch
> demands qualities other than intellectual, such
> as energy, decision, self-reliance, power of
> combination and organisation, of managing men,
> and so on; and also physical activity,
> qualities which are deemed to be as yet
> imperfectly developed in natives. Therefore,
> it seems to be thought preferable to refrain
> from placing natives in the higher class of
> executive posts, which, according to this
> view, had better be reserved for the present
> exclusively for Europeans. But, if this be the
> case, it is a cogent reason for beginning to
> appoint natives to the higher offices in the
> executive branch. For certainly these
> qualities, other than intellectual, are of the
> utmost consequence to the well-being and
> progress of the nation....[52]

Temple believed that executive training would educe "those
moral forces which are summed up in the expression 'manhood'",
though he considered the attainment of true manhood as still

---

[51]Ibid., vol. II, p. 669.

[52]Ibid., vol. II, pp. 667-668.

remote.[53] He warned the Government of India, however, not
to write off the Indians as uncivilized without giving them
a chance to show their paces as bureaucrats -- a role in which
he predicted a happy future for them.

Here at least there was some small agreement between
Temple and Campbell. Campbell enthusiastically supported
the advancement of Indians in the civil service. He viewed
government employment, however, not as nursery training for
some distant adulthood but as a political education in
addition to immediate municipal and village self-rule. In
his opinion India's self-government should be advanced by
building upon those village communities which, he asserted,
still thrived in the South among the Vellallers and in the
North among the Jats, the Rajputs and Punjabis.[54] Having
closely watched panchayets in the Punjab dispensing justice
and establishing regulations, he concluded that although they
were not immune "from the abuses which afflict corporations

---

[53]Ibid.

[54]Campbell, Modern India, p. 85. As a young district
officer stationed between 1846 and 1851 in Wadnee District
near Ludhiana in the Punjab, he observed that "simple village
municipalities" continued to function according to a
traditional pattern. In small villages landowners continued
to choose a patil and panchayet directly; in larger villages
they divided themselves into puttees, or subdivisions, and
selected one representative to the panchayet from each. See
Ibid., p. 90; Memoirs, vol. I, p. 58.

all over the world",[55] they nonetheless functioned far more
effectively than most Western critics were willing to concede.

This was, of course, an approach to the problems of
self-rule quite different in kind from that of Temple. For
Campbell the question was not how the Indians could be
prepared as individuals for self-government at some future
date, but how power could be transferred from the imperial
administration to towns and villages as fast as possible.
He firmly believed that the Government of India's disinterest
in the panchayets and its preference for municipal organizations devised on western lines ("brand-new European sorts
of things, not at all indigenous")[56] was foolish. "Our
present tentatives in the direction of local government", he
asserted

> are too much in the nature of trying to
> introduce new and foreign forms of that
> good thing, and to spread them from above
> downwards, rather than the method which I
> would prefer, viz., to gather together the
> threads of the indigenous system, strengthen
> and improve that system, and from that basis
> work upwards to higher things.[57]

The sanity of building upwards from the "admirable little
village republics"[58] to ever larger units -- "to provinces and
quasi-national areas" --was demonstrated by innumerable

-----

[55]Campbell, _Memoirs_, vol. I, p. 81.

[56]_Ibid_., vol. I, p. 82.

[57]Campbell, _British Empire_, pp. 76-77.

[58]_Ibid_., p. 77.

historical precedents.[59]

> I think all history shows that free govern-
> ments only succeed when the unit of govern-
> ment is small -- when communes, self-governing
> in much, make up small States; and free nations
> are only successful when they are composed of
> a federation of smaller States.[60]

Campbell told the imperial administrators to note the
political instability caused by overcentralization in France
and to consider the benefits derived from tiny political
subdivisions in Switzerland, the United States and ancient
Greece. Small units of government allowed the people to see,
know and easily understand the issues under debate,[61] and
to discern properly their own and their neighbour's self-
interest.[62]

Campbell's proposals for the renovation of the
panchayets as the unit of local government included one idea
of astonishing radicalism. This was that the panchayets
should be staffed, not by the old landowning families, but
by men drawn from the lower ranks of the ryots. To Campbell's
thinking the sturdy ryot was "as good and as intelligent as
we are",[63] unsapped -- like the traditional village leaders --

---

[59]Ibid., p. 76.

[60]Ibid., p. 8.

[61]Ibid., p. 9.

[62]Ibid.

[63]Campbell, Modern India, p. 63.

by years of tax-financed prosperity, uncorrupt. That this
was calculated to annoy the majority of the Indian Civil
Service (and certainly Temple) may be taken for granted; but
at the same time Campbell's radical preoccupation with
social justice and popular democracy was sincere and genuine.
There was, in fact, good reason to review the appointments
to panchayets throughout India and Campbell, an unabashed
opportunist, seized on it. This was that in the early 19th
century British administrators had usurped from the
individuals in many villages the right to choose the
panchayet, and had replaced representatives chosen on merit
and social position with others selected solely on family
connection. The idea was sensible (Campbell conceded): it
was to ensure stability by allowing leading village families
an almost dynastic succession on the panchayet. But it led
to a sharp decline in the calibre of appointees:

> ... native rulers were, in native times,
> selected upon a Darwinian system of the
> survival of the strongest. Under our
> system the great evil is that we are bound
> to insist upon legitimate descent, and have
> little or no power of selection; we have no
> security that the legitimate heir will be a
> good man -- he is very often a bad one.[64]

The immediate consequence, lamented by Campbell, was that
the appointment of men undeserving of the respect of the
village depleted the power of a body whose authority rested
primarily on personal esteem.

---

[64]Campbell, Memoirs, vol. II, p. 87.

His solution -- quite revolutionary in its implications
-- was to abandon the notion of legitimized succession on the
panchayet and to "create a fresh class of leaders"[65] out of
the lowly ryots. To his sadness (as a Whig paternalist) the
older village leaders had been corrupted beyond recall by
extravagance and sloth arising from the economic prosperity
brought by the pax Britannica. "The higher classes cannot
bear prosperity. It causes them to degenerate, especially if
they are born to greatness. Hence the impossibility of adapt-
ing to anything useful most of the higher classes found by
us".[66] Faced with this impasse, he abandoned the historical
caution of Orientalists and paternalists and turned to the
poorest cultivators to create his "fresh class of leaders".
"From the acuteness and aptness to learn of the inferior
classes, this can be done as is done in no other country", he
declared. He strongly rejected the sneers of colleagues
about their incorrigible dishonesty; Indian officials were,
he maintained,

> generally speaking, excellent men. They
> were very acute, wrote with great facility
> and correctness, and thoroughly understood
> their business. Of course they were not all
> immaculate, but I believe that their alleged
> corruption and rascality are very greatly
> exaggerated. Very much of the corruption
> imputed to them consisted of nothing more
> than customary fees and douceurs, such as
> were till very recently received in most
> offices in /‾Great Britain‾/ and are, most

---

[65]Campbell, Modern India, p. 64.

[66]Ibid., p. 63.

> people believe, received in a great many
> offices still. But we are much harder upon
> natives who are found out in little
> peccadilloes of that kind than we are upon
> the officials of municipalities and other
> offices in our own country.[67]

So much of an opportunist was Campbell that the inconsistency all this created at the heart of his thought seems
never to have occurred to him. There was no possible
reconciliation between the paternalist in Campbell, dedicated
throughout his life to preserving traditional institutions,
and the grand radical with a policy to elevate tenant
cultivators over landowners and lower castes over higher ones.
One suspects Campbell was unaware of the dilemma, and for
good reason. His real talent lay in creating administrative
programs, not in devising large-scale theories. If an
immediate problem commanded the abandonment of the paternalist
code, Campbell did not hesitate -- or pause to contemplate
the incongruities occasioned by this pragmatic frame of mind.

It is perhaps surprising that Campbell said nothing
of a need for radical reform in the land revenue system,
since the previous generation of Orientalists had recognized
this as the key to the survival or collapse of India's
village institutions. It can only be said that Campbell's
negativism on the subject was the negativism of his age.
Between 1840 and 1870, controversy over revenue settlement

---

[67]Campbell, Memoirs, vol. I, p. 35.

on the land occurred only where new areas were taken over by

conquest. Elsewhere, no attempt was made to breathe new life

into village institutions in the vast majority of places

where they had collapsed, and the debate on the land revenue

program was effectively over.[68] Campbell's hopes for the

future, however, lay in the panchayets of idealized ryots

rather than in the patils, revived in importance by a new

land revenue program; and like many of his colleagues he

was not exactly sad at the disappearance of the patils, who,

while representing traditional authority, were to his mind

deeply corrupted men.

Equally surprising is the omission, in Campbell's

vision of panchayet-ruled India, of a solution to the prob-

lems of the appellate courts. These courts, relying on

Western law and established in the early 19th century,

provided recourse from the decisions of the panchayet and

thereby diminished its authority. "I have always thought",

Campbell wrote, "that throughout India

> a very great deal of harm has been done by
> the interference of our authorities, both
> executive and judicial (especially judicial),
> with indigenous village corporations.
> Nothing can be perfect in this world, but a
> certain latitude must be given to popular

---

[68]Campbell may well have mistaken the extent of this
collapse across India, for his first service was in the
Punjab, where thanks to late annexation by the British the
decline of patil and panchayet was not well advanced. To
colleagues in the rest of India, his ardor to rebuild on
"existing foundations" seemed naive.

> representatives, and the fabric falls to
> pieces when every litigious person is
> allowed to bring everything into question
> in every court. I think there is a great
> deal too much of that... in India, with
> the result that the small self-supporting
> municipalities, which held their own in the
> worst of native times, have been very much
> weakened and degraded, if not dissolved.[69]

All this had been half-feared by the Orientalists who intro-

duced the appellate courts. By 1850 there was no denying

their role in weakening the customary system of local self-

government.

III. WHEN WILL THE INDIANS BE FIT FOR INDEPENDENCE?

In the 1870's nationalist organizations like the Poona

Sarvajanik Sabha[70] and the British Indian Association[71] began

to push for immediate local self-government and to talk

---

[69]Campbell, Memoirs, vol. I, pp. 81-82.

[70]Poona Sarvajanik Sabha: organized in Poona in 1871
to communicate public opinion on pending legislation to the
presidency government and to suggest ways to improve municipal government. The provision that members hold a power of
attorney for fifty adults, authorizing them to speak on their
behalf in all public matters, gave the Sabha a representative
character. Its membership was composed of landholders,
businessmen, lawyers, teachers and retired government
servants. Led from 1871 to 1878 by M.G. Ranade, it stimulated
political activity throughout the Deccan.

[71]British Indian Association: established in Calcutta
in 1851 by Hindu zemindars to represent their interests to
the presidency and supreme governments. For the next three
decades it relentlessly sent memorials and petitions on
every conceivable topic of public concern to the government
and reviewed all legislation. Because it made no attempt
to attract support from the educated middle classes, it began
to lose its influence in government circles in the 1870's.

dreamingly of eventual independence. The emergence of
these nationalist groups forced a subtle change in British
attitudes. The majority of administrators, for whom we here
take Temple as a spokesman, continued to regard the Indians
as incapable of self-rule, but came to realize that they
might win it nevertheless. They also realized that conceding
the demands of the nationalists for full local self-government
could give birth to demands for full independence.

British fear was greater than Indian imagination, however, and in the 1870's a movement for independence was not
a threat. Nevertheless, panaceas were put forward to stifle
the birth of nationalist fervor and to defuse the campaign
for local self-government. Temple, to whom the thought --
let alone the date -- of full Indian independence was incon-
ceivable, suggested that well-placed jobs in the Indian Civil
Service be offered to some of the principal protestors.
"Highly educated men often fail to obtain employment worthy
of their talents and requirements" and joined nationalist
groups in protest[72]: there was a growing Western-educated
elite without jobs because they had been offered only menial
employment by the government, he pointed out. Prestigious
and well-paid office in the bureaucracy would appease their
desire for power and ensure that their talents were used
constructively under the direction of British officials

---

[72]Sir Richard Temple, Men and Events of My Time in
India, London, 1882, p. 15.

instead of destructively in subversive organizations. In
a similar fashion the threatened disloyalty of the non-
westernized princes could be dissipated by "investing native
worthies with honorary functions and duties in the administration of the country, thereby attaching them to the
government under which they lived".[73]

It also fell to Temple, as Lieutenant-Governor of
Bengal from 1873-76, to respond to demands from the British
Indian Association for local self-government in Calcutta.
He decided to accede, despite the strong illusion among civil
servants of the 70's that the causes of local self-rule and
independence were inextricably linked in nationalist minds.
In this cosmopolitan city, he responded, a limited franchise
was practicable because the Europeans and educated Indians
who would run for office could be trusted to wield power
wisely.[74] But elsewhere Temple refused nationalist demands
for local self-government. In the mofussil towns and
villages the people were too isolated and backward "to offer
sound conclusions on any large or complex question not coming
under their immediate cognisance".[75] Many, he added pessi-
mistically, were incapable of "discerning any kind of

[73]Temple, My Life, vol. II, p. 79.

[74]Sir Richard Temple, "Speeches 1870-1880", Address
of 16 June 1877 to the Poona Sarvajanik Sabha, I.O.L. Eur.
Mss. F 86: 201.

[75]Temple to Wyllie, 16 August 1867, I.O.L. Eur. Mss.
F 86: 209.

generality, even about their own lives".[76] Until his retirement from Indian service in 1880 Temple was adamant that as long as the overwhelming majority of the population remained morally lax, illiterate and politically apathetic, "the realisation of such hopes ∕⎺for an extended system of self-government_7 if it ever be possible, is so remote as to be outside the range of practical politics".[77]

Although Temple doubtless recognized the inevitability of long-term independence, his advice to colleagues in the 1870's was to stand firm "with calmness and self-assurance" against those who "indulge aspirations which cannot be satisfied in the immediate future".[78] He refused to concede any form of local self-government outside the presidency towns, which involved genuinely independent decision-taking. Indians could certainly act as the hands, feet and arms of district magistrates and district officers, and benefit from the experience; but they must be allowed no scope for exercizing initiative. After 1882 and Ripon's Resolution on Local Self-Government, it became obvious that the British would one day capitulate and Temple became an increasingly dated figure.

---

[76]Temple, My Life, vol. I, p. 57.

[77]Temple, Men and Events, p. 19.

[78]Ibid., p. 15.

Campbell responded to the aereal visions of Indian independence with all the sympathy his colleagues lacked; but he, too, began to display the pessimism of age and experience. "We may look forward to a time in the far distant future", he wrote in the still-radical Westminster Review in 1884,

> when the people of India shall no longer be
> held in leading-strings; when education,
> intelligence and public spirit shall have
> become so general that there will no longer
> be place there for bureaucratic Government;
> when the various provinces, and even the
> empire itself, shall be managed on constitu-
> tional principles and by representative methods.
> We believe it to be the lofty mission of
> England in India to make the dawn of that day
> possible.[79]

The paternalist who vied with the radical inside Campbell all his life was beginning to triumph. Independence was desirable (a considerable mental step for any British administrator in India), but so far off as to be beyond present concern. Campbell was not so radical, after his period as Lieutenant-Governor of Bengal, as to argue that independence should come before enlightenment and education of the Indians; and he began to doubt that this could be achieved as quickly as the young Campbell -- with his faith in the "excellent natural intellect" and "industrial energy" of the Indians -- had believed. That the competence of the Indians to rule themselves independently of Britain

---

[79]Campbell, "Local Self-Government", p. 75.

would grow was certain to Campbell the radical, but that the
process of self-education would be tediously slow became
apparent to Campbell the conservative paternalist.

His prescription for the intervening years was the
continuation of paternal despotism above but the institution
of comprehensive local self-government below. His vision
was of immediate power over local affairs for village and
town councils throughout the Empire, and the gradual concession of power to ever larger units until British despotism
had been transformed into popular democracy at all levels of
government. Local self-government would naturally lead on
to higher things, he wrote in 1872, for

> human reason was so constituted that what
> was called patriotism and public spirit were
> the natural accompaniments and result of
> self-government. If you made a beginning of
> self-government, public spirit and patriotism
> would result.[80]

What was necessary in the Indians was an increased realization that individual self-interest was identical to the
interests of the population as a whole -- a theory whose
radicalism has more to do with Rousseau than with any British
source. Clashes between sects and classes in India, and
the hopeless lack of political unity, was seen by Campbell
as a major problem second only to failures in education in
preparing India for independence.

----

[80]Ibid., pp. 69-70.

> The great difficulty in the way of any kind
> of self-government on a large scale is in the
> separation and want of sympathy among the
> different classes, so that they cannot be
> brought politically to amalgamate, and
> individuals of one class can little be
> trusted with authority over the others.
> The inhabitants of villages of the same demo-
> cratic tribes unites, as has been said, in a
> very perfect system of self-government; but
> it cannot be carried beyond this...[81]

This was Campbell in 1852, the young district officer
whose experience suggested that only a foreign power could
reconcile the competing claims of Moslems and Hindus,
Brahmins and Untouchables, Bengalis and Madrasis, to name
only a few of the major divisions which riddled Indian
society.[82] It was the main reason for his advice in 1853 in
India As It May Be that "while everything should be done to
elevate the natives socially and individually, I see no
object in attempting their political elevation beyond the
limits of small municipalities".[83] But the war between
class, caste and region was unabated when Campbell wrote in
1882, seven years after his departure, that abandonment of
Britain's role as referee of India's clashing interests was
"far outside the range of practical politics".[84] His final

---

[81]Campbell, Modern India, p. 262.

[82]Ibid., pp. 260-261.

[83]Campbell, India As It May Be, p. 105.

[84]Campbell, "Local Self-Government", p. 80.

recorded word on the subject, in The British Empire (1887),
was indeed pessimistic. "Again we come to the question: do
we desire to prepare the natives for political freedom? And
again we are not yet prepared to answer it".[85]

IV. CONCLUSION

It is a paradox that Temple, by the grant of self-
government to Calcutta can be said to have done more to
advance the cause of self-rule in India than Campbell, its
strongest proponent. It is a paradox also that Campbell,
by the end of his career, should have exhibited as great a
pessimism for Indian self-improvement as Temple, the man
who mocked it so savagely throughout his career. The moral
to be drawn is that no creed was clear-cut in mid-century
British India and no label accurately hits off its man.

This is perhaps especially true of Campbell, who is
called "the spokesman of enlightened paternalism" in Prof.
Stoke's distinguished book.[86] By this phrase Prof. Stokes
allies Campbell to the majority; and in his account he takes
Campbell as a prototype of those administrators seeking to
preserve the traditional yet admitting the need for change.
It is a label which totally fails to explain Campbell's
fanatical commitment to local self-government, a commitment

---

[85]Campbell, British Empire, p. 78

[86]Eric Stokes, op. cit., p. 341.

quite at odds with the temper of the British majority of his
time. Nor does "paternalist" explain Campbell's impatience
for change or his penchant for tampering with the traditional
-- as, for example, the ruling-family traditions of India's
village panchayets.

This chapter has sought to emphasize that Campbell was
more of a "radical" than a "paternalist", and that neither
label fully describes the man. The two creeds clashed
within his thought throughout his life; and though Campbell
can only be congratulated for his ability to think outside
strict party lines, he must be held guilty of frequent
logical inconsistency. His radicalism is quite surprisingly
ignored by his official biographers, Sir Charles Bernard and
C.E. Buckland, and subsequently by Stokes and other modern
historians of the Raj. It was very much fathered by his
"conversion" to Utilitarianism in the 1840's while a pupil
of Malthus at Haileybury; but in his Memoirs Campbell placed
heavy stress on the devotion instilled by his parents to
radical causes. His father was much acclaimed in his native
Fife for his outspoken support of Parliamentary reform in
the 1820's, and won a knighthood for putting down anti-reform
riots in 1832;[87] Lady Campbell -- no less active in the
cause -- lavished radicalism upon the youthful George. Years

---

[87]Campbell, Memoirs, vol. I, p. 6.

later he wrote: "I don't know whether I was born a radical, or was made one in 1832. I rather think my nature inclines that way".[88] Thereafter he claimed that he was "a good Radical and that in all climes and countries /¯he_7 was for the interests of the masses, and would promote measures for their benefit".[89] It was not calculated to endear him to the British establishment in India; but upon his return there after an unsuccessful general election fight in Dunbartonshire in 1868 as a radical, he was chosen by Mayo to govern Bengal expressly because of his radical leanings.[90] These were demonstrated in his Orissa Famine Commission Report of 1867, his enthusiastic support of Mayo's local tax program, and his public condemnations of the "sleepy hollow" conservatism of the Bengal Civil Service.[91] It was not his last fling as a radical: after retirement from India he sat for the safe Liberal seat of Kirkcaldy (Fife) from 1875 to 1892.

For such a man service in India must have been acutely

---

[88]Ibid., vol. I, p. 7; for Campbell's self-confessed conversion to Utilitarianism at Haileybury, see Ibid., vol. I, p. 10.

[89]Ibid., vol. I, p. 186.

[90]Ibid., vol. I, p. 198.

[91]Buckland, op. cit., vol. I, p. 484.

frustrating. There was precious little room for action for radicals with a contempt for tradition and an anxiety to reform; and in practice most of the youthful Utilitarians who trooped from Haileybury to India learned the practical merits of paternalism when they got there. Most came to look upon the Principle of Utility as no more than a pious slogan to be invoked when it appeared that an oligarchy or a privileged minority might be locally favored at the expense of the majority. They looked upon Bentham's constitutional dicta as guidelines for improving administration rather than for reconstructing Indian society. Accordingly, they looked with favor on Utilitarian programs for codifying the law, registering tenurial rights on a standard plan, and setting up a network of local courts using a simple oral procedure. Adopted in the practical manner of the 1840's, Utilitarianism was not only reconcileable with paternalism but even complementary to it; and though for the historian such an alliance raises theoretical problems and inconsistencies, for most Utilitarians in India they were non-existent on the ground. But not for all. Campbell was the sort of radical who disproves all thought that this might be a "natural alliance" between Tory gentlemen and Benthamite administrators, as G.M. Young assumed. [92] For men of his sort such an alliance

---

[92] G.M. Young, _Portrait of an Age_, Oxford, 1977 (issued with notes by G. Kitson Clark and others), p. 68.

existed faute de mieux, and for much of his career Campbell
resisted alliance of any kind.

But even Campbell, the sternest radical of them all,
had his sharp edges worn down in time, though his later
writings show only a flickering awareness of the degree to
which this occurred. In his own mind he was a radical to
the end, largely unconscious of the conflict of ideas within
him. "I think I have always been prone to fixed and logical
principles of action. But, on the other hand, I have
perhaps been given too much to independent views; too little
apt to follow the current tide of opinion"[93] is as near as
his Memoirs got to recognizing his own contradictions.

Temperamentally, of course, paternalists and radicals
could always tell each other apart, however confused their
views might be in theory. Campbell's urgency to right the
wrongs of Indian society isolated colleagues like Temple
and may well -- from the evidence -- have acutely irritated
them. He is credited even by his friends with an abrupt,
uncompromising manner; and during his 37 months as
Lieutenant-Governor of Bengal (1871-3) he seems to have
dealt heavy blows to bureaucratic morale. This was the
opinion of his close friend and secretary, later his
biographer, C. E. Buckland:

---

[93]Campbell, Memoirs, vol. I, p. 4.

> His views were clear, but his temper was
> uncompromising. He seemed to allow nothing,
> either for native habits of thought, or for
> the weakness of his own officials, and he
> speedily acquired the character of an abrupt,
> uncourteous man. His whole term was characterised
> by contention, not in the sense of wrangling,
> but of disputation. In the Imperial Council,
> where his sound views ought to have had, and
> indeed had, weight, his contentious tone and
> persistence did much to destroy the effect that
> his perception of facts created...[94]

This said, the genial liberal vision of Trevelyan and Macaulay is far more readily seen in the unpopular Campbell than ever so in Temple and his colleagues. One forgets, when reading through the British contempt of the Indians between 1840 and 1870, that a previous generation of administrators had looked upon them with far greater hope and genorosity. In 1836 Trevelyan voiced the prevailing optimism of the age about Indian self-rule:

> The political education of a nation is a
> work of time; and while it is in progress,
> we shall be as safe as it will be possible
> for us to be. The natives will not rise
> against us, we shall stoop to raise them;
> there will be no reaction, because there
> will be no pressure; the national activity
> will be fully and harmlessly employed in
> acquiring and diffusing European knowledge,
> and in naturalising European institutions.
> The educated classes, knowing that the
> elevation of their country on these principles
> can only be worked out under our protection,
> will naturally cling to us... The change will
> thus be peaceably and gradually effected;
> there will be no struggle, no mutual
> exasperation; the natives will have indepen-
> dence, after first learning how to make good
> use of it.[95]

---

[94] Buckland, op. cit., vol. I, p. 570.

[95] C.E. Trevelyan, The Education of the People of India, London, 1838, pp. 194-19.

That was, of course, naive, and the British administrators spoken for by Temple were far harder-headed. But what was lost from the earlier generation was not merely naivete but also kindness and social hope. The latter died, in all but a few of Campbell's sort. In the 1870's, when 25,000 Indian Bachelors of Art -- Macaulay's "class of persons Indian in colour and blood, but English in tastes, in opinions, in morals, and intellect"[96] -- demanded comprehensive local self-government, they drew a negative response, bar Bombay and Calcutta. Their aspirations were dismissed by men like Temple in terms of the incivility, amorality and political ineptitude of the overwhelming majority of the population. The "paternalists" of 1850-70 had lost a liberal spirit. Campbell, at least, was an honorable exception.

---

[96]T.B. Macaulay, Minute on Education, 2 February 1835, in G.O. Trevelyan, The Competition Wallah, London, 1864, p. 411.

Very truly &c
H. S. Maine

CHAPTER SEVEN

INDIAN FITNESS FOR SELF-RULE:
THE VIEWS OF SIR HENRY MAINE

In the years after the Mutiny, the greatest
authority on local self-government and the only thinker
of distinction on the subject was Sir Henry Maine. His
unrivalled reputation was built upon two books, Ancient
Law (1861) and Village Communities East and West (1871),
written on either side of his seven-year term from 1862 to
1869 as Law Member of the Government of India. They were
scholarly; and they were widely read. In comparison to
Maine, Sir George Campbell, his main source of information
on India for Village Communities East and West, was a
secondary mind, while Sir Richard Temple was the stolid and
third-rate representative of a largely inert body of thought.
After 1870, when a genuine debate on local self-government
revived after years of torpid lack of interest, there was
no higher name of appeal than his.

Maine was, before going out to India, the Regius
Professor of Civil Law at Cambridge (1847-54) and Reader
in Roman Law at the Inns of Court (1852-62). He wrote his
books in England and his immense scholarship was not, for

the most part, addressed to readers in India.   Doubtless
he would have been surprised at the extent of his reputation
there (we do not know; for his wife burned his correspondence). His role in the debate on local self-government in
the 1870's was not to participate but to be used: Campbell,
Trevelyan and Frere made known their respect, while Indian
nationalists paid him the doubtful compliment of excerpting
his historical work and quoting it at the British to quite
opposed political ends.   Among senior colleagues in Britain
his chief plea for India was, however, largely rejected.
This was that she should be spared the sort of democratic
self-government introduced to Britain in the Second and
Third Reform Acts, a bogy which loomed increasingly large for
India under Gladstone in the 1880's.   Maine detested the
democratic principle.   He was convinced by the declining
standards of British political life after 1867 that no nation
-- Britain or India -- could be civilized under democratic
government; and he wished for both countries a progressive
aristocracy.   His last work, Popular Government (1885),
argued vehemently against a "barbarous" empire ruled by
the common man.   On this he was, as he came with increasing
bitterness to realize, not to be heard.

Maine's importance to the historian of local self-
government lies in the way he was used in the 1870's to
provide support for plans to devolve power back to the
villages.   The Government of India's decentralization
scheme, introduced by Mayo in 1870, began this process

by offering seats to Indians on the new advisory district
committees; it was followed by the detailed proposals of
Frere in 1871 and, more radically, of Trevelyan in 1873
to restore some of the lost powers of village self-rule.
It was Maine who provided the essential intellectual
justification for policies which reversed forty years of
thinking in Calcutta. His second book, Village Communities,
showed that there had been a long and successful history
of local self-government in India, at times superior to
the forms of self-government displayed in Western Europe;
there was therefore good historical authority for allowing
Indians a say in municipal government while a British
district officer took the final decisions.

Much more important, however, was the new light on
the innate capacities of the Indians for self-rule which
Maine had cast in the writing of Ancient Law (1861). As
an academic Maine had been exposed to the German historical
school of Hugo, von Savigny and Ihering, and to the
philological studies of Max Müller and the investigations
of the Ethnological Society of London.[1] On their search
for anatomic, linguistic and cultural links between
contemporary Anglo-Saxons and their primitive ancestors
he based the most influential assertion of Ancient Law.

---

[1]John Burrow, Evolution and Society, Cambridge, 1966,
p. 143.

This was that ancient India was the nursery of what the
world was coming to know as "Aryan civilization". This
cannot fairly be called a discovery original to Maine:
in the 1850's Müller set out the concept of Aryanism, and
Campbell demonstrated the physical link between ancient
Rajputs and modern Anglo-Saxons. But comparatively few
people read Müller or Campbell, and many read Maine; and it
was Maine who was the first boldly to label Indian civilization as "Aryan" and to show that Indians possessed the
Aryan virtues.

It was a declaration incontestable on the facts,
and it was a justification seized upon throughout the 1870's
as a support for plans to involve Indians in local government.
How far it led to greater respect for the Indians within
the ICS is debatable. Among senior administrators such
as Temple, disdain for the Indians seems to have increased
in proportion to their stubborn refusal to be westernized;
and to them Maine's arguments appeared convenient rather
than convincing. It was, after all, a decade of beating
retreat on Indian self-rule, and of going back on previous
thinking. Whenever we come across a British administrator
in the 70's referring to the long history of local self-
government in India and refraining from a sneer at ancient
barbarism, there is an implicit appeal to Maine. Even if
one wished, it was not possible after Ancient Law to express
contempt for the Indians with the total assurance which
James Mill had made available to the generation before.

Maine not merely offered an unshakeable foundation of learning to those who were willing to be optimistic about the
Indians: he succeeded, even to sceptics, in placing ancient
Indian civilization on a pedestal only a little lower than
the Greeks and the Romans.   To an age newly fascinated by
theories of race and well disposed to regard abilities as
inherited, his demonstration of the noble ancestry of the
Indians was shocking indeed.

Maine's conviction of the Indians' potential to reach
the pinnacles of Aryan civilization did not, however, blind
him to present day realities.   India was demonstrably
unready, to his eyes, for self-government -- national or
local.   His most brilliant argument was devoted to the
insistence that India (and other countries of similar
predicament) must first be moved forward from a traditional
society organized around family "status" to one based on
legal "contract", and that local self-government should
not be granted before this process had taken place.
In this view he had the support of the majority of British
officers in the field in India.   But Parliament, the
Secretary of State, the Prime Minister and the men of
highest influence in India thought differently: and in
1882 Lord Ripon conceded a generous measure of municipal
self-rule.   This was, indeed,a major strategic reverse to
Maine's hopes.   But his highest ambition was to move India
forward to a modern society respecting legal contract; and

by the end of his career he could count his successes, with
the stamp of his reforming mind impressed upon much of the
Government of India's statute book for the 60's and 70's,
most notably in the new laws governing private property.

Ironically, Maine must himself be held responsible,
to a large degree, for the greater favor with which Britons
at home were able to look on Indians and Indian capacities.
To those who had hitherto accepted Mill's withering scorn
of India as barbarous and sub-Chinese, Maine's connection
of India and Aryan civilization entered the unconscious
mind of the age as a new and repercussive fact.   Indian
nationalists cited it as proof that their people's
abilities were higher than the Government of India would
allow, and as evidence of their readiness for self-rule.
Thus was Maine stood on his head; and thus was Maine the
distinguished legal historian, the learned academic,
incorporated into the polemic of his times.

What distinguishes Maine's argument about states
of civilization from those of Mill and Scottish predecessors is his analysis in terms of developing law codes.   He
regarded the judicial structure as the decisive influence
on the political and economic organization of a society
at differing stages of its history.   It was a novel
approach, received with respect, but denied popular
acceptance in Maine's time or since.   It is the key to

his claim that India could only be granted modern Aryan political institutions when its legal system had been advanced to harmonize with them.   On that critical step did India's entitlement to local self-government rest.

———————————

I.   ARE THE INDIANS CIVILIZED?

Like Campbell, Maine assumed the Indians to be capable of climbing to the pinnacle of James Mill's ladder of civilization by virtue of their Anglo-Saxon kinship and their common -- if distant -- Aryan heritage.[2] What distinguished the Aryan world from China, Eastern Europe and Africa for Maine was its capacity for progress, an attribute which he lauded as precious and rare in the history of the world.   "It is indisputable", he asserted in Ancient Law, "that much the greatest part of mankind has never shown a particle of desire that its civil institutions should be improved....   The stationary condition of the human race is the rule, the progressive the exception".

> Vast populations... detest that which in the language of the West is called reform.   The entire Mahommedan world detests it.   The multitudes of coloured men who swarm the great continent of Africa detest it, and it is detested by that large part of mankind which we are accustomed to leave on one side as barbarous or savage.   The millions upon millions of men who fill the Chinese Empire loathe and (what is more) despise it.[3]

———————————

[2] Sir Henry Maine, Ancient Law, 10th ed., London, 1920, p. 17.

[3] Ibid., p. 27.

To Maine's mind -- as to Campbell's -- the attainment of
civilization was unique to the Aryan peoples as a consequence
of their peculiar zeal for self-improvement. As he explained
to an Oxford audience in 1871, "civilization is nothing more
than a name for the old order of the Aryan world, dissolved
but perpetually reconstructing itself under a vast variety
of solvent influences".[4] Mid-Victorian India had all the
capacity for progress of any other Aryan country. It
possessed "a whole world of Aryan institutions, Aryan
customs, Aryan ideas, Aryan beliefs, in a far earlier stage
of growth and development than any which survived beyond
its borders". It was, in short, an embryonic civilization
which could mature under the guiding hand of British lawyers
and administrators.[5]

In his attempt to gauge how far Indian civilization
was retarded, Maine calculated that no less than one and a
half millennia of social change separated India from Britain.
Contemporary Indian behavior seemed to him to parallel that
of the Romans of the 6th century before Christ.[6] At the
beginning of remembered history, he conjectured, Indians
and Romans together had passed through an "era of heroic
kings". During this period, which was recorded in the West

---

[4]Sir Henry Maine, The Effects of Observation of India
on Modern European Thought, London, 1875, p. 30.

[5]Ibid., p. 2.

[6]Maine, Ancient Law, p. 12.

in the poems of Homer, law took the form of _themistes_, or
isolated judgments passed by the kings on specific topics
of dispute.[7]   Subsequently, both branches of
the Aryan world had progressed to an "era of oligarchies",
during which narrow aristocratic bodies, claiming expert
knowledge of past _themistes_, interpreted the dictates of
custom to the people.[8]   As early as this second stage of
development an important divergence occurred between
East and West.   Whereas the Mediterranean Aryans became
dissatisfied with a feeble line of hereditary monarchs and
transferred their allegiance to councils of military and
political chiefs, the Eastern branch remained loyal to
kings allied to priestly elites.   The conservatism of
these ecclesiastical cliques became irrevocably impressed
on Indian notions of law and retarded internally-generated
legal development ever thereafter.

Before stagnation set in, however, India like the
West entered what Maine called the "era of codes".[9]   The
invention of writing having facilitated the transcription
of customary rules onto stone tablets, the law became a
public document accessible for reference by the literate.[10]

---

[7]_Ibid._, p. 8.

[8]_Ibid._, p. 9.

[9]_Ibid._, p. 12.

[10]_Ibid._, p. 13.

Maine believed that the timing of codification was of the
utmost importance.   The possibility of all future social
development depended entirely upon how accurately the new
codes reflected the norms of social behavior at the time
of transcription.   In the West codification occurred
between 451 and 449 BC, when fortuitously the plebeian demand for written law was met with the Twelve Tables of Rome.
This was a transcription of customary law which so exactly
coincided with existing practice that it regulated Roman
society effectively.[11]   In the East the plebeian element was
too weak to wrest a code from the priestly oligarchy until
the beginning of the Christian era.   The Law of Manu which
resulted -- a Brahminical compilation of prescriptions for
ideal behavior -- was as far from actual social forms as
could be.[12]   The time-lag proved catastrophic for India.
Customary rules which had once been acceptable guides were
now out of date;   and the Brahmins invented superstitions to
justify precepts which reason could not sanction.[13]
The best example of this distortion, to Maine's mind, was
the survival of caste, a division of social classes
appropriate to a past crisis of social history but
degrading when prolonged indefinitely without good cause.
India would remain backward and uncivilized, he predicted,

---

[11]Ibid., p. 14.

[12]Ibid., p. 15.

[13]Ibid., pp. 16-17.

so long as religious transgressions were punished by civil
penalties, religious censure was incurred by civil crimes,
the individual's status was defined by religious categories,and his actions were circumscribed by religious
proscriptions.[14]

Whereas Indian society had been frozen by an
inflexible code, progress had been achieved in the West
through three legal mechanisms -- fictions, equity and
legislation -- which bent the inevitable rigidity of codified
law to the reforming influence and which made legal precepts
adaptable to the needs of changing society.[15]   First,
legal fictions provided a means of maintaining the letter
of the law while changing its substance, thus satisfying at
once the needs for stability and improvement.[16]   Secondly,
the principle of equity modified the law to conform to
abstract notions of social justice.[17]   And third, legislation enabled the Emperor and Senate to frame new laws
meeting the demands of progressive public opinion.[18]   Maine
believed that without these instruments progress would have
been impossible in the West and would continue to be so

---

[14]Ibid., pp. 17-18.

[15]Ibid., p. 29.

[16]Ibid., pp. 30-32.

[17]Ibid., pp. 32-33.

[18]Ibid., pp. 33-34.

elsewhere. He therefore conceived the mission of the British in India as reforming the long stagnant society of the Brahmins by introducing this three-fold apparatus, thereby modernizing traditional beliefs and institutions.

II. HOW CAN INDIAN SOCIETY BE REFORMED?

That the elevation of Indian society depended entirely upon infusing an occidental spirit of progress among an oriental people was axiomatic. As Maine stated so elegantly and memorably in 1875, "except the blind forces of Nature, nothing moves in this world which is not Greek in origin.

> A ferment spreading from that source has vitalized all the great progressive races of mankind, penetrating from one to another and producing results according to its hidden and latent genius, and results, of course, often far greater than exhibited in Greece itself.
>
> Not one of those intellectual excellencies which we regard as characteristics of the great progressive races of the world -- not the law of the Romans; not the philosophy and sagacity of the Germans; not the luminous order of the French; not the political aptitude of the English; not that insight into physical nature to which all races have contributed -- would, apparently have come into existence if these races had been left to themselves. To one small people covering in its original seat no more than a hand's breadth of territory, it was given to create the principle of progress, of movement upwards and not backwards or downwards -- of destruction tending to construction. That people was the Greek.[19]

---

[19]Maine, Observation, p. 40.

Once an Aryan nation like Britain had itself been infused
with the Greek spirit of progress, it could not help but
pass it on to whomever it ruled; for "whatever be the
nature and value of that bundle of influences which we
call 'Progress'", Maine observed, "nothing can be more
certain than when a society is touched by it, it spreads
like a contagion".[20]

Maine held that the fundamental goal of the British
in India was to impart the spirit of reform. This was
the means to progress in Indian society and among the
Indians as individuals: blue prints for progress of the
Utilitarian sort were useless. Change could not be planned
or predicted in society. "It is by its indirect and for
the most part uninterested influences", he asserted, echoing
the Scottish Enlightenment before him, "that the British
power metamorphoses and dissolves the ideas and social
forms underneath it".[21] Law codes and school books were
necessary to hasten the pace and direct the course of reform,
but the British presence on the sub-continent was what was
essential to prompt the Indians to adopt the spirit of
progress. "It is this principle which we Englishmen are
communicating to India", he reminded imperial legislators
in Calcutta:

_____

[20]Ibid., p. 39.

[21]Sir Henry Maine, Village Communities in the East
and West, 2nd ed., London, 1872, pp. 27-28.

> We did not create it. We deserve no special
> credit for it. It has come to us filtered
> through many different media. But we have
> received it, and as we have received it, so we
> pass it on. There is no reason why if it has
> time to work, it should not develop in India
> effects as wonderful as in others of the socie-
> ties of mankind.[22]

With the lofty assurance of the mid-Victorian
evolutionist, Maine proclaimed that the principle of progress was as clear as its mechanism. "The movement of
progressive societies has hitherto been a movement from
Status to Contract".[23] A generalization as sweeping as
Darwin's observation about the survival of the fittest,
this maxim never entered the vocabulary of popular social
Darwinism because its legal connotations were unintelligible
to the general reader. Nevertheless, it rapidly became,
and has remained, a cliché of legal history. In Ancient
Law Maine clearly defined his terms and traced the path
from status to contract which India, like any other Aryan
nation, would have to follow to attain civilization:

> Starting, as if from one terminum of history,
> from a condition of society in which all the
> relations of Persons are summed up in the
> relations of Family, we seem to have steadily
> moved towards a phase of social order in which
> all these relations arise from the free agree-
> ment of individuals....
> The word Status may be usefully employed
> to construct a formula expressing the law of
> progress thus indicated, which, whatever be its
> value, seems to me to be sufficiently ascertained.

---

[22]Maine, Observation, pp. 37-38.

[23]Maine, Ancient Law, pp. 174.

> All the forms of Status taken notice of in
> the law of Persons were derived from, and to
> some extent are still coloured by, the powers
> and privileges anciently residing in the
> Family. If then we employ Status, agreeably
> with the usage of the best writers, to signify
> these personal conditions only, and avoid apply-
> ing the term to such conditions as are the
> immediate or remote result of agreement, we may
> say that the movement of the progressive
> societies has hitherto been a movement from
> Status to Contract.[24]

Because of its law code India had never moved beyond the
early stage at which each family was ruled by an omniscient
chief or paterfamilias. The rights and possessions of the
individual were tied to those of the village community,
which was regarded by its members as a corporate family even
if representing many families in reality.[25] In the West,
by contrast, the transition from status to contract was
made as soon as the legal identity of men, women and slaves
was distinguished from that of the corporate family and
tenurial rights were transformed from co-proprietary to
separate holdings.[26]

Maine, like Bentham and James Mill before him,
envisioned a society respecting individual freedoms as the
most civilized form of social organization and as the best
guarantee that the greatest good would be achieved for the

---

[24]Ibid., pp. 172-173.

[25]Maine, Village Communities, pp. 107-108.

[26]Maine, Ancient Law, p. 172.

greatest number. His ambitions to destroy the provisions of law and custom restricting the individual were well advanced during his tenure as Member of the Viceroy's Council from 1862 to 1869. He therefore set about the wholesale revision of Indian law codes to segregate the individual from the family and from the religious group, and to free property from the restrictions of joint tenure. He enthusiastically endorsed the recommendations of a Crown Commission set up in 1861 to devise a law of succession because the proposed legislation secured the right to private property in India even more stringently than in England. Besides abolishing the distinction between the devolution of movable and immovable property, it declared that no person should acquire by marriage an interest in the property of the spouse.[27] Maine also urged the passage of a bill to make legitimate the marriage and offspring of those who, like members of the Brahmo Samaj, did not belong to any of the recognized religions of India (Christian, Jewish, Hindu, Muslim, Parsi, Buddhist, Sikh and Jain).[28] He supported a bill to legalize the remarriage of Christian converts who had been deserted or

---

[27] Sir Mountstuart Elphinstone Grant Duff, Sir Henry Maine, London, 1892, "Speech on The Law of Succession", pp. 192-207.

[28] Ibid., "Speech on Civil Marriage of Natives", pp. 285-293.

272

repudiated by their spouses as a consequence of conversion.[29]
He also sponsored a series of measures enforcing specific
perfomance of contract. Criminal penalties had
traditionally been meted out for non-performance: the
defendant had been bankrupted and sent to jail without the
plaintiff being properly compensated. To aid the plaintiff
Maine proposed that the civil courts be empowered to insist
that a contract be performed the moment evidence of laxity
was brought to its attention. In this way unsatisfactory
penalties would be avoided and the fulfilment of business
commitments ensured.[30] All of these measures defined the
rights and obligations of the individual in free, contractual
relationships.

Moving India on from status to contract required,
for Maine, a gradual displacement of the backward elements
of customary law and the abolition of the incoherent and
unwieldy codes compiled by the Orientalists. Like
Bentham, he regarded a progressive civil code as the most
effective means of reforming society. For Bentham, this
meant devising an universally applicable code on the
principle of a constant human nature, unvarying in time

[29]Ibid., "Speech on Re-Marriage of Native Converts",
pp. 130-163.

[30]Ibid., "Speech on Specific Performance of Contracts",
pp. 170-178.

or place: for Maine, on the other hand, it meant compiling

a code which reconciled and blended existing Indian and

English law.   An appreciation of cultural differences

acquired from the German historians and a keen sense of

an "unprogressive" society's resistance to change prompted

his rejection of abstract notions of human behavior and of

all thought of sudden reform.   The Utilitarians had erred,

he contended, in assuming that law could be transplanted

from one society to another without modification.[31]

"When we are transferring a system from England to a country

so far removed from it, morally and mentally, as India", he

observed,

> we cannot be quite sure that all the propositions
> which are roughly true of one people and of one
> state of society are in the same degree true of
> another people and of another social state.
> Still less can we be sure that the relative truth
> of rules founded on propositions of this sort
> is the same in the two countries.[32]

The glaring fault which Maine discerned in Fitzjames

Stephen's Indian Evidence Act -- which he praised as an

otherwise admirable attempt to introduce the finest

aspects of English jurisprudence to India -- was its

failure to provide for substantial local amendment.[33]

---

[31]George Feaver, From Status to Contract: A Biography of Sir Henry Maine, 1822-1888, London, 1969, p. 103.

[32]Sir Henry Maine, "Mr. Fitzjames Stephen's Introduction to the Indian Evidence Act".   Fortnightly Review,
XIII, January 1873, pp. 51-67.

[33]Ibid., p. 66.

Like the presidency officials who supported financial
and administrative decentralization in the 1860's, Maine
realized that unless allowance were made for ethnic and
linguistic differences, imperial legislation could not
be effectively implemented.

Maine therefore urged that the code being drawn up
by the Indian Law Commission in the 1860's be based on the
best customary practice, improved by progressive law.
It should avoid the Orientalist mistake of sacrificing
simplicity and intelligibility by haphazard patching of
modern English law onto traditional ways. To clarify
the law Maine recommended that the Law Commissioners
"set forth fundamental principles with as much simplicity
as was compatible with accuracy", confirm "wholesome"
Indian usage whenever possible, but rely primarily on "the
good sense and logical coherence" of English law."[34]
When the ever-cautious Secretary of State, Sir Charles
Wood, alleged that India was becoming "abnormally law-
ridden" as a consequence of this methodical codification,[35]
Maine replied: "When the constitution is spoiled by
overdoses of law, the remedy is not to defy law but to

---

[34]Grant Duff, op. cit., "Speech on Over-Legislation",
p. 231.

[35]Wood to Maine, 25 February 1865, quoted by Feaver,
Op. cit., p. 72.

administer the poison more scientifically".[36]

Maine was pleased to find evidence of Indian progress from status to contract in the decline of the authority of the panchayet after 1830. From that date the number of cases taken to the mofussil courts by villagers dissatisfied with the verdicts of their panchayets had increased dramatically. Significantly, a large proportion of these cases involved property disputes: these lay outside the competence of the panchayet because customary law did not recognize private property. Whereas Campbell lamented the transfer of power from village elders to British civil servants and urged the creation of a new class of village leaders capable of leading rural people back to traditional methods of adjudication, Maine welcomed the displacement of the panachyet as a sign of progress.[37] Nevertheless, he became so dismayed at the low level of justice dispensed by the poorly-staffed, overworked mofussil courts that he drew up a bill to relieve the strain. The resulting legislation provided for "a regular, fair-dealing, and incorrupt Panchayet" incorporated into the Western judicial system. The indigenous tribunals were transformed into small cause courts presided over by itinerant registrars,

[36]Maine to Wood, 5 July 1864, Ibid.

[37]Grant Duff, op. cit., "Memorandum on Mr. Caird's Report on the Condition of India", p. 426.

and resident judges were set up in mofussil towns to hear
all appeals arising from them. To Maine's delight this
statute destroyed the last stronghold of pure customary
law in India, for the modified panchayets relied on English
rather than Indian law.[38]

By the time Maine left India in 1869 society could
be seen to be moving rapidly from status to contract.
By establishing Western courts of justice in every
administrative district, imperial administrators had
introduced the three essential mechanisms of legal reform
(fictions, equity and legislation). Custom articulated
by the panchayet had given way to fixed law passed by the
legislature and to judgments decreed by the courts; the
ultimate legal sanction of disapproval or even ostracism
by the village community had been replaced by the implicit
command of the sovereign behind the law; and specific
penalties for crime had been substituted for ill-defined
punishments.[39] Reforms which had been instituted over
centuries in Western Europe had been compressed into a
few decades in India. Before departing from Calcutta,
Maine proudly announced to the Imperial Legislative
Council that "the sense of personal rights /was_7 growing
everywhere into greater strength" and that "the sacredness

[38]Ibid., "Speech on Small Cause Courts", pp. 209-217.

[39]Maine , Village Communities, p. 72.

of personal obligation arising out of contract" was
replacing a debilitating sense of obligation to the
community.[40]   Despite these incontrovertible signs of
progress, however, individual freedom was still inhibited
by the patriarchal joint family, the village community and
caste.   Until these barriers to the formation of
contractual relationships were completely broken down,
civilization as Maine understood it would remain out of
reach.

III.   HOW   ADVANCED   ARE   INDIAN   VILLAGE   INSTITUTIONS?

During his seven years in India Maine acquired
his knowledge of village government through his work on
the Imperial Executive and Legislative Councils as well as
from personal observations of rural life made on his
semi-annual trips between Calcutta and Simla.   In addition
he gained valuable information from Lord Lawrence, the
oldest and arguably the greatest living authority on the
customs of Northern India, and from Sir George Campbell,
the most notable expert of the day on the village community.[41]
Upon returning to England in 1869 he used this material to
elucidate Aryan social development at stages later than those
treated in Ancient Law.

---

[40]Ibid., pp. 112-113.

[41]Ibid., p. vii.

Recent research by the German historians Von
Maurer and Nasse suggested that the Teutonic mark or
township -- which scholars had previously believed to have
sprung ex nihilo upon medieval Europe -- had actually grown
quite naturally out of the ancient Roman vicus or village.[42]
Maine at once noticed similiarities between these townships
and the Indian village community, "resemblances too strong
and numerous", he decided, "to be accidental".[43]   In 1871
he analyzed these intriguing parallels in a series of
lectures delivered at Oxford and later published as Village
Communities East and West: these addresses riveted the
attention of scholars and imperial administrators on the
contemporary Indian village and its institutions of self-rule.

The most obvious characteristic which linked the
Indian village with the pre-medieval German mark was a
communal pattern of living. In both settlements arable
land was divided into separate lots but was cultivated
according to customary rules observed by all; it was
periodically redistributed on an equal basis to the
householders; and the common land or waste was accessible
to the entire community. Each family was ruled by a
despotic paterfamilias, and the group as a whole was

---

[42]Ibid., pp. 10-11.

[43]Ibid., p. 12.

governed by a council of family heads.[44]   But here the
resemblances ended; for the Germans, unlike the Indians,
were a bellicose people given to feuding with their
neighbours and coveting their land.   The constant threat
of war necessitated changes in the Teutonic village
communities which, according to Von Maurer and Nasse, led
them forward to feudalism.   Family heads who had
traditionally sat on the governing council -- and who had
always been awarded a higher status than other males in the
community -- banded together to lead their clansmen in combat.
In recognition of this the community allowed them to enclose
their land from the communal holdings and to grant access
to it in return for the performance of specific duties,
usually military.   Soon the rights and obligations of
their tenants became hereditary.[45] In this way democratically
organized village communities were replaced by manorial
groups of military overlords and subservient tenants, and
communal holdings were surrendered to individual noble
proprietors.

Maine agreed with Von Maurer and Nasse that the
emergence of a new aristocracy powerful enough to introduce
novel forms of land tenure was an important event in the
history of Western Europe.   He went on to rank them as

------

[44]Ibid., pp. 107-108.

[45]Ibid., p. 132.

the very progenitors of progress with the political and
military oligarchies who codified ancient law.   "The true
authors of human improvement are aristocracies", he boldly
told his democratic age; but the word 'aristocracy' had to

> be properly understood. A privileged class
> arises because it is stronger and wiser than
> the others. Rejoicing in its strength, it
> instructs and civilises itself. Very often,
> the knowledge and skill which it has acquired
> is diffused beyond its limits. It constantly
> happens that this larger portion thus obtains
> new strength, at the same time it becomes
> conscious of new appetites; and then it excludes
> its predecessors from their monopoly, or insists
> on sharing it. But the old process only
> recommences. Aristocracy rises on the decay
> of aristocracy, and the world makes progress
> by one privileged class pushing another from
> its seat.[46]

Displaying competence to reform the law -- the essential
characteristic of the progressive Aryan elite as Maine
understood it -- the feudal lords of the West inaugurated
the all-important legal separation of private property
from communal tenure, and thereby advanced European society
well along the path from "status" to "contract".

In India an aristocracy of this type never appeared
and the advance to feudalism never occurred. No changes
took place on the land, for the alien kings who swept the
subcontinent for centuries left the cultivators undisturbed
in ownership, being content to demand agricultural rent
and to recruit young men for their armies. Nor were there

---

[46]Sir Henry Maine, "Radical Patriarchalism", St.
James's Gazette, I, 18 June 1880, p. 260.

changes in village institutions.[47]   The military organization
in self-defence which in Germany gave birth to new village
hierarchies and feudal institutions was unknown in India,
where the peace-loving villages submitted without resistance,
and where the aggression of meat-eating Germans in search
of wasteland for grazing was absent (the Indians were largely
vegetarian).   Nor, without an aristocracy to lead it on,
was there any change in the tenure of the land.   The
Teutonic penchant to experiment with techniques for
improving crop yield, encouraged by a progressive code and
the spirit of innovation engendered by it, was not shared
by the Indians.   Trapped by an outmoded and inflexible
code, they were content to till the soil by the inefficient
means sanctioned by tradition.[48]

Maine had no doubt that India, if left alone,
would never reach the stage of feudalism, much less that
of modern civilization.[49]   But a century of British
dominion had already loosened the deadening grip of
custom which kept India locked in the ancient world.
By defining individual proprietary rights in most of the
subcontinent through the permanent and the ryotwari land
settlements, the British had created freedom of contract --

---

[47]Maine, Village Communities, pp. 159-160.

[48]Ibid., p. 164.

[49]Ibid., p. 12.

however limited by traditional concepts of ownership --
and an open land market -- however distorted by the
constraints of the moneylender.   By the 1860's it was
possible to hope that a landowning class would emerge which
would display the aristocratic wisdom, strength and imagination in regenerating society described by Maine in
Village Communities, although it had become clear that the
pleasure-loving zemindars of Bengal and Northern India
would never fulfil this role.   Campbell held that the
lowest peasant proprietors possessed these characteristics,
while Temple put his trust in the urban middle class with
rural connections.   Maine, however, failed to discern the
necessary qualities of leadership in any of these groups.[50]
His hopes for India's early attainment of civilization were
therefore not high; but his belief in her potential to
reach this goal in time -- with the essential aid of
progressive English law -- was unimpaired.

IV.   WHEN WILL THE INDIANS BE FIT FOR INDEPENDENCE?
It follows from the above that Maine should be
utterly dismayed when the first demands of the Indian National
Congress for self-government were expressed as demands
for democracy.   "The language of political aspiration,
in India itself", he lamented,

----

[50]Feaver, op. cit., p. 203.

283

> seems to me to savour of the new political
> philosophy which has spread of late years
> over the West, and which has substituted
> for the old maxim that government should be
> carried on for the good of the community,
> the new assumption that it should be
> carried on by the community itself, that is,
> by the numerical majority of the adult male
> portion of it.[51]

Democracy offered the highest guarantee that India would
remain steeped in primitivism.   Only the despotism of the
British could advance a modern contractual society.
In his essay on India in Sir Humphrey Ward's Diamond
Jubilee celebrations, Maine set out the curious co-existence
there of the modern and the primitive.   Since 1850, he
allowed, Indian society had been immeasurably improved
by government-sponsored education programs, four law codes
and the spread of the free market economy along hundreds
of miles of new roads, railways, canals and navigable rivers.
In contrast, most Indians remained backward, stationary and
even barbarous.   In 1886 only one male in sixteen could
read;   fewer still ventured more than a mile or two beyond
their villages to trade or seek justice in the British courts;
and even fewer embarked on long train journeys to India's
major cities.   The vision of the average Indian extended
no further than his family, his hut and his plot of land;
and his way of life continued to resemble that of an

_____

[51]Sir Humphrey Ward, The Reign of Queen Victoria,
London, 1887, vol. I, p. 519.

Etruscan peasant during the Republic.[52]   To trust self-
government into such hands was to surrender the value of one
hundred years of British rule.

Where also was the enlightened elite which could bring
India forward to the civilization of other Aryan countries?
By Maine's definition only those who had acquired a Bachelor
of Arts degree could be considered educated; and on this basis
he calculated that no more than 25,000, or 1 per cent of the
total population of British India, was capable of voting or
governing responsibly.   How could so tiny a minority, mainly
urban in its tastes and Western by education, "democratically"
represent the interests of the rural masses?[53]   The difference
in their respective life styles was too great, and contact
between the two groups was too limited, for any representative
arrangement to be effective.

> If the effect of employing in an Eastern society
> the political mechanism growing into favour in
> the West were to lift into administrative and
> legislative supremacy a small group of men
> numbering about 5,000 or 10,000 or 100,000 --
> a particular class or race or caste educated in
> a particular way -- the government thus established
> might have merits or demerits, but it could not,
> without violent straining of language, be called
> a popular government or democracy.   Ruling over
> 2,000,000 or 250,000,000 men, it would be one of
> the narrowest oligarchies which the world has
> ever seen.[54]

Democracy in India would not merely be self-destructive: it
was a nonsense in its own terms.

---

[52]Ibid., pp. 527-528.

[53]Ibid.

[54]Ibid., p. 513.

Far more detrimental to India's long-term prospects of local self-government, however, was the unprogressive outlook of the educated minority. The barons of medieval Europe had been a numerically small and culturally isolated group; but they had nonetheless qualified as progressive Aryan aristocrats by identifying their interests with the reformation of society as a whole. Maine condemned the complacency which, in contrast, allowed India's educated classes to reform their own outlooks and behavior and to improve their own standard of living, while ignoring the educational and material needs of their fellow-countrymen.[55] Somehow -- and Maine never explains how or why -- educated Indians had been exposed to Western thought without being infected by the spirit of progress. "There is in India a minority", he pointed out,

> educated at the feet of English politicians and
> in books saturated with English political ideas,
> which has learned to repeat their language;
> but it is doubtful whether even these, if they
> had a voice in the matter, would allow a finger
> to be laid on the very subjects with which
> European legislation is beginning to concern[56]
> itself, social and religious usage.

To those who aspired to their transformation into so-called "black Englishmen", India's educated elite was a disappointment. It had, worst of all, remained passive before the palpable absurdities of the caste system -- the social

---

[55]Ibid., p. 527.

[56]Sir Henry Maine, Popular Government, London, 1885, pp. 132-133.

system which asserted men's permanent inequality through any
number of worlds in which they might be reincarnated.
Maine, observing that caste survived as a social force
even after its religious significance had been undermined
by Western education, and noting that instead of withering
away in India's major cities, it had constantly redefined
itself and adapted to changing circumstances,[57] blamed the
intellectual spinelessness of the educated classes.
They themselves dared not risk the renunciation of caste
or the social consequences of diffusing Western learning
throughout Indian society, he concluded with contempt.

Maine's response to the limited demands for local
self-government which arose during his term as Law Member
(1862-69) and after his return home, when he sat on the
Council of India in the 1870's, was more detailed but no
less negative. He offered two fundamental grounds for
opposition. First, he declared that the ryots were
insufficiently liberated from barbarism and superstition
to govern themselves with reason and enlightenment in the
foreseeable future. Secondly, he contended that plans to
invest the panchayets with new responsibilities (put
forward by Campbell, Trevelyan and Frere) would retard
progress by preventing the disintegration of the village
community, an essential step in India's movement from

---

[57]Ward, op. cit., p. 519.

"status" to "contract".

The locus classicus of Maine's objections to local self-government is his "Speech on Indian municipalities", made to the Imperial Legislative Council in 1868 when a bill was introduced providing for the appointment of municipal committees in the North-West Provinces. (The objects of this measure were three-fold: one, to set up municipal committees wherever they did not already exist in the province; two, to substitute popular election for nomination as the mode of selection after two years; and three, to treat these committees as the foundation of a system of popular government). The speech, if reactionary in its effect, nonetheless contains a fashionable admixture of comparative and evolutionary argument.[58] The former showed the Indians as unregenerate members of a stationary society; outside -- for the most part -- the influences for progress in the world. On such ground they exhibited not even a latent aptitude for responsible self-government. Considered from an evolutionary standpoint, however, they possessed the capacity for self-government but not (as yet) the civilization to justify it. Until society advanced, he told the Council, local self-government would prove abortive.

---

[58]Burrow, op cit., pp. 156-157.

Maine's speech opens with a series of damning
references to the consequences of popular municipal
government in Britain -- and a warning of the likely fate
for India.   Municipal corporations at home, he declared
roundly, were variously corrupt, tyrannous, extravagant
or parsimonious.   How much worse, therefore, these
"temptations and misleading influences" would be in India,
where the overwhelming majority of the voters would be
illiterate, superstitious and non-progressive in their
views.[59]   The municipal committees proposed for the North-
West   Provinces, he adamantly assured the Council, could
not possibly be based on popular representation.   It
was almost impossible in England to create constituencies
in which one class or group did not oppress another: and
in India?   "Considering how Native Society was divided
into castes, and sects, and religions, and races, it was
surprising that there should be practicable, anywhere, a
system of municipal election at once fair and free".[60]
Further, it was impossible to transplant to India in a mere
two years (as demanded by the bill) municipal institutions
which had existed in Europe for 2000 years.[61]

---

[59]Grant Duff, op. cit., "Speech on Indian Municipalities", p. 264.

[60]Ibid.

[61]Ibid., p. 263.

He would concede, he told the Council, that in the presidency towns "contract" was replacing "status", that caste was gradually breaking down, that Western education was preparing the people to vote intelligently; he believed that Calcutta, Bombay and Madras could be entrusted to elect representatives to municipal corporations.[62] But elsewhere, outside these cities, local self-government would be wrecked by communal rivalry between the unprogressive and unenlightened. A Hindu council in the North-West Provinces might try to exclude the Muslim minority; the Lieutenant-Governor would veto this; new elections would be held; next time a Muslim majority might attempt to exclude the Hindus. "Surely," Maine pleaded, "it would be seen that this perpetual submission and rejection might cause a chronic irritation and fret which would constitute a grave political danger".[63]

As support grew for local self-government among Liberal politicians in the 1880's, Maine became more

[62]Ibid., p. 267.

[63]Ibid., p. 266. Reports from local officials supported Maine's suspicion that in most parts of the mofussil educated, public-spirited men could not be persuaded to stand for office; in some areas worthy representatives could not be found at all; in other areas councillors would be chosen on the basis of religion of caste rather than ability. In Maine's opinion any of these contingencies would weaken the calibre of popular representatives and doom any experiment with local self-government to certain failure. Ibid.

outspoken in his disapproval of their folly. "Sentimen-
tal Liberalism", he agreed with Fitzjames Stephen,[64] his
fellow Law Member on the Viceroy's Council, took no
account of weighty historical evidence of physical, mental
and social inequalities.[65] Maine supported Stephen's
jeers at Liberals for pandering to the British working class
and his jibes at Gladstone as "the people's William", and
added harsher words of his own: Lord Ripon, the Liberal
Viceroy, was guilty of "nigger-worshipping to an accursed
degree".[66] India, he warned, could not be transformed from
despotism to democracy at the speed which Liberals hoped:
they, and the Utilitarian fathers of their thought on
human nature, were guilty of serious miscalculations. Their
fictitious assumption that men everywhere were capable of
discerning their self-interest paid "insufficient or no
attention to custom, ideas, and motive in various places
and time."[67] Bentham, and Liberals with him, had "grossly

---

[64]Sir James Fitzjames Stephen (1829-1894): called to
the bar at the Inner Temple; Secretary to the Education
Commission, 1858-1861; Recorder of Newark, 1859-1869; Law
Member of the Supreme Council of India, 1869-1872; Judge of
the High Court, 1879-1891; wrote for The Saturday Review,
The Cornhill Magazine, and The Pall Mall Gazette; Liberty,
Equality and Fraternity, 1873.

[65]Sir James Fitzjames Stephen, Liberty, Equality,
Fraternity, ed. by R.J. White, Cambridge, 1967, p. 16.

[66]Quoted by Feaver, op. cit., p. 204.

[67]Maine, "Radical Patriarchalism", p. 260.

underestimated human stupidity".   They had ignored the
incontrovertible fact that

> most of the elements of human society, like
> most of that which goes to make up the
> individual man, come by inheritance.   It is
> true that the old order changes, yielding place
> to new, but the new does not wholly consist of
> positive additions to the old; much of it is
> merely the old very slightly modified, very
> slightly displaced, and very superficially
> recombined.[68]

To Maine's understanding the Indian ryot was a dull
and hapless creature, who had successfully resisted change
for thousands of years and would reform now only at the
slowest pace, persistently prodded by British officials.
His reformation was liable to be further blocked by the
phenomenon which historians have since labelled as "Young
Bengal": the movement which had begun at Hindu College,
Calcutta in 1824 to defend religious orthodoxy and caste
against westernization and which had since given birth
to other cultural resistance movements like the Ramakrishna
Mission[69] and the Arya Samaj[70].

---

[68]Maine, Observation, p. 31.

[69]The Ramakrishna Mission: founded by the guru Ramakrishna Paramahansa(1836-1886) and organized by Swami Vive-
kananda (1863-1902) as a religious and social reform movement,
dedicated to improving the living conditions of the ryots and
arousing national pride by asserting the superiority of Hindu
culture and civilization over those of Western Europe.

[70]Arya Samaj: founded by Swami Dayananda Saraswati
(1824-1883) as a Hindu reform movement dedicated to unifying
India nationally, socially and religiously by converting the
non-Hindu and Hindu masses alike to a simple religion based
on the Vedas and emancipated from restrictions of caste,
child-marriage and prohibition of female education and widow
remarriage.

In 1868 Maine lamented that

> if ever India was perfectly ductile and plastic
> body under the hand of the Legislator, it has
> ceased to be so now.   We may have untaught the
> natives much, but we have also taught them that
> any custom, not immoral or dangerous to the
> public peace, which they choose to make a stand
> for, cannot be easily invaded.   Where thirty
> years ago there was unhesitating submission to
> an order of government, there is now an appeal to
> the courts or to a dangerous agitation.[71]

Hostility to progress, Maine concluded, had
restricted the creation of a free, contractual, self-
governing society to the three presidency towns.   He
warned Liberals that "beyond the fringe of British civilization on the coast, the social state there to be observed
can only be called Barbarism....   This is the real India".[72]

---

[71]Maine, Observation, pp. 15-16.

[72]Ward, op. cit., p. 518.

CHAPTER EIGHT

INDIAN FITNESS FOR SELF-RULE AND
THE ORGANIZATION OF GOVERNMENT :

MERGING THEMES

1870 - 1882

Between 1870 and 1882 the controversy over Indian self-rule was revived by the debate on decentralization. But it need not have been. Self-rule had no essential part in a discussion of administrative and financial devolution. It was, however, made part by several senior officials in the Government of India and by those in the Indian Civil Service who believed that self-governing Indians were the best people to control local finances and administration -- a task they regarded as being increasingly beyond the resources of British officials. This was the conclusion of a minority in the Indian Civil Service. But it was an influential minority which commanded the prestigious East India Association as its public forum; and it was backed by a well-organized body of educated Indians who edited the vernacular press. By 1882, when Lord Ripon drafted his Resolution on Local Self-Government, it had grown from a small nucleus inside the Indian Civil Service to a sizeable body of opinion.

It was a slow growth to influence. In the decade

after the Mutiny, believers in decentralizing government to
self-ruling Indians were lone voices in the wilderness.
Samuel Laing, the architect of decentralization, was also
the most notable proponent of local self-government.
Recognizing that presidency and provincial officals could
not control the collection and distribution of local taxes
in the thousands of mofussil towns and villages in British
India, he advocated the creation of "municipal institutions"
relying on the Indians' "self-help and self-guidance" to
manage them. In 1862 he astonished the imperial Legislative
Council by describing his "vision" of a self-ruling Empire,
"where ... the native population are gradually trained in
the management of their own affairs for those of a wider
area; so that India may have what it has never yet had --
a political life, and at length be, what it has never yet
been -- a nation"[1]. Few in Laing's audience shared his conviction that local self-government could be allied with decentralization to such advantage. The majority, like Temple,
had never been entranced by dreams of a self-governing
dominion; and many of those who had been captivated by such
fantacies in the 1840's and 50's had foresaken them during
the Mutiny.

------

[1]Laing, Budget Speech, 27 April 1861, Proceedings of
the Legislative Council of India, Jan. - Nov., 1861,
vol. VII, p. 358.

Laing's "vision" of Indian self-rule did, however,
appeal to the most prominent members of the Punjab civil
service. With Campbell they were impressed by the unique
vitality of the province's self-governing village communities
and were convinced of the Indians' capacity to manage municipal government independently of British control. In 1861
the Divisional Commissioners urged that committees be
erected in district headquarter towns to administer the
collection and expenditure of local /¯municipal_7 taxes.
The Commissioners of Amritsar and the Cis-Sutlej recommended
that the government nominate a few officials to sit on these
committees and that the rate-payers elect the rest.[2] But
even this bold step towards local self-government seemed too
tentative to the Commissioner of Peshawar, who urged that all
delegates be chosen by popular election. The government's
decision that one-half of the members of each committee be
elected and the other half be nominated was greeted enthusiastically by the Commissioner of Jullunder, who commented
that he saw "no reason for denying to the natives of India
that which we so fondly cherish for ourselves. I disbelieve
altogether in the theory that foreign administrators know the
wants of the people better than they do themselves".[3] The

---

[2] Amar Nath, The Development of Local Self-Government
in the Punjab 1849-1900, Lahore, 1930, p. 16.

[3] Ibid.

Punjab experiment of the 1860's proved so successful that
the Lieutenant-Governor, Sir Robert Montgomery, lauded this
"policy which, mindful of our position, and of the paucity
and costliness of our agency, seeks to devolve on the people
as much of the business of administration as can safely and
prudently be confined to them".[4]

Trevelyan and Frere -- the two most prominent spokes-
men for bringing government as close to the people as
possible after the Mutiny -- shared Montgomery's admiration
for village self-rule and pressed for the extension of
decentralization from the local governments to the towns and
villages. In 1864 Trevelyan rhapsodized in Orientalist
strains on the glories of the "village republic" and urged
the ICS to entrust the municipal committees created in that
year with real power and responsibility:

> The people of this country are perfectly capable
> of administering their own local affairs. The
> municipal feeling is deeply rooted in them.
> The village communities, each of which is a
> little republic, are the most abiding of
> Indian institutions. They maintained the
> framework of society while successive invaders
> swept over the country. In the cities, also,
> the people cluster in their wards, trade guilds
> and panchayets, and show much capacity for
> corporate action.[5]

---

[4]Montgomery, Minute of 7 June 1865, Home Department
General Proceedings, 1865, no. 437.

[5]Gazette of India Extraordinary, 14 September 1864,
Resolution of the Government of India in Finance Department,
31 August 1864, no. 2245.

Nine years later he proclaimed that "representation must be commensurate with taxation" and proposed that a federal system of government be instituted at once[6]: building up from the municipal fund committees, half a dozen zillah committees (composed of local worthies, elected by the rate-payers and/or nominated by the government) would be set up in each presidency and province; and a "quasi-representative" council (one-third of its members nominated by government and two-thirds by the zillah committees) would be attached to each local government.[7] Frere put forward a similar plan in 1871. But as usual his presentation was marred by ambiguous terms: the village panchayets would elect delegates to district councils; these councils would in turn select representatives to "provincial councils" (defined not according to geography but according to linguistic groups -- i.e. one for the Sindhis, one for the Gujeratis, one for the Marathas, etc.); these would elect men to sit on local legislative assemblies in the presidency and provincial capitals.[8] Trevelyan predicted that such a union of

---

[6] Trevelyan, evidence submitted to the Select Committee on Indian Finance, 28 February 1873, Parliamentary Papers (House of Commons), 1873, vol. 12.

[7] Trevelyan, evidence of 4 March 1873, Ibid.

[8] Frere, "Public Opinion in India", East India Association Journal, 1871, vol. V, p. 167 (Speech of 19 July 1871).

decentralization and Indian self-rule would create "a school
of self-government for the whole of India, the longest step
yet taken towards teaching its two million people to govern
themselves".[9]

Throughout the 1870's the majority of British administrators in India opposed Trevelyan's and Frere's plans for
the union of decentralization with local self-government.
They clung to the traditional belief that civilization should
precede self-rule and insisted that because the reformation
of Indian society would take many years to complete, the
grant of local self-government should be postponed indefinitely.
Maine, it will be remembered, predicted that Indian society
would not pass from "status" to "contract" for at least a
century. The Commissioner of Orissa -- to name but one
prominent local official -- was even less sanguine: "We
cannot as yet expect natives of India in the mass to exhibit
the feelings and intelligence of European nations", he
hautily announced in 1872. "Did they possess European
instincts, there would be no difficulty, but they do not, and
cannot for centuries to come be completely molded to
European institutions...."[10]

---

[9]Trevelyan, evidence of 28 February 1873, Parliamentary
Papers (House of Commons), 1873, vol. 12.

[10]Mr. Pritchard, Speech of 9 June 1871, East India
Association Journal, 1871, vol. V, p. 136.

In equally strident tones Sir Mordaunt Wells, the notorious
Calcutta judge, urged the imperial authorities to resist
demands to introduce representative institutions until the
people attained a far higher "intellectual and moral culture".[11]
Temple joined the disapproving chorus: in his opinion the
Indians of the 1870's were no more fit to run town councils
than Rugby schoolboys. Almost to a man the many opponents
of local self-government chose one word -- "premature" -- to
assess its prospects when the Government of India queried the
feasibility of expanding the scope of decentralization to
towns and villages in 1871, 1877 and 1881.[12]

The supporters of local self-government launched a
three-pronged attack on this negative judgment. First, they
straightforwardly opposed it. They claimed that a century
of British rule had, without question, prepared the Indians
for municipal self-rule. For example, the Commissioner of
Patna observed that under British tutelage the Indian had
been transformed from "a submissive and unquestioning child"
who was incapable of governing himself, to an educated and
self-assertive adolescent who was ready to assume some of
the responsibilities of representative government.

---

[11]Sir Mordaunt Wells, Speech of 19 June 1871, East
India Association Journal, 1871, vol. V, p. 149.

[12]See Financial Proceedings, Accounts, January 1871
and January 1877; Parliamentary Papers (House of Commens)
1883, vol. 51, part II.

> The relationship between England and India ...
> has been very much like that between a kind but
> rather rough and careless parent, and an unruly,
> sharp, but somewhat ricketty boy. The father
> cuffs the boy on the head, gives him orders,
> stuffs him with whatever he thinks wholesome,
> whether suited to his constitution or not,
> and carries out a rough paternal despotism,
> without dreaming of opposition or cavil; but
> the boy somehow or other, picks up scraps of
> information, and all of a sudden the father finds
> that the lubberly and obedient boy has grown
> into an educated, thinking young man. That
> passive submission to the father's will which
> led the boy to obey the father's orders
> without questioning has passed away; the boy
> has learned to think, and with thought he has
> learned to criticise his father's actions and
> scrutinise his commands. That is the position
> now of India.[13]

In the same vein the Commissioner of the Punjab contended that

the Indians should no longer be treated "like children or

imbeciles": they had been liberally educated, taught their

rights and encouraged to think for themselves; under the

circumstances, their request to play a limited role in

government could neither reasonably nor honorably be denied.[14]

Those educated Indians who clamored for a voice in local

government in the 1870's condemned the majority of the ICS

for refusing to admit that Indian society had been markedly

regenerated in the past half century by the British, and

for dismissing all Indians -- regardless of education,

sophistication and westernization -- as childlike, morally

feeble and even barbarous. Further, they accused them of

mindlessley repeating the opinions held by James Mill and

---

[13]William Taylor, Speech of 9 June 1871, East India
Association Journal, 1871, vol. V, p. 119.

[14]Sir Donald McLeod, Memorandum of 1861, Nath. op. cit.,
Appendix I.

Macaulay in 1833 as if they were still valid. W.C. Bonerjea, an attorney of the Calcutta High Court, suggested that the ICS would do better to quote J.S. Mill, whose Considerations of Representative Government advanced three criteria which to his mind demonstrated the Indians' preparation for self-government. These were a willingness and ability to adopt representative institutions, to fulfill the duties and discharge the functions which they imposed, and to do whatever was necessary for their preservation.[15] Pherozeshah Mehta, a distinguished Parsee barrister of Bombay, pointed out that no one was demanding "full-blown representation"; educated Indians were simply asking for "the slow introduction of the representative principle". In his opinion even James Mill and Macaulay would have condoned cautious experiments in the presidency towns and major settlements of the mofussil in the 1870's.[16]

Next, supporters of local self-government countered the charge that the introduction of representative institutions was "premature" by re-examining the relationship between civilization and self-rule and modifying it in two important ways. They began by challenging the notion that

[15]W.C. Bonerjea, "Representation and Responsible Government for India", East India Association Journal, 1867 vol. I, p. 197, (Speech of 25 July 1867).

[16]Pherozeshah Mehta, "Bombay Municipal Reform", Speech of 29 November 1871, C.Y. Chintamani,ed., Speeches and Writings of The Hon. Sir Pherozeshah Mehta, Allahabad, 1905, p.99.

self-rule should be reserved for the civilized. They conceived that the Utilitarian concept of enlightened self-interest, Maine's definition of contract, and the ICS standards of education and morality as articulated by Temple to be too abstract to be of any practical value and too lofty to be attained by most of mankind. This conviction led them to abandon the traditional criteria of civilization and to embrace the convenient radical belief that all nations -- regardless of their positions on Mill's ladder of civilizations -- were equally capable of managing representative government. "Let us not be frightened by that bugbear incapacity", advised Chisholm Anstey, a Bombay High Court Judge:

> there is no nation unfit for free institutions. If you wait for absolute perfection the world will come to an end before you have established your free institutions -- but you must take the world as it is, and there is no nation so ignorant but knows its wants, or some of its more pressing wants; there is no nation so poor, but it has some proprietary or possessory interests for the perfection of which it is solicitous; and there is no nation which is not entitled, therefore, with a view to its own interests and its own wants, or to what it conceives to be its wants and interests, to be heard in its own defence.[17]

W.C. Bonerjea expressed the educated Indians' contempt for the notion that particular forms of government were suited to particular societies at different stages in their historical development: "the doctrine that all nations are

---

[17] Chisholm Anstey, Speech of 19 July 1871, East India Association Journal, 1871, vol. V, p. 183.

not made for representative government may be disregarded.
I never yet knew a nation made for one thing in particular".
Sadly, he predicted, if the introduction of representative
government were "left to the determination of those who are
resolved not to give it to her, our people will never be
ripe enough".[18]

To replace civilization as a guide to the introduction
of representative government, the supporters of municipal
self-rule substituted that of historical precedent. This
was a criterion first used by Campbell in the 1850's, and
its adoption by the Britons and Indians who publically
campaigned for local self-government in the 1870's was a
decisive turning point in the debate on how to govern India.
It enabled them to ignore the Indians' disqualification for
self-rule on the basis of abstract norms of economic,
social and cultural achievement, and to assert their qualification on empirical evidence. The Indians, they boasted,
had successfully conducted town and village government for
centuries: the "municipal spirit" had infused the village
community; the panchayet had embodied the "germ" of representative government; and "the instincts of self-government" had
thrived "in every community in India".[19] To buttress these

---

[18]Bonerjea, op. cit., p. 169.

[19]Dadabhai Naoroji, Speech of 25 July 1867, East
India Association Journal, 1867, vol. I, p. 186; Bonerjea,
op. cit., p. 172.

assertions they combed the works of Munroe, Metcalfe, and Elphinstone in search of passages extolling the village community; they discovered emotive phrases like "village republic" and "indestructable atom", and repeated them reverently and often.[20] No one captured the Orientalist imagery or sense of awe at ancient institutions more success-fully than Sir Charles Trevelyan, whose ode to the village community delivered to the Fawcett Committee on Indian Finance in London in 1873 quickly passed into the corpus of quotable scripture:

> The foundation of Indian society is the village
> municipality, that has been the salvation of
> India. One foreign conqueror after another
> has swept over India but the village
> municipalities have stuck to the soil like
> their own kusa grass, which they liken it to;
> it is a kind of grass which it is impossible
> to tear up by the roots, because it grows in
> bunches, and they say the village constitution is
> like that grass. They have been nursed in it, it
> is perfectly familiar to them, and even in large
> towns, for instance Delhi, although there is no
> official municipality, yet the people acted in the
> municipal spirit.[21]

The advocates of local self-government also cited Maine extensively and elevated him to the pantheon of prophets supporting Indian self-rule -- an altogether curious phenomenon. Nothing could have been clearer to the reader of _Ancient Law_ or _Village Communities East and West_ than

---

[20] J.M. Ludlow, Speech of 19 July 1871, _East India Association Journal_, 1871, vol. V, p. 165; Dr. Leitner, "Native Self-Government in Matters of Education", Speech of 27 January 1875, _Ibid._, vol. IX, p. 4; Bonerjea, _op. cit._, p. 171.

[21] Trevelyan, evidence of 28 February 1873, Parliamentary Papers (House of Commons) 1873, vol. 12.

Maine's unbridled contempt for the village community as a
primitive institution whose destruction was essential to
India's progress from status to contract and thus to civilization;   but the supporters of local self-government shamelessly ignored his conclusions and seized his evidence of
resemblances between the Indian village and the medieval
German township as conclusive proof of Indian expertise in
operating representative institutions. The first and most
illustrious person to quote Maine's words out of context was
Sir Bartle Frere, who informed the East India Association in
London three months after the publication of Village
Communities East and West that the former Law Member and
eminent legal historian regarded the Indian "genius" as "one
of representation",

> --not ... representation by election under
> Reform Acts, but representation generally
> by castes, and trades, and professions,
> every class of that community being represented;
> and that where there is any difficulty, anything
> to be laid before the Government, anything to
> be discussed among themselves -- a fellow-
> citizen to be punished, or a fellow-citizen to
> be rewarded -- there is always a public
> meeting of the caste, the village, or the
> district;   and this is an expression, it seems
> to me, of the genius of the people as unmistakable
> as that which is arrived at by our Saxon method
> of gathering together in assemblies of different
> kinds to vote by tribes, or by hundreds, or by
> shires.[22]

Frere merely embellished Maine's assertion of the Aryan potential for self-rule. But Chisholm Anstey, in his anxiety to

---

[22]Frere, "Public Opinion in India", East India
Association Journal, 1871, vol. V, p. 115.

prove India's impressive and lengthy record of municipal
government, utterly mangled Maine's thought by losing sight
of the crucial distinction between progressive Aryan societies
and stationary non-Aryan ones. "We are apt to forget", he
observed, "that the East is the parent of municipalities.

> Local self-government, in the widest accep-
> tance of the term, is as old as the East itself.
> No matter what may be the religion of the
> people who inhabit what we call the East, there
> is no portion of that country, there is not a
> portion of Asia, from west to east, from north
> to south, which is not swarming with municipalities;
> and not only so but like unto our municipalities
> of old, they are all bound together as in a
> species of work, so that you have ready made to
> your hands the framework of a great system of
> representation.[23]

Thus did the supporters of local self-government distort
Maine's ideas to demonstrate that the Indians -- despite
their uncivilized state -- had governed themselves remarkably
well for centuries.

To strengthen their case the supporters of local self-
government amended the relationship between civilization and
self-rule in another important way. This second redefinition
was totally inconsistent with the first, but it was nevertheless advanced simultaneously; for its exponents were
empassioned men, whose enthusiasm for what they regarded as
a just cause frequently obscured their logic. Reversing the
accepted chronological sequence of civilization and self-rule,
they argued that if self-rule preceded civilization, it
would promote rather than impede India's progress up the

---

[23] Quoted by Mehta, op. cit., p. 101.

ladder of civilization. This was a startling proposition,
one which flatly contradicted the familiar hypotheses of the
Utilitarians, Maine and Temple. It was reached by reinterpreting the concept of political education. In the 1830's
Macaulay and Trevelyan had used this term to refer to the
Indians' preparation for full independence from Britain
through the institution of self-government in towns and
provinces, and ultimately in the imperial capital itself.
Since the Mutiny Temple and most of the ICS had used it in a
far more limited sense to mean instruction in administration
and finance through employment in the civil service. In 1861
Sir Donald McLeod of the Punjab resurrected the older usage
when he defined political education as "allowing $\sqrt{\ }$the Indians$\sqrt{\ }$
a share in the management of their own affairs".[24] Having
enlarged the classroom from the bureaucracy to town councils,
and having expanded the student-body from the Western-educated
elite to the great mass of rate-payers, he contended that
political education of this broader sort offered what no other
type of education could. It "infused its pupils" with "self-
respect and a spirit of progress" and inspired them to
improve their manners, morals and minds in order to earn a
voice in local politics. It thereby promoted manliness,
honesty and courage -- the essential attributes of civilized
people. "England has attained to a foremost place in the
scale of nations", he stated, "owing to the republican spirit
of its institutions, which gives a large portion of the

---

[24]Sir Donald McLeod, quoted by Dr. Leitner, op. cit.,
p. 2.

community a voice in the administration of the affairs of the body politic, and thus induces, on the part of all those who are well disposed, a desire to show themselves worthy of consideration". India, he concluded, could follow Britain's illustrious example by adopting local self-government.[25]

Finally, the supporters of local self-government contended that whatever the relationship between civilization and self-rule, the Government of India should link municipal self-rule to decentralization because it was expedient. They cited the recent passage of the second Reform Act in Britain as a classic -- if embarrassing -- example of enfranchising people who were neither civilized nor prepared for representative government according to traditional standards, but who had nevertheless been given the vote because it was politically opportune. Anstey stated that the British lower middle classes "are not fit for it if philosophers are to judge, if school-masters are to judge, and if men of religion are to judge; but we do not go upon that foundation here ...."[26] Bonerjea observed that no one could reasonably claim "that when Disraeli first proposed to bring in a Reform Bill this session the nation was prepared for household suffrage, 'pure and simple'; and yet a bill for household suffrage

---

[25]Ibid.

[26]Chisholm Anstey, op. cit., p. 184.

has passed ...."[27]

Advocates of municipal self-rule defended its
expediency on two grounds. First, they declared that the
indefinite continuation of absolute despotic government
risked a second Mutiny because it afforded the Indians no
means of expressing opposition to imperial policy except
armed rebellion. Frere argued that representative government, alone, provided the Indians with a constitutional
framework for voicing grievances peaceably.[28] Pherozeshah
Mehta developed this theme by labelling representative
institutions a "safety valve for the peaceful emission of
popular irritation, discontent, and disaffection" and by
asserting that "the instincts and habits induced by the
experience of local self-government always assist in preventing the violent and revolutionary overthrow of the states
in which it has been practised and fostered and favour
gradual and well-considered and constitutional changes".[29]
W.C. Bonerjea conjectured that besides minimizing the threat
of internal violence, representative government would
diminish the possibility of foreign conquest; for should
Russian troops descend from the Khyber Pass onto the plains

---

[27]Bonerjea, op. cit., p. 170.

[28]Frere began arguing this point as early as 1860.
See Martineau, op. cit., vol.I, p. 335 (Minute of March 1860).

[29]Mehta, op. cit., p. 103.

of North India -- as many feared they might throughout the
latter half of the 19th century -- the Indians would display
greater allegiance to a government in which they participated
than one from which they were excluded.[30]

Secondly, they explained its expediency in terms of
its potential for solving a seemingly intractible administrative problem. This was the destruction of the traditional
system of collecting information from the mofussil after the
Mutiny and the failure of the ICS to devise a viable
alternative. It was a common complaint in the 1860's that
the policy of "centralisation by department" (to use Frere's
term) had transformed the district magistrate from a ruler-
on-horseback, who spent a large part of the year touring the
countryside, settling the villagers' disputes and discovering
their needs, into a bureaucrat who was enshrouded in paperwork, tied to his desk, and available only to the comparatively
few Indians who were capable of filling out the appropriate
forms and presenting them at district headquarters. Wistfully,
one old Punjab official described the demise of the old-
fashioned Burra Sahib. "Things have completely changed", he
lamented.

> In the first place, we all know that in the
> old times it was a very common thing for the
> officer in charge of a district to be a sort
> of patriarch who patted the people on the

---

[30]Bonerjea, op. cit., p. 176.

> back, went through their little villages,
> heard their tales of sorrow or wrong, and
> helped them where he could. But those happy
> days -- and those of us who know what they
> were will agree with me in calling them happy
> days -- are, I am sorry to say, now rapidly
> passing away.... Officials now have no time
> to enter into the feelings of the people, and
> inquire into their prejudices. They are not
> allowed to go out of the established beaten
> road. They cannot go about as they used to
> do; and they are tied to a mass of routine
> desk work; so that it is impossible to get
> at the feeling of the natives in the same
> way as it used to be accomplished.[31]

Believers in municipal self-rule recommended that if the
district officer could no longer enjoy direct access to the
rural population, he should elicit their opinions through
their representatives on local councils.[32] They regarded
the erection of new channels of communication between the
panchayet and the kutcherry as a primary asset of the
various decentralization schemes discussed in the 1860's, as
well as Mayo's plan of 1870. The Indian members of the
district and municipal fund committees would, they calculated,
offer the foreign bureaucracy useful advice and enable it to
govern more knowledgeably and thus more efficiently.

The opponents of local self-government were swift to
refute all of the supporters' arguments in favor of uniting
decentralization and municipal self-rule. They took particular pleasure in pointing out the folly of scrapping the

----

[31]William Forsyth, Speech of 9 June 1871, East India
Association Journal, 1871, vol. V, p. 129.

[32]Sir George Campbell, Speech of 18 March 1871,
Proceedings of the Legislative Council of India, Jan.-Nov. 1871.

assumption that civilization must precede self-rule. They
contended that one attribute of civilization -- if no other
-- was essential to the success of representative government
in India (or anywhere else). This was independent political
thought. And this, they alleged, the Indians had never
displayed. One noted Anglo-Indian pointed out

> that they require a long course of political
> training to educate them up to that standard
> of independence of thought that will induce
> them to believe that they can express their
> opinions freely upon public questions with
> impunity. I am sorry to say that I cannot
> think our present system of administration
> is calculated, as a general rule, to impart
> that education of which I speak.[33]

Observing that "a native heading a council would be ten times
more impatient of free expression of opinion than any English
official", he concluded that representative institutions
should not be introduced in India before this minimum
qualification for civilization -- and thus self-rule -- had
been achieved.[34] Next, the opponents attacked the proposition that the Indians were capable of running independent
municipal committees in the 1870's because they had managed
self-ruling village communities for centuries past. Remind-
ing the Government of India that good village government had
been destroyed by oppressive headmen, they predicted that the
new town councils would be destroyed in a similar fashion by
the urban elites: anglicized Indians would dominate council

---

[33]Pritchard, op. cit., p. 136.

[34]Ibid.

proceedings, exploit the rate-payers and re-enact the tyranny of the patils on a grand scale.[35] Finally, they condemned the supporters' rationale for the expediency of local self-government as being not only wrong, but dangerous. They contended that it was built on a misunderstanding of the nature of imperialism -- on a belief that the Raj rested ultimately on consent, when in fact it rested on force; on the false expectation that representative bodies could be soldered onto the base of the despotic Government of India without threatening the military security which sustained British rule. Their thoughts were most cogently and memorably articulated by Sir James Fitzjames Stephen at the end of the period under discussion:

> The Government of India is essentially an
> absolute government, founded, not on consent,
> but on conquest. It does not represent the
> native principles of life or of government, and
> it can never do so until it represents heathenism
> and barbarism. It represents a belligerent
> civilization, and no anomaly can be more striking
> or so dangerous, as its administration by men,
> who being at the head of a Government founded
> upon conquest, implying at every point the
> superiority of the conquering race, of their
> ideas, their institutions, their opinions and
> their principles, and having no justification
> for its existence except that superiority,
> shrink from the open, uncompromising straight-
> forward assertion of it, seek to apologise for
> their own position, and refuse, from whatever
> cause, to uphold and support it....[36]

Equally fatuous to their reckoning was the idea that Indian

---

[35]Wells, op. cit., p. 148.

[36]Sir James Fitzjames Stephen, letter to The Times, 1 March 1883.

participation in local administration would enhance bureaucratic efficiency. They compared the ICS to an elite
military corps and reasoned that just as civilians were ill-
equipped to join in army maneuvres, Indian councillors were
unfit to assist professional civil servants in managing local
government. Lacking administrative expertise and a commitment to moral and material progress, they would impede the
reformation of traditional society and thereby defeat the
ostensible goal of the British in India.[37] The majority of
the ICS concluded that there were no advantages whatsoever
to the alliance of local self-government with decentralization
and no compelling reason to renounce the principle that self-
rule should be withheld indefinitely from the uncivilized.

In rebuttal the supporters of local self-government
dismissed the prediction that the Westernized elite would
behave like arrogant, extortionate patils as bigoted nonsense.
They did not, however, deny that years of despotic government
in India had stiffled public opinion, sapped the people's
will to criticize their rulers, and prevented them from
taking independent political stances. One enthusiast forthrightly admitted that the "spirit of submission and subser-
vency ... almost of toadyism" bred of despotism made it
difficult for the British to elicit "any honest and independent opinion" from the Indians who had been appointed to sit

---

[37]Cunningham to Temple, 7 May 1879, I.O.L. Eur. Mss.
F 86-188A.

on the district and municipal committees set up after 1870.[38]
Other supporters were no less concerned that the obsequiousness
of the educated Indians and the humility of the illiterate
impeded an open discussion of local issues with government
officials. They advocated a daring solution to help the
Indians overcome the mentality of a conquered and dependent
people: they urged the imperial goverment to force Indian
councillors to "learn to swim" by leaving them alone to make
decisions for themselves and by letting them "sink" in a mire
of mistakes -- if need be -- so that they might learn to keep
politically afloat.[39] They dismissed as preposterous the
assumption that people who had rarely been near the water
would never learn to swim. And they roundly condemned the
popular belief that the ultimate advantages of such an
experiement in political education were not worth the
immediate risks.[40]

　　　Throughout the 1870's the supporters of local self-
government agreed that political education should be encouraged by substituting municipal elections for government
nomination as the method of selecting Indian delegates to
municipal and district committees and by replacing district

---

[38]Taylor, op. cit., p. 121.

[39]Naroroji, op. cit., p. 186.

[40]Trevelyan, evidence of 28 February 1873,
Parliamentary Papers (House of Commons), 1873, vol. 12.

officers with non-official chairmen as leaders of the committees.
But neither of these suggestions was heeded outside the presidency towns; for the ICS district officers -- whom the local
governments had empowered to decide if and when elections and
non-official chairmen should be introduced -- remained
implaccably opposed. Their refusal to implement reform
voluntarily provoked those who believed in the necessity of
linking municipal self-rule to decentralization to implore the
local and imperial governments to impose change by fiat.

Significantly, the leadership of the campaign for
municipal reform passed in the mid-1870's from senior British
civil servants -- airing their views through official channels
and the East India Association -- to educated Indians --
pressing their case in the vernacular press. In belligerent
tones the Indians condemned the existing system of representative local government as a "sham"[41], a "charade"[42] and "a
mockery of self-government"[43]. Many committee presidents,
they claimed, obstructed political education by discouraging
Indian representatives from expressing their views on
municipal affairs and by formulating policy without consulting

---

[41] Som Prakash, 28 June 1875, Bengal Native Newspaper
Report, 1874-1875.

[42] Ibid.

[43] Sahachar, 7 June 1875, Ibid.

them[44]: some failed to circulate agenda prior to meetings,[45]
while others refused to allow rate-payers to attend meetings,[46]
neglected to publish minutes of the proceedings,[47] introduced
new taxes despite the unanimous opposition of Indian
delegates,[48] and spent a greater proportion of municipal
funds on European residential areas than on Indian ones[49]; a
few -- they alleged -- actually dismissed Indian representatives
who dared to criticize them.[50] Members of the vernacular
press were equally vociferous in denouncing the committee
presidents for selecting Indian delegates whom they regarded
as unqualified to serve as popular representatives. They
accused the British of appointing rich landowners who were

---

[44]Shivaji, 8 March 1878, Bombay Native Newspaper
Report, 1878; Sadharani, 18 April 1875, Bengal Native Newspaper Report, 1874-1875.

[45]Hitechchhu, 10 January 1878, Bombay Native Newspaper
Report, 1878.

[46]Dnyan Prakash, 19 July 1881, Bombay Native Newspaper Report, 1881.

[47]Vivekanvardhani, October 1879, Madras Native Newspaper Report; Behar Bandhu, 2 February 1876, Bengal Native
Newspaper Report, 1876.

[48]Dnyan Prakash, 19 July 1881, Bombay Native Newspaper Report, 1881.

[49]Subabha Samachara, 15 June 1878, Bengal Native
Newspaper Report; Kalpatani, 4 July 1880, Bombay Native
Newspaper Report.

[50]Hindu Hitoishini, 20 May 1876, Bengal Native Newspaper Report, 1876.

ignorant of the peoples' needs, unwilling to oppose government officials, and unable to speak English with sufficient
fluency to participate in committee debates; they condemned
them for disregarding those educated and public-spirited
members of the Westernized middle classes who repeatedly
expressed a desire to sit on the committees.[51] When rate-
payers associations and pressure groups began to petition for
the introduction of municipal elections at the end of the
decade, the press was swift to publish their demands and
chronicle the growing strength of popular support for real
representative government. The Bombay papers, for example,
were assiduous in recording the repeated attempts of the
Poona Sarvajanik Sabha to persuade Sir Philip Wodehouse,
Governor from 1874 to 1876 and Sir Richard Temple, Governor
from 1877 to 1880,to grant the franchise to Poona, Ahmedabad,
and the other large towns in the Bombay mofussil; and they
were outspoken in condemning the government for declining all
of their petitions on the grounds of the peoples' lack of
preparation for representative government.[52] In 1876 one

[51]Suthashab Nimani, November 1877, Madras Native Newspaper Report, 1877-1887; Samsher Bahadur, 6 October 1876,
Bombay Native Newspaper Report, 1876; Amrita Bazar Patrika,
7 January 1875, Bengal Native Newspaper Report, 1875.

[52]Shivaji, 8 March 1878, Bombay Native Newspaper
Report, 1878; 11 June 1881, Bombay Native Newspaper Report,
1881; Dnyan Prakash, 31 October 1876, Bombay Native Newspaper Report, 1876; 26 November 1877, Bombay Native Newspaper Report, 1877; Poona Waibhaw, 22 June 1881, Bombay
Native Newspaper Report, 1881.

Bengali newspaper editor became so infuriated by the
Lieutenant-Governor's refusal to extend the franchise to
rate-payers and to order the appointment of non-official
committee chairmen that he issued a bold ultimatum to the
presidency government: admit that the Indians are ready,
willing and able to rule their own municipalities; or face
a boycott of committee proceedings by all Indian delegates.[53]
His courage in risking official censure was exceptional.
But his impatience with British officialdom was shared by
a significant minority of the ICS and an impressive body of
educated Indians. By 1880, when Lord Ripon became the
Viceroy, their campaign for the union of local self-
government and decentralization could no longer be ignored.

[53]Hindu Hitoishini, 23 September 1876, Bengal Native
Newspaper Report, 1876.

EPILOGUE

LORD RIPON'S RESOLUTION ON
LOCAL SELF-GOVERNMENT :

MAY 1882

In 1882 Lord Ripon attempted to answer the century-
old question of how India should be governed with his famous
Resolution on Local Self-Government.[1] This document met the
demands of the previous decade's reformers by replacing
British officials with non-official Indians as municipal
committee chairmen and by enfranchising the ratepayers to
elect a majority of the committee representatives. Further,
it extended decentralization by devolving three-fifths of
the revenue and one quarter of the expenditure of the imperial
government to the local governments, and by requiring the
presidencies and provinces to transfer as many taxes and
services as possible to district and municipal committees.
Through these momentous innovations the Viceroy instituted a
system of popular municipal government whose magnitude and
vitality were unprecedented in the history of India.

Ripon linked local self-government with decentralization
because he accepted the argument -- first posed by Laing in

---

[1]Resolution of 18 May 1882, Finance Department
Proceedings, June 1882, Accounts no. 616.

1861 and repeated by the supporters of local self-government throughout the 1860's and 70's -- that a small British bureaucracy possessed neither the men nor the money to promote the moral and material progress of this huge, sprawling and remarkably diverse Asian population.[2] Having served briefly at the India Office in London in the 1860's, he knew from personal experience how much the scope of government activity had expanded since the Mutiny and how little actual control the overworked ICS could exert over these increasingly ambitious and rapidly proliferating programs. In his opinion the alliance of decentralization and local self-government offered much-needed relief "from the ever increasing mass of details by which $/$ local officials_$/$ are becoming more and more overwhelmed" by devolving responsibilities -- petty in themselves but cumbrous in total -- to municipal committees.[3] The Resolution's key provision was that district officers review the decisions taken by the elected committees and give advice when requested, but not attend committee meetings unless invited.[4] Its aim (in Ripon's words) was to transform the district officer from "'a Burra Sahib', which may be freely translated 'big swell'", who directed all activities

---

[2]Ibid., para. 5.

[3]Ripon to Hughes, 12 June 1882, Correspondence in England, vol. III, no. 86.

[4]Resolution of 18 May, para. 17.

and stiffled all Indian initiative in his zeal to transact
business quickly and efficiently, into a sympathetic and
patient advisor, remaining outside the boardroom, "urging
/ the committee_7 forward if it is supine, checking it if it
goes wrong, and generally supervising its proceedings from
the independent position of one who has no part in them".[5]

Ripon hoped that besides freeing the ICS from niggling
worries, the withdrawal of British officials from the
committee chambers would facilitate the political education
of the Indian peoples.[6] He believed that it would "induce
the people themselves to undertake, as far as may be possible,
the management of their own affairs" and thereby plunge them
into the deep end with a life-guard nearby but without a
life preserver, as supporters of local self-government so
often put it in the 1870's. "No substantial advance will be
made in training the natives to take a larger share in the
management of their own local affairs", he remarked on
several occasions, "so long as they are compelled to conduct
their business, not only under the supervision and control
(of that I approve), but in the actual presence of the chief
executive officer of the District".[7] According to his

---

[5]Ripon to Hughes, 12 June 1882, Correspondence in
England, vol. III, no. 86.

[6]Resolution of 18 May 1882, para. 5.

[7]Ripon to Forster, 19 May 1883, Correspondence in
England, vol, IV, no. 60.

calculations, Mayo's admirable attempt to encourage local
self-government had been foiled by those members of the ICS
who "deprived /⁻the committees_7 of any shadow of independence and made them mere machines for registering official
orders"[8]; who rendered the committees "shams"[9] of popular
government, "where selected natives say ditto to the proposals
of the executive officers".[10]

Ripon justified his decision to institute local self-
government not on the Indians' attainment of civilization and
their resulting qualification for self-rule on economic,
social or moral grounds, or, indeed, on the basis of
historical precedent -- on these he was remarkably silent --
but on naked expediency. He accepted the argument, often
repeated by the policy's supporters during the 1870's, that
sufficient numbers of rate-payers were suited by self-interest,
if not by education as well, to run their own local affairs,
and that these public-spirited people would become enemies of
British rule if the imperial government continued to deny
them this privilege. Writing to Gladstone in 1881, he
explained in a lengthy and important letter why the introduction of representative government was opportune:

---

[8]Ripon to Gladstone, 6 October 1882, Ibid., vol. III
no. 118.

[9]Ibid.

[10]Ripon to Hughes, 12 June 1882, Ibid., vol. III,
no. 86.

... we have entered upon a period of change in
India; the spread of education, the substitution
of legal for discretionary administration, the
progress of railway, telegraphs, etc., are now
beginning to produce a marked effect upon the
people; new ideas are springing up; new
aspirations are being called out; and a process
has begun which will go on with increasing
rapidity and force from year to year. Such a
condition of affairs is one in which the task
of government, and especially of practically
despotic government, is beset with difficulties
of no light kind: to move too fast is dangerous,
but to lag behind is more dangerous still; and
the problem is how to deal with this new-born
spirit of progress, raw and superficial as in many
respects it is, so as to direct it into a right
course, and to derive from it all the benefits
which its development is capable of ultimately
conferring upon the country, and at the same time
to prevent it from becoming, through blind
indifference or stupid repression, a source of
serious political danger. It is considerations
such as these which lead me to attach much
importance to measures which, though small in
themselves, are calculated to provide a
legitimate outlet for the ambitions and
aspirations which we have ourselves created by
the education, civilization, and material
progress, which we have been the means of
introducing into the country; such measures
will not only have an immediate effect in
promoting gradually and safely the political
education of the people, which I hold to be a
great object of public policy, but will also
pave the way for further advances in the same
direction as that education becomes fuller and
more widespread.[11]

In describing "the men whom our education is raising up in

India in yearly increasing numbers... who ... unless we

gradually provide /¯them_7 with outlets for their political

aspirations, ... will become most naturally our bitter and

---

[11]Ripon to Gladstone, 6 October 1882, Ibid., vol.
III, no. 118.

very dangerous opponents"[12], Ripon singled out the English-educated city dwelling elite, the 25,000 Bachelors of Art, to whom even Maine and Temple were prepared to concede the vote and a place on municipal committees. He failed to consider the other 99% of the population, the illiterate ryots of the mofussil, whose inbred resistance to change had preserved the village community for centuries, whose stubborn conservatism was no less an obstacle to the reformation of Indian society in the 19th century than in any previous age, whose "unenlightened" ways had led the Utilitarians to pronounce them unfit for self-rule, and whose "barbarous" economic, moral and cultural state led Maine, Temple and the majority of the ICS to reach the same verdict. It is curious that Ripon did not embrace the line of defence staked out by the Orientalists at the beginning of the century and built up by Campbell, Trevelyan and Frere after the Mutiny: that the village community was a "little republic" through which the peoples' aptitude for self-rule had developed and flourished over the centuries. Ripon did refer to the village community as the forerunner of modern municipal institutions; but he did so not to prove the Indians' capacity for self-rule on the basis of their experience of representative government through the village panchayet, but rather to demonstrate the conservative

---

[12]Ripon to Forster, 19 May 1883, Ibid., vol. IV, no. 60.

nature of his local self-government scheme, its continuity
with the past and its roots in "the indigenous system /‾which‾7
we have done a great deal to destroy, but remnants of /‾which‾7
exist to a greater or lesser extent in most parts of the
country, and upon /‾which‾7 I hope to build up my edifice of
local self-government".[13] With W.C. Bonerjea (appealing to
J.S. Mill) Ripon despised all tests of civilization and
capacity for self-rule and believed that the urban elite's
readiness and eagerness to undertake the responsibilities of
representative institutions was sufficient cause to
institute local self-government.

Candidly, Ripon admitted that in basing his decision
to inaugurate local self-government on expediency alone, he
was making a "political" rather than an "administrative"
decision.[14] He rejected the popular "administrative" argument
that efficient bureaucratic rule was a better guarantor of
the public welfare than representative government. He
conceded that the transfer of power from professional civil
servants to amateur committee members would lower administrative standards and slacken the pace of reform. "I
have no doubt", he confessed publically,

> that there are in India, just as there are in
> England, municipal bodies that are not always

---

[13]Ripon to Hughes, 12 June 1882, _Ibid._, vol. III,
no. 86.

[14]Ripon to Gladstone, 6 October 1882, _Ibid._, vol. III,
no. 118.

> wise, who are sometimes found to obstruct
> measures of importance, and possibly even
> seriously to neglect their duties. I very
> well recollect, a good many years ago, the
> late Lord Palmerston, telling the House of
> Commons, when he was advocating sanitary
> reform, that there was always in every
> town in England a clean party and a dirty
> party -- a party that was in favour of a
> good water supply and good drainage, and a
> party opposed to measures of that kind. I
> have not the least doubt that there is a clean
> party and a dirty party in the towns and
> cities of India, and I can quite understand
> that, to men zealous for improvement, it may
> often be trying to see important schemes,
> calculated to confer great benefits on a
> large community, postponed, or marked, or
> laid aside from ignorance, or apathy, or
> indifference.[15]

In making this overtly "political" decision, he adopted

McLeod's argument that political education possessed one

asset which outweighed all of these liabilities -- its

potential to instruct the Indians in the difficult art of

self-rule and prepare them to govern themselves independently

of foreign assistance; and he claimed that political

education was an important part of the Liberal party's plan

for India. "The policy which I have been pursuing on this

subject of local self-government is a broad question of

political principle", he informed Gladstone. "What", he

asked rhetorically, "is the nature of the policy which we

ought to pursue in India?

> Is it to be the policy of those who have
> established a free press, who have pro-
> moted education, and who have admitted
> natives more and more largely to the

---

[15]Ripon, "Address to the Delhi Municipality", 5
November 1881, K.A.S. Gupta, ed., Speeches of the Marquis of
Ripon, Calcutta, 1883, vol. I, p. 116.

> public service in various forms; or is it to
> be that of those who hate the freedom of the
> Press, who dread the progress of education,
> and who watch with jealousy and alarm every-
> thing which tends, in however limited a
> degree, to give the natives of India a larger
> share in the management of their own affairs ?
> I cannot doubt which of these two policies is the
> right one; in all events I am quite sure which
> of them alone I could be content to follow.[16]

Ripon thus reduced local self-government to an issue of

party politics. The Tories offered "repressive measures

/̅the Vernacular Press Act_/ and tinsel shows /̅the Delhi

Durbar of 1876, at which the Queen was proclaimed Empress of

India by the Conservative Viceroy, Lord Lytton, at the

behest of Disraeli_/" and denied the Indians a voice in the

administration: the Liberals promised "education", "free

public discussion", and the chance to participate in

government.[17] Proudly, Ripon boasted that in introducing

local self-government he was applying to India "those broad

liberal principles to which I have been attached all my

life"[18]; that "I get more Radical every day, and am

rejoiced to say that the effect of despotic power has so

far been to strengthen and deepen my liberal convictions"[19];

that "the old fogies in the India Council /̅like Maine_/ are,

---

[16]Ripon to Gladstone, 6 October 1882, Correspondence in England, vol. III, no. 118.

[17]Ripon to Hughes, 8 December, Ibid., vol. III, no. 138.

[18]Ripon to Bright, 19 July 1882, Ibid., vol. III, no. 97.

[19]Ripon to Forster, 26 May 1881, Ibid., vol. II, no. 56.

I suspect, very much inclined to look upon me as a dangerous radical, second only in wickedness to Gladstone..."[20]; that the Government of Bombay's Resolution against local self-government (the only public denunciation of this policy in India) read "more like a Tory pamphlet than the utterance of a responsible Government"[21], and that the Governor, Sir James Fergusson, was "a Tory of Tories".[22]

Ripon correctly anticipated that the majority of the ICS -- most of whom were conservative in their approach to constitutional change, and some of whom (like Temple) were Tories as well -- would resist the Liberal policy of surrendering power to self-governing Indians. "It is natural", he wrote Gladstone,

> that many district officers should view with
> dislike an alteration of system which will
> to some degree diminish their present absolute
> supremacy. India is governed by a bureaucracy
> which, though I sincerely believe it to be the
> best bureaucracy that the world has ever seen,
> has still the faults and dangers which belong
> to every institution of that kind; among
> those faults is conspicuously a jealousy of
> allowing non-officials to interfere in any

---

[20]Ripon to Hughes, 8 December 1882, Ibid., vol. III, no. 138.

[21]Ibid.

[22]Ripon to Gladstone, 6 October 1882, Ibid., vol. III, no. 118.

way whatever with any portion, however
restricted, of the administration of the
country.[23]

Ripon vindicated his decision to transfer duties from the

civil service to municipal committees despite overwhelming

official opposition by asserting that the "best men" in the

ICS and at home supported him.[24] This was an ingenious and

highly effective ploy. It enabled him to calculate support

according to arbitrary criteria (i.e., anyone who was a

Liberal or who was for him was good; anyone who was a

Conservative or against him bad) and to persuade the

parliamentary Liberal party and the prime minister that

virtue and social justice were on his side even if the ma-

jority of the Indian administration was not. It allowed him

to dismiss critics on the Council of India in London (a

"deadweight of opposition", he complained)[25] as "philistines"[26]

and to ignore all but the "best men" in India like Aitchison,

the Lieutenant-Governor of the Punjab ("a real good man of

the best Scotch type, with a strong infusion of Puritan force

[23]Ibid.

[24]The phrase is used no fewer than five times in his
letter to Gladstone of 6 October 1882; see also Ripon to
Kimberley, 10 July 1883 (Quoted by Lucien Wolf, The Life
of the First Marquis of Ripon, London, 1921, vol. II, p. 101;
Ripon to Hughes, 12 June 1882, Correspondence in England,
vol. III, no. 86; Ripon to Baxter, 6 December 1882, Ibid.,
no. 137.

[25]Ripon to Gladstone, 10 August, 1883, Ibid., vol.
IV, no. 95.

[26]Ripon to Kimberley, 10 July 1883, quoted by Wolf,
op. cit., p. 102.

and righteousness about him", who enthusiastically backed local self-government)[27]; and at home men like Henry Fawcett, the chairman of the House of Commons Select Committee on Indian Finance in 1873 (who agreed with Ripon "that some loss of administrative efficiency may be far more than compensated by bringing into operation an agency calculated to improve the political and social education of the people")[28] and Gladstone himself (who reassured Ripon that "administrative perfection is not always, at all costs, to be pursued when the alternative is local self-government")[29]. With the "best men" supporting him, Ripon felt able to face the ICS opposition as an evil to be suffered and overcome in the name of Liberal principles.

The introduction of local self-government in 1882 did not transform the base of the imperial government from a foreign despotism into a popular democracy.[30] Indeed, the franchise was everywhere limited to property-holders, and in most parts of the Empire the ICS maintained a firm hold over Indian committee members until after the first World War, when members of the Indian National Congress began to

---

[27]Ripon to Hughes, 25 May 1883, Correspondence in England, vol. IV, no. 63.

[28]Fawcett to Ripon, 26 January 1883, Ibid., no. 12.

[29]Gladstone to Ripon, 24 November 1881, Ibid., vol. II, no. 151.

[30]See Appendix B.

resist their authority and demand not simply genuine
municipal self-rule, but national independence as well.
Nevertheless, it signalled a change of far-reaching importance in the governance of India. It acknowledged that in
theory if not in practice Indian ratepayers -- educated or
illiterate, enlightened or superstitious, civilized or
barbarous -- should run their own municipal affairs. That
this vital concession should be presented in the language
of partisan rivalry and debated after the founding of the
Indian National Congress in 1885 in terms of nationalist
aspirations marks yet another turning point in the debate
on how to govern India, one which -- as Maine, Temple and
Campbell all foresaw -- led to the complete withdrawal of
the British from India.

APPENDIX   A

FOUNDATIONS   OF   MUNICIPALITIES   IN   INDIA :

1864 - 1868

1864

Bombay: Nasik

Bengal: Dacca, Chittagong, Patna, Comillah

North-West   Provinces: Meerut, Almora, Etawah

Central Provinces: Jubbalpore

1865

Bengal: Burdwan, Gaya, Serampore, Arrah, Midnapore, Hooghly

1866

Madras: Trichinopoly

1867

North-Western Provinces: Saharanpur

Punjab: Lahore, Rawalpindi, Ferozepore

1868

Bengal: Brahamanbaria

North-West   Provinces: Benares

Punjab: Amritsar

Total numbers of municipalities : 1870

Bombay: 100

Madras: 44

Bengal: 65

North-West   Provinces: 67

Punjab: 127

Central Provinces: 40

APPENDIX B

COMPOSITION OF MUNICIPAL BOARDS

	Total number of Municipalities		Those with Elected Members		Those with Nominated Members	
	1881	1885	1881	1885	1881	1885
Bengal	138	147	3	118	135	29
Bombay	162	162	10	40	152	122
Madras	47	54	12	43	35	11
North-West Provinces	107	109	75	101	35	8
Punjab	197	197	5	122	192	75
Central Provinces	61	58	61	58	--	--
Burma	7	13	--	8	7	5

SELECT BIBLIOGRAPHY

I.   India Office Library

A. Official Records

Selections from the Revenue Records of the North-West Provinces, 1818-1820.

Selections from the Records of the North-West Provinces, vol. IV.

Selections from the Records of the East India House, Relating to the Revenue, Police, and Civil and Criminal Justice under the Company's Government in India, vol. IV, 1826.

Revenue Letters from Bombay, vol. VIII, 1829-1830.

Official Correspondence on the System of Revenue Survey and Assessment in the Bombay Presidency, 1859 (revised ed.).

Government of India:
 Finance Department Proceedings, 1858-1882.
 Home Department Proceedings, 1858-1882.
 Legislative Council Proceedings, 1861-1882.

Annual Presidency and Provincial Administration Reports, 1860-1882.

B. Official Publications

Gazette of India Extraordinary

Parliamentary Papers (House of Commons): 1830, vol. 49; 1831, vol. 5; 1832, vol. 3 and vol. 4; 1853, vol. 3; 1860, vol. 49; 1865, vol. 40; 1873, vol. 12; 1883, vol. 51.

C.   Manuscript Collections

Wood Papers

Temple Papers

D.   Periodicals

East India Association Journal.

Native Newspaper Reports, 1860-1882.

II.   The British Library

Lord Ripon, Correspondence in England; Correspondence in India.

Periodicals: The Westminster Review; The Edinburgh Review; The Fortnightly Review; The St. James's Gazette; The Times; Asiatick Researches; The Cambridge Journal.

III.   Other Works

Baden Powell, B.H., The Indian Village Community, London, 1896.

Ballhatchet, Kenneth, Social Policy and Social Change in Western India, 1817-1830, Oxford, 1957.

Banerjea, Pramanath, Provincial Finance in India, London, 1929.

Barrington, Emily Isabel, The Servant of All, London, 1927, 2 vol.

Beaglehole, Timothy, Thomas Munro and the Development of Administrative Policy in Madras 1792-1818, Cambridge, 1966.

Bhattacharyya, S., Financial Foundations of the British Raj, Simla, 1971.

Bowring, Sir John, ed., The Works of Jeremy Bentham, Oxford, 1910.

Brown, Ford K., Fathers of the Victorians: The Age of Wilberforce, Cambridge, 1961.

Buckland, Sir Charles, Bengal under the Lieutenant-Governors, Calcutta, 1901, 2 vol.

Burrow, John, Evolution and Society, Cambridge, 1966.

Campbell, Sir George, The British Empire, London, 1887.

India as it May be, London, 1853.

Memoirs of My Indian Career, ed. by Sir Charles Bernard, London, 1893, 2 vol.

Modern India, London, 1852.

Chintamani, C.Y., ed. The Speeches and Writings of the Hon. Pherozeshah Mehta, Allahabad, 1905.

Choksey, R.D., The Aftermath of Revolt, Bombay, 1950.

Clive, John, Macaulay: The Shaping of the Historian, New York, 1973.

Coupland, Reginald, The Indian Problem, 1833-1935, London, 1943.

Cross, Cecil M.P., The Development of Self-Government in India 1858-1914, Chicago, 1922.

Dutt, Romesh Chandra, Economic History of India in the Victorian Age, London, 1950.

Embree, Ainslie, Charles Grant and British India, New York, 1962.

Feaver, George, From Status to Contract: A Biography of Sir Henry Maine 1822-1888, London, 1969.

Forrest, G.W., Selections from the State Papers of the Governors-General of India: Warren Hastings, Oxford, 1910.

Gleig, George Robert, The Life of Sir Thomas Munro, London, 1830, 3 vol.

Gopal, Sarvepalli, British Policy in India, 1858-1905, Cambridge, 1965.

Grant Duff, Sir Mountstuart Elphinstone, Sir Henry Maine, London, 1892.

Gupta, K.A.S., ed., Speeches of the Marquis of Ripon, Calcutta, 1883, 2 vol.

Halevy, Eli, The Growth of Philosophic Radicalism, London, 1928.

Hunter, Sir William Wilson, A Life of the Earl of Mayo, 4th Viceroy of India, London, 1875.

Hutchins, Francis, The Illusion of Permanence: British Imperialism in India, Princeton, 1967.

Ilbert, Sir Courtenay Peregrine, The Government of India, Oxford, 1915.

Kopf, David, British Orientalism and the Bengal Renaissance, Berkeley and Los Angeles, 1969.

Kumar, Ravinder, Western India in the Nineteenth Century, London, 1968.

Lovett, Sir Verney, India, London, 1923.

Maclagen, Michael "Clemency" Canning, London, 1962.

Maine, Sir Henry Sumner, Ancient Law, London, 1920, 10th ed.

   The Effects of Observation of India on Modern European Thought, London, 1875.

   Popular Government, London, 1885.

   Village Communities in the East and West, London, 1871, 2nd ed.

Marshall, Peter J., The British Discovery of Hinduism in the Eighteenth Century, Cambridge, 1970.

Martineau, John, Sir Bartle Frere, London, 1895, 2 vol.

Metcalf, Thomas Richard, The Aftermath of the Mutiny, Princeton, 1964.

Mill, James, History of British India, London, 1840.

Misra, B.B., The Central Administration of the East India Company, 1773-1834, Manchester, 1959.

   The Administrative History of India, 1834-1947, Oxford, 1970.

Moon, Penderel, Warren Hastings and British India, London, 1947

Moore, Robin, J., Sir Charles Wood's Indian Policy, 1853-1866, Manchester, 1966.

Morris, Henry, The Life of Charles Grant, London, 1904.

Mukherjee, Soumyendra Nath, Sir William Jones: A Study in Eighteenth Century British Attitudes to India, Cambridge, 1968.

Muller, F. Max, India, What Can It Teach Us?, London, 1883.

Nath, Amar, The Development of Local Self-Government in the Punjab, 1849-1900, Lahore, 1930.

Norton, John Bruce, Topics for Indian Statesmen, London, 1858.

Pritchard, Iltudus Thomas, The Administration of India, 1859-1868, London, 1869, 2 vol.

Rosselli, John, Lord William Bentinck: The Making of a Liberal Imperialist, 1774-1839, London, 1974.

Sen, Surendranath, The Administrative History of the Mahrattas, Calcutta, 1925, 2nd ed.

Smith, Reginald Bosworth, The Life of Lord Lawrence, London, 1885, 6th ed., 2 vol.

Stephen, Sir James Fitzjames, Liberty, Equality, Fraternity, ed. by R.J. White, Cambridge, 1967.

Stokes, Eric, The English Utilitarians and India, Oxford, 1959.

Strachey, Sir John, India, London, 1888.

        and Col. Richard St. .chey, Finance and the Public Works of India from 1869-1881, London, 1882.

Temple, Sir Richard, India in 1880, London, 1881, 3rd ed.

        The Story of My Life, London, 1896, 2 vol.

Thomas, Patrick Jones, The Growth of Federal Finance in India, Being a Survey of India's Public Finances, 1833-1939, London, 1939.

Thompson, Edward and G.T. Garratt, The Rise and Fulfilment of British Rule in India, Allahabad, 1966.

Tinker, Hugh, The Foundations of Local Self-Government in India, Pakistan and Burma, London, 1954.

Trevelyan, Sir Charles, The Education of the People of India, London, 1838.

    Statement by Sir Charles Trevelyan on the Circumstances Connected with His Recall from the Government of Madras, London, 1860.

Trevelyan, George Otto, The Competition Wallah, London, 1864.

    The Life and Letters of Lord Macaulay, London, 1876, 2 vol.

Trevelyan, Sir Humphrey, The India We Left: Charles Trevelyan, 1826-1865; Humphrey Trevelyan 1929-1947, London, 1972.

Ward, Sir Humphrey, The Reign of Queen Victoria, London, 1887, 2 vol.

West, Sir Algernon, The Administration of Sir Charles Wood, London, 1867.

Wilkes, Mark, Historical Sketches of the South of India, Mysore, 1810.

Wilson, James, Speech delivered before the Legislative Council of Calcutta, 18 February 1860, London, 1860.

Wolf, Lucien, The Life of the First Marquis of Ripon, London, 1921, 2 vol.

Woodruff, Philip, The Men Who Ruled India: The Guardians, London, 1954.

Worsfold, Sir William, Sir Bartle Frere, London, 1923.

Young, G.M., Portrait of an Age, Oxford, 1977 (issued with notes by G. Kitson Clark and others).

5 34

INDEX

Anstey, Chisholm, 302, 305, 308.
Arnold, Thomas, 211, 213, 215, 216, 231, 232.
        at Rugby: 215, 232, 290, 299.
Arya Samaj, 21, 291.
Asiatick Researches, 17, 18.
Asiatick Society (of Bengal), 17-19.

Bagehot, Walter, 166.
Baji Rao II, 53.
Beadon, Sir Cecil, 195.
Bengal Presidency, 62.
        relation to London, Bombay and Madras: 106-109.
        indigo disturbances of 1859: 118-121.
Bentham, Jeremy, 31, 34-36, 39, 57, 75, 252, 270, 272, 290.
Bentinck, Lord William, 38, 39, 82, 213.
Bible Society, 28-30.
Bombay Presidency, 45, 55, 64, 75-78, 83, 91, 103, 105,
        107, 108, 118, 134, 141, 144.
        struggle against the Public Works Department: 142,
        167-180.
Bonerjea, W.C., 301, 308-310, 326.
Brahmo Samaj, 21, 271.
Bright, John, 104-105.
British Indian Association, 125, 242, 244.
Burke, Edmund, 213.

Calcutta bureaucracy, 106-109, 127, 134, 142-180, 190.
Campbell, Sir George, 108, 214-215, 218-228, 235-242,
        246-257, 259, 262, 275, 277, 286, 303, 332.
        leader of the Madras Revolt against the Government of
                India: 143, 159-167.
Canning, 1st Earl,
        supporter of administrative centralization: 99, 101,
        102, 109, 112, 127, 129, 130, 140-142.
        supporter of financial centralization: 145, 147, 152.
        opponent of the Madras Revolt of 1860: 159, 165-167.
Central Provinces, 103, 195.
Charter Acts,
        of 1813: 28, 29.
        of 1833: 29, 103, 128, 145, 146.
        of 1853: 103, 145, 146.
Christian views on Indian society,
        evangelical: 12, 13, 23, 28-30.
                Macaulay's evangelical views: 38, 42, 213.
        'muscular': 213, 216.
Church Missionary Society, 28, 30.